YOUNG STUDENTS

Learning Library®

VOLUME 6

Concrete—Dog

NEWFIELD
PUBLICATIONS

MIDDLETOWN · CONNECTICUT

PHOTO CREDITS

ALLSPORT page 743(bottom right). AUSTRALIAN NEWS & INFORMATION BUREAU page 645(bottom righ); 658(center left). BBC HULTON PICTURE LIBRARY page 646(top left). BARNABY'S PICTURE LIBRARY page 685(top right). THE BETTMANN ARCHIVE page 657(bottom right); 718(bottom left); 725(top right). BIBLIOTHEQUE NATIONAL, PARIS page 638(top left). BIRKBECK COLLEGE page 683(top right). JANET & COLIN BORD page 696(bottom right). BRITISH MUSEUM page 679(top left). RICHARD BRYANT page 722(top right). BUREAU OF SPORT FISHERIES & WILDLIFE page 670(bottom left/Luther C. Goldman). J ALLAN CASH page 636(top left); 661(bottom right). CZECH TOURIST OFFICE page 689(top right). BRUCE COLEMAN LTD page 721(top right). STATE OF CONNECTICUT DEVELOPMENT COMMISSION page 634(top right). GENE COX page 737(bottom right); 738(top left). ARMANDO CURCIO EDITORE, SPA page 601(bottom left & center top); 638(bottom left); 644(top); 653(top right); 656(bottom); 657(center); 660(bottom); 662(bottom right); 670(top left); 673(top right); 675(bottom right); 677(center right); 681(both pics); 688(top left); 696(top left); 698(top right); 701(bottom right); 703(bottom left); 707(top right); 711(all pics); 712(bottom left); 723(top right); 725(bottom right); 726(top right); 744(bottom left); 745(center right). DANCE NEWS page 697(bottom right). JESSIE DAVIS page 698(top right). DELAWARE STATE TRAVEL SERVICE page 713(right center); 714(top left). DEPT OF DENTAL ILLUSTRATION, GLASGOW DENTAL HOSPITAL page 718(top left). EDITORIAL PHOTOCOLOR ARCHIVES page 695(center right); 703(top right). FRENCH TOURIST OFFICE page 634(top left). GIRAUDON page 627(top right). GREENPEACE page 640(top left). SONIA HALLIDAY page 668(bottom left). ROBERT HARDING & ASSOCIATES page 667(bottom). BRIAN HAWKES page 639(bottom right). RUSSELL F. HOGELAND page 691(top right). ALAN HUTCHISON page 668(top right). IMITOR page 733(center & bottom right). INDUSTRIAL INSTITUTE FOR COTTON page 665(top right). INTERFOTO MTI page 677(bottom right & top right). JAPAN NATIONAL TOURIST OFFICE page 685(bottom right). MOMO page 690(bottom right); 721(bottom right). MANSELL COLLECTION page 737(top right); 738(bottom left). MERCKE SHARP & DOHME page 739(top right). PAT MORRIS page 624; 709(bottom right). MARTYN MOXON page 672(bottom left). NHPA page 669(bottom right); 710(bottom left/Brian Hawkes); 721(top left). NATIONAL DAIRY COUNCIL page 692(top left). NATIONAL FILM ARCHIVES page 696(bottom left). NATIONAL GALLERY page 640(bottom left). NATIONAL LIBRARY OF MEDICINE, BETHESDA page 686(top left). NATURE PHOTOGRAPHERS LTD page 706(top left/B. Burbidge). NEVADA COMMISSION ON TOURISM page 694(top right). PHOTOSOURCE page 712(top left). POPPERFOTO page 647(center left). RTHPL page 719(top right). SATOUR page 697(top left). FRANK SPOONER PICTURES page 722(bottom). SWISS TOURIST OFFICE page 686(bottom left). THE ART GALLERY MAGAZINE (MARCH 1973 ISSUE) page 690(bottom left/ Karen Breschi). JANE TWOMEY page 67(bottom right). UNITED STATES CAPITOL HISTORICAL SOCIETY page 628(bottom left); 630(top left). UNITED STATES DEPARTMENT OF AGRICULTURE page 660(top). UNITED PRESS INTERNATIONAL page 741(top left). UNITED STATES DEPARTMENT OF ACRICULTURE/AGRICULTURAL RESEARCH SERVICE page 664(bottom). UNITED STATES AIR FORCE OFFICIAL PHOTOGRAPH page 701(top right). UNITED STATES SECRET SERVICE page 665(bottom). VIRGINIA CHAMBER OF COMMERCE page 626(bottom right). C.R. WARNE page 670(bottom right). WASHINGTON CONVENTION & VISITORS BUREAU page 741(bottom). ZEFA page 631(bottom right); 632(top right); 634(bottom left); 640(top right); 653(bottom right); 663(bottom right); 684(top left); 693(bottom left); 704(top left); 715(top right); 717(top right); 722(top left); 723(bottom right); 736(top left).

Young Students Learning Library is a federally registered trademark of Newfield Publications, Inc.

ISBN 0-8374-0476-2

1993 Edition

CONTENTS

CONCRETE All kinds of structures—houses, skyscrapers, bridges, dams, oil rigs, and more—can be built of concrete. Many buildings contain concrete beams and slabs in the walls and floors, and some are constructed on top of huge blocks of concrete buried in the ground to provide strong foundations. Roads are often made of layers of concrete beneath a surface of tar and gravel.

The reason that concrete can be used in so many different ways is that it can be formed into any shape required, yet is very strong. A whole arch or dome, for example, can be made in one piece using concrete. Large panels and slabs of concrete can be made in a factory and then taken to the building site and fixed together.

Many of the modern buildings and structures in towns and cities are made of concrete, unlike older houses built of brick or stone. However, concrete is not a new building material. It was invented in ancient times. The Romans used concrete to build aqueducts and even the Colosseum.

Concrete is made by mixing sand, cement, and water together with small stones such as gravel or crushed rock. The wet concrete is poured into a mold and sets hard in the shape of the mold. *Cement* is made by burning a mixture of limestone or chalk and clay in a kiln, and then crushing it into powder. On adding water, cement sets hard. In concrete, the cement binds the sand and stones together to produce a hard material.

Concrete, however, is not very strong when used alone. It tends to crack if subjected to heavy loads. To increase its strength, it is reinforced by putting steel rods in the concrete to take the strain. Prestressed concrete contains steel bars that squeeze or compress the concrete, making it much stronger.

ALSO READ: BUILDING MATERIAL, CONSTRUCTION.

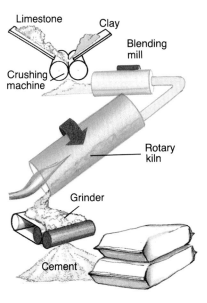

▲ *The making of cement, the most important material used in making concrete. The ingredients are heated for several hours in the kiln at about 2,700° F (1,500° C).*

CONDENSATION see WATER CYCLE.

CONDUCTION see HEAT AND COLD.

CONFEDERATE STATES OF AMERICA A group of Southern states withdrew from the United States during 1860 and 1861. These states joined together after Abraham Lincoln was elected President of the United States in 1861. Many people in these states disagreed strongly with Lincoln's ideas and believed he would make slavery illegal. They formed their own country, named the Confederate States of America.

Six states—South Carolina, Mississippi, Florida, Alabama, Georgia, and Louisiana—originally formed the Confederacy. Representatives from each of the states held a meeting in Montgomery, Alabama, early in 1861. They chose Montgomery as the capital of the Confederacy. They elected Jefferson Davis of Mississippi

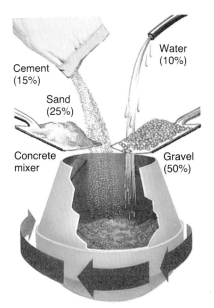

▼ *The ingredients used in making concrete. One of concrete's great advantages as a building material is that it can be easily made on site.*

Water (10%)

Cement (15%)

Sand (25%)

Concrete mixer

Gravel (50%)

◄ *The California Redwood is the world's tallest tree. It has reached 370 feet (112 m) in its native California. See* CONIFERS.

▲ *Jefferson Davis announces the secession of the South from the Union in Montgomery, Alabama, the first Confederate capital. Shortly after, the Civil War broke out.*

▲ *A soldier proudly holds the most famous of Confederate flags. The flag is still flown today outside homes and public buildings in many parts of the South.*

as president. Judah Benjamin became the attorney general. Alexander Hamilton Stephens of Georgia was elected vice-president. Davis chose six advisers for his cabinet. The representatives then drew up a constitution. They established an elected congress, made up of representatives from the states as well as the nonvoting members of the cabinet. The president and vice-president had six-year terms of office. They issued their own money. A permanent army was put under the control of the government. Slavery was declared legal.

Rivalry had existed for a long time between the Northern and Southern parts of the United States. The North now refused to allow the secession of the Confederate States, and the Civil War broke out in April 1861. Texas, Virginia, Arkansas, North Carolina, and Tennessee joined the Confederacy later that year, and the capital was moved to Richmond, Virginia. The counties of northwestern Virginia wanted to remain loyal to the union. They created their own new state, West Virginia, in 1863.

The Confederates had very little money to pay for the war and very few soldiers to fight it. Large taxes were levied, and the people gave generously. But the Confederates were

soon in serious financial trouble. They were unable to get enough aid from the foreign countries—France, Great Britain, the Netherlands, Spain, and Brazil—who agreed to trade with them. Moreover, many of their ships were blockaded by the Union navy. The South won several battles, but after two years, the wealthy, industrial North began to win the war. The Confederacy not only lacked the needed supplies, but its leaders disagreed over how the war should be fought. In April 1865, Davis and his cabinet were forced to escape from Richmond, which was under attack by Northern armies. Later that month, the Confederate States of America collapsed and the war was over.

ALSO READ: CIVIL WAR; DAVIS, JEFFERSON; LINCOLN, ABRAHAM; SLAVERY; WEST VIRGINIA.

CONFUCIUS (about 551–479 B.C.)
Confucius was an early great Chinese philosopher. He was born in what is now the province of Shantung, China. His family was very poor. When Confucius was only three, his

▼ *The White House of the Confederacy in Richmond, Virginia. Richmond replaced Montgomery, Alabama, as the Confederate capital in May 1861.*

father died. His mother did her best to see he got a good education. When he was 21, students began to come to listen to him.

Confucius taught that men should be honest, loyal, thoughtful toward others, and obedient. He said that life has five main relationships. These are between ruler and subject, father and son, elder and younger brother, husband and wife, and friend and friend. Each of these relationships includes certain duties and responsibilities that should be carried out as well as possible. Each person must do his duty to the other. The two most important ways to make these relationships work, he said, were *jen* (love) and *li* (manners or etiquette). Confucius had many wise sayings. The most familiar of all was "What you do not wish done to yourself, do not do to others." Jesus Christ taught this philosophy—the Golden Rule—500 years later.

When Confucius was 52, he was made governor of his state, Lu. It is said that he did such a good job of ruling it that a neighboring governor became jealous, so Confucius gave up his post. He spent the next 13 years searching for a prince who would listen to his ideas, so that he could demonstrate the principles of good government. But China was governed by many dishonest leaders in those days.

Confucius died almost unknown, but his ideas have since come to be followed by millions of people. He taught a way of looking at life and the universe, not a religion. But his teachings slowly became mixed with old Chinese customs to form a religion. Confucianism has played an important part in the culture and history of China, Korea, and Japan.

ALSO READ: CHINA, PHILOSOPHY, RELIGION.

CONGO The People's Republic of the Congo is a Central African nation that used to be called Congo (Brazzaville). Brazzaville is the name of the country's capital. This name was used because the country's neighbor, Zaire, was until 1971 also called the Congo. Congo (Brazzaville) was a French colony until it received independence in 1960.

Congo is approximately twice the size of Washington state. It is bordered on the west by Gabon, on the north by Cameroon and the Central African Republic, and on the east and south by Zaire. The Atlantic Ocean forms the southwestern boundary. The equator runs through the country.

Congo has three geographical regions. The narrow coastal plain extends 40 miles (64 km) inland. Highlands form the central part of the country. In the north lies the basin of the Congo River. This river, called the Zaire River in Zaire, separates

▲ *Confucius was born in the 6th century B.C. in China. He tried to bring people back to peace and order through the wisdom of the past.*

CONGO

Capital City: Brazzaville (600,000 people).
Area: 175,676 square miles (454,999 sq. km).
Population: 2,250,000.
Government: People's republic.
Natural Resources: Petroleum, lumber, minerals, natural gas.
Export Products: Crude petroleum, lumber, coffee, cocoa, sugar, diamonds.
Unit of Money: Franc of the African Financial Community.
Official Language: French.

▲ *The badge of members of the U.S. Congress, the law-making branch of the federal government.*

Congo from Zaire. It is a major transportation route.

Congo has a tropical climate. Rain falls throughout the year in most of the country. The coastal plain is cooler and drier than the rest of the land.

Over one-half of the Congolese live by raising only the crops they need for their own use. Others also raise crops that can be exported, such as peanuts, coffee, cocoa, palm kernels, and tobacco. Some people earn a living by fishing and lumbering.

Congo has little industry. The waterfalls on several rivers may someday be used for hydroelectric power, however. Oil is now by far the leading export. Lead, gold, and diamonds are also mined.

The Congolese belong to several ethnic and language groups. Almost half of the people are members of the Bakongo group. Others belong to the Bateke, M'Bochi, and Sangha. Many of them speak French, the nation's official language, in addition to their local languages.

The country is a transport hub of central Africa. The Congo River system and the Congo-Ocean Railroad connect inland areas with Pointe-Noire, the country's main seaport.

ALSO READ: AFRICA, ZAIRE RIVER.

▼ *The U.S. House of Representatives has 435 members. The public is allowed to watch the House in session from the balcony.*

CONGO RIVER   see ZAIRE RIVER.

CONGRESS, UNITED STATES

"All legislative powers herein granted shall be vested in a Congress of the United States, which shall consist of a Senate and a House of Representatives." These words establish the U.S. Congress for the purpose of making the nation's laws.

The government of the United States is divided into three branches so that no one person or group can acquire too much power. This is called the "check and balance" system of government. Each branch has specific powers to check (stop) the others if one tries to become too powerful. The powers of each branch balance the powers of the other two branches.

The President of the United States and the people who work with him form the *executive* branch of the government. The Supreme Court and the federal court system form the *judicial* branch of the government. Congress makes up the *legislative* branch of the government. This branch is called legislative because "to legislate" means "to make laws," and making laws is the main job of Congress. The English word "congress" comes from a Latin word meaning "come together." When the U.S. Congress holds a session (meets), members of Congress get together in the Capitol building in Washington, D.C.

The United States Congress is a *bicameral* legislature. This means that it has two houses (parts), the *Senate* and the *House of Representatives*. The powers of Congress are divided between these two houses. This is another example of the check and balance system. The Senate and the House of Representatives must work together to make new laws.

The House of Representatives
The House of Representatives has

HOW A BILL BECOMES LAW IN CONGRESS

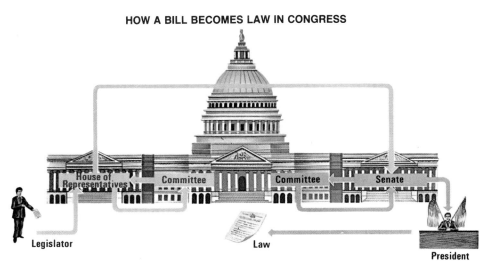

Legislator

House of Representatives

Committee

Committee

Senate

Law

President

◀ *Laws go through many stages before they are made. In the United States a law is discussed first in a committee of the House of Representatives, and then on the "floor" of the House. If it is passed in the House, the law is then sent to the Senate, where it is studied by a committee and then discussed on the "floor." If everybody agrees that the proposal is a good one, it is sent to the President. If the President approves the proposal, it becomes a law.*

been called the *lower house* of Congress, and the Senate has been called the *upper house*. These names were chosen when Congress was first set up. The House of Representatives at that time was less powerful than the Senate. Now both houses are about equal in power, but the old names are sometimes still used.

Members of the House of Representatives are called *representatives*. They represent the people who elect them. Members of the House are also sometimes called *congressmen* or *congresswomen*. A representative is elected for a two-year term, usually by people of a particular area in his or her home state. (A few representatives are elected by all the people of their state. These people are called "representatives at large.") Each area, called a *congressional district*, is set by the legislature of each state according to population. A representative may be reelected by the people of the district every two years. If they are not satisfied with the job being done, they elect someone else. The House is said to be the chamber closest to the people, because voters express their opinion every two years.

The first meeting of the House was held in 1789 with 65 representatives. The number of representatives increased steadily until 1911. The House then decided that adding more members would be impractical, so the number of representatives was set at 435. The number of people represented by each representative is constantly growing. The number of congressional districts in each state depends on the number of people living in that state, but each state has at least one.

Each representative, according to recent statistics, represents about 550,000 people. The number of congressional districts in each state is adjusted after each census (a count of the population taken every ten years) to make sure that no state has more or less than its fair share of representatives.

The leader of the House of Representatives is called the *Speaker of the House*. The Speaker is chosen at the beginning of each new Congress by representatives of the political party that elects the majority of congressmen. The members hold separate meetings, by party, to choose four other leaders: the House Majority Leader and the Majority Whip and the House Minority Leader and the Minority Whip. Majority and minority leaders, or *floor leaders*, as they are often called, try to keep the lawmaking process running smoothly. The whips help them by making sure that all the representatives are present for important votes.

The House of Representatives has many special powers. It is allowed to

Article 1 of the United States Constitution tells us who shall or shall not sit in Congress:

A Representative must have reached the age of 25 and been a citizen of the United States for seven years. A Representative must also be an inhabitant of the state in which he or she sits.

A Senator must be 30 years of age and must have been a United States citizen for nine years. A Senator must also be an inhabitant of the state in which he or she is chosen.

The President has to be a natural born citizen of the United States. He must be at least 35 years of age and must have been a U.S. resident for 14 years.

▲ *The Senate of the United States. Great Americans have spoken in this chamber, and some of the most important decisions in U.S. history have been made here.*

impeach (bring charges against) the President or other federal officials if the representatives think they are guilty of wrongdoing. The House also has the power to introduce *bills* (proposals for new laws) concerning revenue (money that the government collects from taxes and other sources). The Senate must approve any new revenue bill after the House passes it, but only the House can begin the process of making a new revenue law. The House forms committees that study problems and hold hearings to help in deciding whether a new idea should become a law. Each committee specializes in studying certain subjects important to the nation, such as agriculture or education.

The Senate   Members of the Senate are called *senators*. Two senators are elected from each state, whether it is large or small. All the voters in a state elect that state's senators, who serve for six years. The United States now has 50 states, so Congress has 100 senators. Not all senators run for election at the same time. Instead, one-third of the Senate is elected every two years. The Vice-President of the United States presides over the Senate. When the Vice-President is busy elsewhere, a senator called the *president pro tempore* ("temporary presi-

dent") presides. The president pro tempore is elected by the other senators.

Like the House, the Senate has some special powers. The Senate must *ratify* (approve) all treaties with foreign governments. If the President or some other official is impeached by the House, the Senate becomes a court. Whoever is impeached must stand trial before the Senate. If found guilty, that person is removed from office. The Senate must also *confirm* (approve) the President's choices for Cabinet members and Supreme Court justices. These people cannot be appointed to their jobs unless they are approved by the Senate. Like the House, the Senate forms committees to help in its work. One of the most important committees is the one on foreign affairs. Most of the real work of Congress is done "in committee." This is why the Senate and House are often deserted, even when Congress is in session.

Congress has other powers that both houses share. Only Congress can declare war or raise and support an army and navy. Congress can set up federal courts, make laws regulating certain kinds of business, and borrow money for the government. Congress can provide money to help foreign nations in need, to build weapons for national defense, to pay for medical research, and to build highways. It can propose amendments to the U.S. Constitution and decide when to admit new states into the Union. Congress ran the city of Washington from 1878 to 1974, when home rule was enacted.

How Congress Makes Laws   Any member of either house may start the process of making a law, except for a bill concerning revenue, which must begin in the lower house. Suppose a member of the House of Representatives wants to pass a new law that will provide money for a school health program. He or she begins by "drafting" a bill. This means writing a suggestion for a new law in legal language for other representatives to read and think about. This bill is put into the "hopper," a box for new bills on the desk of the clerk of the House of Representatives.

The clerk sends the bill to a committee for study. In this case, the clerk would probably send the bill to the House Education and Labor Committee because it is about money for schools. The members of the committee read the bill. They may hold hearings, meetings at which experts come to Congress to discuss the bill. The experts might include teachers, school principals, parents of schoolchildren, doctors, and nurses. The committee members listen and think. If they decide the bill is a good one, they "report it out to the floor." This means that they present the bill to all the other members of the House. On the "floor" of the House, the other representatives discuss the bill. All those who want to speak about the bill have a chance to do so. The House then votes on it. The bill is sent to the Senate if the majority of the House passes it.

The bill is now studied by a Senate committee. New hearings are held. Experts come again to give their opinions of the bill. Afterwards the bill is debated on the "floor" of the Senate. If most senators vote for the bill, it is sent to the President.

The President has the power to approve or disapprove a bill. A bill signed by the President becomes law. The President's power to disapprove of a bill is called the *veto power*. If the President vetoes the bill, it is sent back to Congress. The members of both houses think about the bill some more. They try to understand why the President disapproved of the bill. They may change the bill to try to gain the President's approval. If they do not agree with the President, they can again vote in favor of the bill. A bill becomes a law even though the

President has vetoed it if two-thirds of the members of each house vote in favor of it.

ALSO READ: CAPITOL, UNITED STATES; CONSTITUTION, UNITED STATES; COURT SYSTEM; PRESIDENCY; SUPREME COURT; UNITED STATES GOVERNMENT.

CONIFER The world's oldest, tallest, and heaviest living things are *conifers*—cone-bearing trees. So are the trees that grow at the highest places—at the timberline among mountains—and the trees growing in the coldest places—at the treeline in the snowy wastes of the Arctic and Antarctic. Nearly all the paper and three-fourths of the world's lumber come from conifers.

The greatest assortment of conifers in the whole world grows in the western United States. But the huge redwood, the 3,000-year-old sequoia, the beautiful Monterey pine, and the rare pygmy cypress are all in danger of becoming extinct. People are cutting them down ruthlessly because they need the timber and want the land it grows on.

Nearly 500 kinds of conifers exist, grouped in seven different families. The pine is probably the best known. Spruces, hemlocks, cedars, and firs are other familiar coniferous trees.

Conifers are easy to recognize by their leaves. The leaves of many coni-

The oldest conifer and also the world's oldest living thing is a bristlecone pine growing on Wheeler Peak in east Nevada. This ancient tree is probably 4,900 years old, having been alive for over 2,900 years before the birth of Christ.

▼ *Conifers can withstand cold, snowy winters and short, cool summers. They are therefore typically found in a broad belt covering northern North America, Europe, and Siberia (in Russia).*

Douglas fir

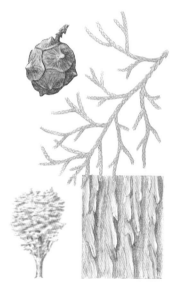

Monterey cypress

Wellingtonia

fers are not broad and flat, like an oak leaf, but long, slim, and pointed. They are thus called "needles." Pine needles grow out from the branch in bunches of two to five, depending on the type of pine tree. Some needles grow nine inches (23 cm) long. Other kinds of conifers have scaly leaves. Almost all conifers are *evergreens*, trees whose branches are never bare of leaves. The leaves of many coniferous trees remain on the branches for several years before they are replaced.

Conifers have special seeds, too. The seeds of other trees are enclosed in a hard or fleshy fruit. The seeds of an apple tree, for example, are in the center of the fruit. Coniferous trees have seeds that are not covered. Instead they are carried on the upper surfaces of the scales that make up the cone. Some trees have seedcones that ripen in a year, but other varieties take two years to develop fully. Botanists classify conifers as *gymnosperms*, or naked-seeded trees. All other trees are *angiosperms*, or trees with covered seeds.

The Pines The pines may be the conifer family you know best. The *white pine* grows all across the northern United States. In colonial days, the British made a law that the big white pines, 60 feet (18 m) high, must be saved for masts for ships of the British navy. Pines are useful in the timber and paper industries. In southern states, turpentine is produced from pine trees. In the eastern states, important pine trees are *longleaf* and *loblolly*. The *lodgepole* and *ponderosa* pines are important in the West. In the Southwest, there is the *pinyon* pine, which produces delicious pine nuts. Blobs of gum from pine trees often drop to the ground. After thousands of years these blobs turn into gemlike amber.

Some pines grow as high as 240 feet (73 m). They also live very long lives. Experts say that more than a dozen *bristlecone* pines have survived for over 4,000 years in the White Moun-

▲ *Giant sequoias are vast conifers. Their bark is reddish brown, thick, fibrous and so soft it can be punched without hurting your fist!*

tains of California.

The *Douglas fir* of the northwestern mountains is not a true fir, but a pine closely related to the hemlock. It is among our largest trees, sometimes reaching 200 feet (60 m) in height, although the average is closer to 100 feet (30 m). Millions of young Douglas firs are cut each year.

Hemlocks, also part of the pine family, are very common in the mountains of the East and Northwest. They grow best in cool, damp climates. Hemlocks reach heights of 60–100 feet (18–30 m) and are important in the timber industry. Four different types are found in the United States. They are the eastern, Carolina, mountain, and western hemlock. The bark of the hemlock is rich in *tannin*, used in tanning leather.

Balsam fir is a very popular Christmas pine. It grows in New England, around the Great Lakes, and in Canada. Blisters on the bark of the balsam produce a resin. The cement made from this resin is useful in cementing glass. Balsam firs provide shelter for wildlife—birds feed on the seeds and deer and rabbits eat the bark and young branches.

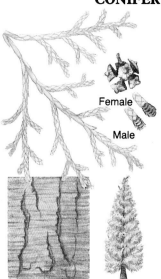

Birds and animals also feed on *spruce*, another kind of pine. Grouse and rabbits eat the needles, deer feed on the twigs, and songbirds enjoy the seeds. Spruce trees are harvested for lumber for the building industry and for pulpwood, used in making paper. The *red spruce*, *white spruce*, and *black spruce* grow in the cool forests of the eastern mountains. *Blue spruce* is one of the western varieties. The *Norway spruce*, brought here from Europe, is another popular tree.

■ LEARN BY DOING

You may get to know one pine tree very well each year—at Christmastime. You may want to get a live Christmas tree planted in a large pot. You can decorate it like any other tree, but when the holiday is over your tree will still be green and fragrant. Keep it in the pot the rest of the winter. If you live in a house with a yard, you can plant the tree when spring comes. ■

Other Conifer Families The *araucarians* are one conifer family of which few species have survived. We know that this family is very old. The trees that turned to stone in the Petrified Forest of Arizona are araucarians.

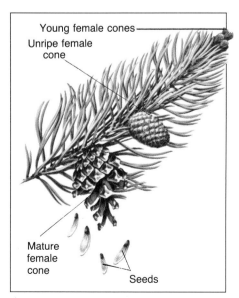

▲ *Conifers reproduce through their cones. Here we see three stages of the development of cones.*

Young female cones
Unripe female cone
Mature female cone
Seeds

Some of those ancient trunks are 200 feet (60 m) long.

Most surviving araucarians are found in the Southern Hemisphere. One you may know is the *Norfolk Island "pine."* It is often grown in pots as a house plant in northern climates, although it comes from a warm place in northern New Zealand. The *monkey-puzzle tree* of Chile has hard, spiky needles and branches that interlock.

The hugest trees in the world belong to the *bald cypress* family. The *dawn redwood* belongs to this group, along with the *giant sequoia* and the *"big cypress"* of Mexico. One sequoia, called General Sherman, is 272 feet (83 m) tall and 101½ feet (31 m) around the base. The "big cypress" in Santa Maria del Tule, Mexico, has a base circumference of 112 feet (34 m). Either of these trees—and others in this family nearly as big—contains enough wood to build a dozen houses, with plenty left over to make roof shingles and fill all the houses with furniture! The seed of the *redwood*, in a cone an inch (2.5 cm) long, would fit on top of a pinhead!

The cypress family includes the many kinds of *juniper*. The beautiful *arborvitae*, often used as hedges, also belongs to this family. The *red cedar* also is a cypress.

The *yews* are another conifer family. Soldiers of William the Conqueror's time knew that wood from the *English yew* made the best bows. Other species of yew grow as small trees or shrubs with handsome needles. The *Canada yew* grows as shrubbery in the United States.

The *podocarps* are a strange conifer family. Most grow in remote places in the Southern Hemisphere. Australia has a *blackpine* in this family, and New Zealand a brown timber which the Maori called *"miro-miro."* Some podocarps would hardly be recognized as conifers—except that they produce cones. The tiniest conifer of all is a podocarp—the New Zealand

Female
Male

Lawson cypress

Noble fir

Grand fir

One of Connecticut's nicknames is Nutmeg State. This name comes from a story told about early Connecticut traders. People say that they made wooden nutmegs and sold them as real ones: this shows how valuable nutmegs once were.

pygmy pine. It grows cones when three inches (7.6 cm) tall.

The *phylloclads* of Tasmania, New Zealand, and the South Pacific islands shed their tiny leaves. They are one exception to the general rule that a conifer is an evergreen and needle-leaved.

ALSO READ: EVERGREEN TREE, FOREST FIRE, FORESTRY, LUMBER AND LUMBERING, PAPER, TREE.

CONJUNCTION see PARTS OF SPEECH.

CONNECTICUT In area, Connecticut is a very small state. Only Delaware and Rhode Island are smaller. But in its contributions to the United States, Connecticut is very large indeed.

Nautilus, the world's first atomic-powered submarine—and many other submarines, too—was built in the huge shipyard at Groton. Until about 100 years ago, Connecticut's shipbuilders turned out sturdy sailing ships and whalers. Connecticut today is a leading manufacturing state—not only of submarines, but of helicopters, airplane engines, machine tools, and ball and roller bearings. Other

▲ *Connecticut has beautiful rural and urban areas. Constitution Plaza is a spacious shopping and business center in Hartford.*

important goods made in the state are electrical products such as switches, outlets, and appliances; hardware such as nuts, bolts, valves, and pipes; cutlery and silverware; clocks and watches; pins, needles, and thread; clothing; firearms; chemicals; plastics and rubber goods; optical instruments; and even brooms. Without the factories of Connecticut, you might well have to do without something you take for granted.

The northeastern region of the United States is called New England. Connecticut is the southernmost New England state. All this manufacturing would be a surprise to a Connecticut Yankee who lived 150 years ago. (A Yankee is a New Englander.) Until the 1850's, almost all the people of Connecticut were farmers. But in 50 years, the scene in the state changed from one of quiet farms to one of busy factories. You will see how all of this came to happen after you read about the area and the people of this state.

The Land Connecticut is bordered on the west by New York State, on the north by Massachusetts, and on the east by Rhode Island. The southern side, however, is coastline, where

▶ *The State Capitol building in Hartford, Connecticut.*

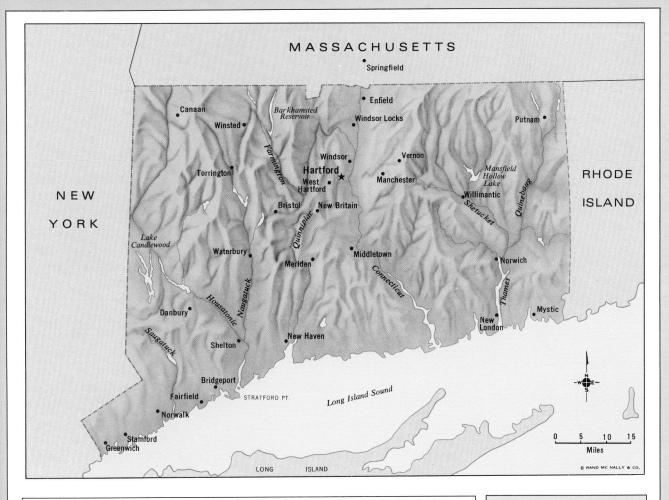

MASSACHUSETTS

Springfield

Canaan
Winsted
Barkhamsted Reservoir
Enfield
Windsor Locks
Putnam

NEW YORK

Torrington
Farmington
Windsor
Hartford
West Hartford
Vernon
Manchester
Mansfield Hollow Lake
Willimantic

RHODE ISLAND

Bristol
New Britain
Quinnipiac
Shetucket
Quinebaug

Lake Candlewood

Waterbury
Meriden
Middletown
Connecticut
Norwich

Housatonic
Naugatuck

Danbury
New Haven
Thames
New London
Mystic

Shelton

Saugatuck

Bridgeport
Fairfield
STRATFORD PT.
Long Island Sound

Norwalk

Stamford
Greenwich

LONG ISLAND

0 5 10 15
Miles

© RAND MC NALLY & CO.

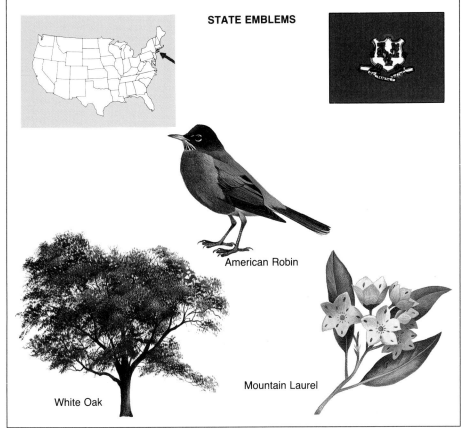

STATE EMBLEMS

American Robin

White Oak

Mountain Laurel

CONNECTICUT

Capital: Hartford (136,000 people).

Area: 5,009 square miles (12,592 sq. km).

Rank: 48th

Population: 3,250,000 Rank: 28th

Statehood: January 9, 1788 (Fifth of the 13 original states to ratify the Constitution)

Principal river: Connecticut 407 miles (655 km)

Highest Point: Mount Frissell 2,380 feet (725 m)

Largest City: Bridgeport (142,000 people)

Motto: Qui Transtulit Sustinet ("He who transplanted still sustains")

Song: "Yankee Doodle"

Famous People: Ethan Allen, P.T. Barnum, Katharine Hepburn Harriet Beecher Stowe

▲ *There are many attractive buildings in Connecticut like this white, wood-framed house.*

the waves of Long Island Sound splash the shore. Long Island Sound is an arm of the Atlantic Ocean. It lies between the mainland of Connecticut and Long Island, part of New York State.

The southwest corner of Connecticut lies very close to New York City. Highways and railroads link the busy city of Bridgeport and the university town of New Haven with New York. Thousands of people who work in New York City live in Connecticut. They travel (*commute*) to work each day by car or by train.

The Connecticut River, which is 407 miles (656 km) long, flows south through the center of the state into Long Island Sound. Small ships can sail up the river as far as Hartford. Farther north, at Windsor Locks, water tumbling from one level to another provides power, and the broad river valley is good for farming.

Seventy percent of Connecticut is forested. Its hills are smooth and green. The state has quiet towns, many with shaded "greens" and white, high-steepled churches. Connecticut also has many lakes. Winters are cold, but not too cold. Summers are hot, but not too hot. The state is poor in most natural resources, but stone, sand, and gravel are found in abundance.

History Several tribes of Algonkian-speaking Indians lived in Connecticut. One was the Mohegan, a branch of the Pequot tribe. *Quonecktacut* was the Algonkian name for the river. It meant "beside the long tidal river." Early settlers—*immigrants*—turned the word into "Connecticut" and called both the river and the land by this name.

A Dutch sea captain, Adriaen Block, discovered the Connecticut River in 1614. The Dutch set up a fort and trading post in Connecticut, but they never settled there permanently. English colonists, however, came from Massachusetts and founded the towns of Saybrook, Wethersfield, and New Haven. The English made the land their own. They defeated the Pequot Indians in a short, bloody war. They then drew up a plan of government believed to be the first formal constitution ever written by a self-governing people. Connecticut was a British colony until 1776. In that year it became one of the 13 original states of the United States of America.

Also in 1776, David Bushnell of Connecticut built a one-man submarine. He named it the *American Turtle*. His craft was the first submarine ever used in the war. However, it was never successful in sinking British warships because it was not easily maneuvered.

Manufacturing in Connecticut Up to the time of the American Revolution, nearly all manufacturing had been done by hand. But people now began to invent machines for manufacturing goods. England led the world in this work, but New England was not far behind.

Eli Whitney did much for the new manufacturing. This inventor was born in Massachusetts, but he lived and worked in Connecticut. His first invention was the cotton gin, a machine that removed the seeds from raw cotton. He built a factory for making cotton gins near New Haven, Connecticut.

Whitney set up a factory for making guns for the U.S. Army in 1798. Firearms had always been made slowly, one at a time. Only skilled gunsmiths, using hand tools, could make them. But Whitney invented machines that could manufacture all the parts of guns, and workers did not have to be highly skilled to use his machines. And his machines produced *interchangeable* parts for his guns, too. If a part broke, it could be easily, quickly, and cheaply replaced. Before Whitney's machines, a handmade part from one gun usually did not work in another gun of the same type.

Simeon North of Connecticut invented machines to make parts for pistols, and other Connecticut inventors did the same thing for making the parts of clocks. Soon even factory machinery could be made by machines, so factory machinery was produced faster and more cheaply. These advances made it easier to start factories, and manufacturing became the leading business in Connecticut.

Manufacturing helped spur the growth of cities throughout the state. Many persons left their farms and moved to cities to work in factories, where they could earn a better living. Factory jobs attracted many persons from other states and countries to settle in Connecticut. Today, the state has many small cities and more people for its size than almost any other state.

Insurance is also an important business in Connecticut. Hartford, the capital, is one of the world's biggest insurance centers, with the headquarters of about 50 major insurance companies located there.

Tourism is a thriving business in Connecticut. The Long Island Sound shoreline is a popular resort area. Tourists are also attracted to Mystic Seaport and Marinelife Aquarium, Yale University's Art Gallery and Peabody Museum, and the Mark Twain and Harriet Beecher Stowe homes. The state has many fine colonial buildings. Agriculture is still part of Connecticut's economy, too. Poultry, eggs, fruit, and shade-grown tobacco are the main items. The state's broadleaf tobacco is used as the wrapper on cigars; it is world-famous.

ALSO READ: STATE; WHITNEY, ELI.

CONQUISTADOR "This land is a whole new world," Amerigo Vespucci wrote of the Americas in the early 1500's. European explorers were soon challenged by the new territory. It would belong to the country whose flag flew over it. Spanish conquistadors (conquerors) claimed much of the land for Spain.

The conquistadors were explorers sent out by Spain to claim and govern territory in the New World. Many of these explorers heard stories of treasure and of cities built of gold. Only Indian tribes stood between them and fortune.

Spanish conquests of the Indians were bloody and violent. Their steel armor, gunpowder, and horses struck terror in the natives. In many cases, a few hundred Spanish soldiers overthrew ancient empires numbering tens of thousands of warriors. In Mexico, Hernando Cortés conquered the powerful Aztec kingdom of Montezuma. Francisco Pizarro, with fewer than 200 men, brutally gained control of the vast Inca empire of South America.

Some conquistadors failed to find wealth but made very important explorations. Vasco Núñez de Balboa crossed Panama and discovered the Pacific Ocean. Juan Ponce de León marched into Florida. Francisco Coronado and Hernando de Soto searched tirelessly for the fabled Seven Cities of Cibola. They found only Indian villages, but they were the first Europeans to explore what is

▲ *A Spanish helmet, sword, and crossbow of the 1500's. The conquistadors defeated the American Indians because of their superior armory.*

▲ *The* conquistadors, *as the Spaniards who conquered South and Central America and the West Indies are known, soon needed men to work on the land and in the mines. Here a group of conquistadors, on the left, watch slaves brought from Africa at work in the silver mines of Haiti.*

now the southwestern United States. Jiminez de Quesada and Francisco Orellana combed the Andes and the Amazon for El Dorado, the Spanish name for an Indian king (and for his country). El Dorado was so rich—stories said—that he took a bath in gold dust each year at a special festival. It is not surprising that the king was never found.

The ruthless and daring conquistadors destroyed entire civilizations in their quest for fame, gold and power. They carried the Spanish language, laws, and religion to two continents. They also took rich treasures back to Spain.

ALSO READ: AZTEC INDIANS; BALBOA, VASCO NÚÑEZ DE; CIBOLA, SEVEN CITIES OF; CORONADO, FRANCISCO; CORTÉS, HERNANDO; DE SOTO, HERNANDO; EL DORADO; INCA; PIZARRO, FRANCISCO; PONCE DE LEÓN, JUAN; SOUTH AMERICA.

CONRAD, JOSEPH (1857–1924) Joseph Conrad is considered one of the greatest English novelists. His writings, marked by detailed descriptions, are realistic and romantic.

He was born of Polish parents in what was then Russian Poland (now the Ukraine). His original name was

▼ *Joseph Conrad, the Polish-born author of great tales about the sea and distant lands.*

Teodor Josef Konrad Watecz Korzeniowski. At age 17 he left Poland to begin 20 years of seafaring life, serving first in the French and then in the British merchant marine. He learned English and worked his way from seaman to captain in the British Merchant Navy. The year he became captain, 1884, he also became a British citizen and changed his name to Joseph Conrad.

In 1894, Conrad retired from the sea, married, settled down in England, and began writing. He could then speak and write English almost as if he had used it all his life. His first novel, *Almayer's Folly*, was published in 1895.

Almost all of Conrad's tales were based on the experiences that he had had at sea, but his stories are about problems that many people must face. He wrote about the many people he had met and the lands he had visited—Africa, the South Seas, and the East Indies. Some of his most famous books are *Nostromo*, *An Outcast of the Islands*, *Lord Jim*, *Chance*, *Under Western Eyes*, *Victory*, *The Arrow of Gold*, and *The Rover*. Conrad wrote many brilliant short stories, too. Perhaps his greatest short story is "Heart of Darkness," based on a voyage up the Congo River, in which the narrator learns about the evil in man's nature.

ALSO READ: LITERATURE, NOVEL, SHORT STORY.

CONSERVATION "We treat our Earth as though we had a spare," someone once said. Human beings have used soil, water, plants, animals, and minerals for nearly everything they make. Often we have wasted and destroyed these natural resources. *Conservation* means protecting resources and using them wisely. It also means preserving areas of natural beauty so that they can be used for recreation.

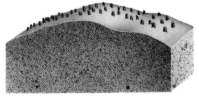

People did not bother much about conservation when North America was first settled. The continent was a land of great natural wealth. It had vast forests, sparkling lakes and rivers, fertile soil, plentiful minerals such as coal and oil, and animals of all kinds. The early colonists thought that they would always have these resources because they were so plentiful. They were not careful about using them. When they wanted to clear land for farming, for example, they often burned down entire forests. This not only destroyed trees and killed many animals, but damaged the soil as well. Trees and plants help to hold soil in place. When a forest is destroyed, rain can wash away the topsoil. This washing away, or *erosion*, spoils land for farming. The practice of one-crop farming in North America also harmed the soil. Many farms in the South, for instance, grew only tobacco, or only cotton. The plants used up certain minerals in the soil, and it quickly became worn out and useless. Nowadays people avoid this by using the system of *crop rotation*, whereby different crops are grown each year so that the soil is not depleted.

Americans have done great harm to our wildlife, too. Millions of bison once roamed the Great Plains. Before the white man came to North America, the Indians hunted bison. They killed only as many animals as they needed for food and clothing. Many white hunters carelessly shot them for sport, leaving the carcasses to rot on the prairie. In the 1880's, only 550 bison could be found!

Another example of what harm humans can do to wildlife is the story of the bald eagle. This courageous and powerful bird was chosen by Congress in 1782 as the official symbol of the United States. At the time, there were many bald eagles in North America. But hunters and farmers over the years killed nearly all of them because they endangered their livestock. The bald eagle is nearly extinct today. Pollution has also harmed these birds. Dumping sewage, garbage, and industrial wastes into our lakes and rivers has polluted the water. The pollution has poisoned the fish that live in the water. When the eagles feed on the fish, they are slowly poisoned, too.

Theodore Roosevelt, as President early this century, began programs to save the country's natural resources. He set aside millions of acres of forest lands. Gifford Pinchot became head of the newly created Forestry Service. The Bureau of Mines was established to find new mineral resources and better methods of mining. The U.S. Department of Agriculture began to teach farmers how to prevent erosion and how to restore worn-out soil through the use of fertilizers and efficient farming. During the Great Depression of the 1930's, the Civilian Conservation Corps was set up. It provided jobs in conservation for young men in national forests and parks across the country. Millions of seedlings planted by the CCC have grown up into beautiful forests.

▲ *Conservationists are concerned about soil erosion. This often happens when people clear away forests to make land for growing crops. At first the soil is fertile (top), but soon it is worn away by wind and weather (middle and bottom).*

▼ *Smoke from chimney stacks is a great foe of nature. Many countries have conservation measures to control it.*

▼ *Oil spilled from ships kills untold millions of seabirds and fish every year. This guillemot is covered in oil. It cannot fly. If it tries to pick off the oil with its beak it swallows the sticky poison. It will die unless bird-lovers clean it with detergent.*

▲ *One of the boats owned by Greenpeace, the international conservation group. It sends these boats out to try to stop people killing whales or spilling poisonous wastes (e.g., nuclear wastes) at sea. The crews risk their lives to help make this world a better place.*

The conservation of our environment and its resources is now one of the greatest concerns of mankind. All over the world governments have passed conservation laws. They have set up national parks and started programs to correct the damage that has already been done. There are also private organizations which work to "save the world".

Conservationists tackle many different problems. For example, in Brazil they must stop the destruction of the rainforests. They have to deal with disasters such as the oil spills. In 1989, the *Exxon Valdez* supertanker spilled 11 million gallons of crude oil into the fertile waters off Alaska. During the Gulf War, Saddam Hussein deliberately poured millions of gallons of oil into the sea.

Conservation is not only about big, international problems however. You can play a part too. For example, you can help by using a little less water when you shower, wash dishes, or brush your teeth. You can save electricity by turning off your lights, radios, and other appliances when they are not being used. By recycling bottles, cans, and newspapers, you help to conserve space in your town landfill (dump). Never throw trash on the street. When you go on a picnic or camp out, always clean up before you leave. Be especially careful with

▲ *Terraced rice paddies in the Philippines. Here is a sensible use of nature's resources.*

matches and campfires because forest fires cause a great deal of damage. Trees can be harmed by carving, too, so never carve the bark of a living tree.

ALSO READ: AIR POLLUTION; ECOLOGY; EROSION; FLOOD; FOREST FIRE; IRRIGATION; MINES AND MINING; NATIONAL FOREST; NATIONAL PARK; POLLUTION; ROOSEVELT, THEODORE; SOIL; WATER POLLUTION; WATER SUPPLY.

▼ *John Constable's painting,* The Haywain, *created a sensation when first shown. See how he has transformed a normal country scene into a beautiful vision.*

CONSTABLE, JOHN (1776–1837)

"I never saw an ugly thing in my life, for let the form of an object be what it will—light, shade, and perspective will make it beautiful." So said John Constable, the famous English artist. His painting, *The Haywain*, shown here, proves what he says. A hay wagon crossing a stream could be an ordinary scene. But he has made it beautiful with the use of light in a glorious sky and by flashes of light and patches of shade in the water. He has used shade beautifully in the trees, and his use of perspective and balance draws you into the scene.

Constable was born in East Bergholt, England. He was the second son of a miller. He painted from his own experience, but he depended on his rich imagination to make ordinary scenes interesting and beautiful. He knew farmers' carts, because he had played in them as a little boy. He had seen the barge horses on the Stour River wearing scarlet fringes on their collars, such as those that draw your eye into the picture. Young John's parents had expected him to join his father in the milling business, but John loved drawing and painting. At age 24 he went away to London to study at the Royal Academy schools. He had a long, slow start. He was so poor that he had to wait five years to marry Maria Bicknell, the love of his life. He kept on working, and the turning point in his career actually came with the painting shown here. *The Haywain* created a great sensation in 1824, when exhibited in France. Constable influenced French painters some years before the English realized he was a great artist. His ideas of changing light and shade were taken up 40 years after his death by the Impressionists.

ALSO READ: IMPRESSIONISM.

CONSTANTINE see ROMAN EMPIRE.

CONSTELLATION For many people, the sky is a map of fairy tales and old legends. "Animals" hide among the stars. People and monsters from ancient myths "live" forever in the nighttime heavens. The stars seem to form patterns in the sky. A constellation is a group of stars that make a shape or picture.

Since earliest times, people have looked at the stars and found familiar patterns. One group of stars seems to look like a four-legged animal. Another group forms the shape of a royal throne. Look north and see if you can find the seven stars that some people call the Big Dipper, part of the constellation called the Great Bear. Orion is the mighty Hunter, placed in the sky by Artemis, goddess of hunting, who loved him. Pegasus is the Winged Horse of the hero Perseus, who also shines in the sky. The ancient Chinese thought that the constellation we call Pisces, the Fishes, was evil and caused great trouble on Earth.

Every constellation has its own legend. In ancient times, when people saw a group of stars in the shape of a horse, a bear, or a man, they wanted to know how such shapes got into the sky. So they made up stories to explain the shapes. Greek mythology tells about many constellations. The story of Orion actually tells how two constellations began.

The Greek god Zeus had twin children named Artemis and Apollo. Artemis was the goddess of hunting. She often traveled with Orion, a great hunter. This made Apollo jealous. One day Apollo tricked Artemis into shooting Orion. Her arrow killed him, and she was heartbroken. She changed Orion into stars. Another version is that Orion accidentally touched Artemis, and that she therefore summoned a huge scorpion to sting him to death. The constellation of the Scorpion is now on the far side of the sky from Orion.

Astronomers recognize 88 different constellations. Some can be seen only from the northern half of the world, others only from the southern half. The Little Dipper is such a constellation. The star at the end of the Little Dipper's handle is Polaris, the North Star. Polaris always seems to be almost exactly due north. Navigators in the Northern Hemisphere can use the North Star to find their way at night. The constellation Crux, the Southern Cross, is visible mainly from the Southern Hemisphere. (It can be seen just north of the equator, too.) It

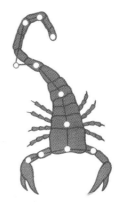

▲ *The ancients imagined that the constellations were like pictures in the night sky. The white dots here represent the stars of the constellation Scorpio, the scorpion. Would you have seen a picture of a scorpion when looking at this constellation?*

▼ *The Big Dipper is part of a constellation called the Great Bear. Go out one clear night and look north. You should see the Big Dipper very easily. Its two brightest stars (the "Pointers") seem to point toward Polaris, the North Star. Polaris is at the end of the Little Dipper's handle.*

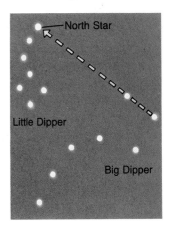

North Star

Little Dipper

Big Dipper

CONSTELLATION

Cancer, the Crab

Taurus, the Bull

1 Equuleus, Colt
2 Delphinus, Dolphin
3 Pegasus, Flying Horse
4 Pisces, Fishes
5 Cetus, Sea Monster
6 Aries, Ram
7 Triangulum, Triangle
8 Andromeda, Chained Maiden
9 Lacerta, Lizard
10 Cygnus, Swan
11 Sagitta, Arrow
12 Aquila, Eagle
13 Lyra, Lyre
14 Cepheus, King
15 Cassiopeia, Lady in Chair
16 Perseus, Champion
17 Camelopardus, Giraffe
18 Auriga, Charioteer
19 Taurus, Bull
20 Orion, Hunter

21 Lynx, Lynx
22 Polaris, Pole Star
23 Ursa Minor, Little Bear
24 Draco, Dragon
25 Hercules, Kneeling Giant
26 Ophiuchus, Serpent-Bearer
27 Serpens, Serpent
28 Corona Borealis, Northern Crown
29 Boötes, Herdsman
30 Ursa Major, Great Bear
31 Gemini, Twins
32 Cancer, Crab
33 Canis Minor, Little Dog
34 Hydra, Sea Serpent
35 Leo, Lion
36 Leo Minor, Little Lion
37 Canes Venatici, Hunting Dogs
38 Coma Berenices, Berenice's Hair
39 Virgo, Virgin

▲ *The constellations seen in the Northern Hemisphere. Those nearest the center of the circle can be seen every night of the year. You can see the others only in certain seasons.*

helps navigators in that part of the world.

Constellations have Latin names. Astronomers call the Little Dipper *Ursa Minor,* or "Little Bear." The Big Dipper is part of *Ursa Major,* or "Great Bear." Each star in a constellation also has a name, and Greek letters identify the stars according to brightness. The brightest star in the constellation *Pisces* (the Fishes) is Alpha Piscium. The next brightest star is Beta Piscium, and so on. The brightest star in our skies is Alpha Canis Majoris, better known as Sirius. It is in the constellation Canis Major ("Great Dog").

Constellations appear and disappear from our skies as the Earth travels around the sun. During the winter, the Northern Hemisphere faces Orion at night. But six months later, on the opposite side of Earth's orbit around the sun, the part of Earth that faces Orion is in the daylight. As Earth moves around the sun, the constellations rise and set a few minutes earlier and slightly lower in the sky each day. Some constellations (such as Orion) do not rise (come above the horizon) during nighttime for several months each year.

■ LEARN BY DOING

Next time you are out on a clear night, see if you can identify some of the constellations. The pictures on these pages will help you. You will have to use your imagination to recognize some of the shapes. Find the Big Dipper. What direction are you facing when you see it? What direction do you face when you look at it two months later? ■

Twelve of the constellations follow paths near the section of sky traveled by the planets. This band across the sky is called the *zodiac.* The star shapes inside the band are the *constellations of the zodiac.* The planets appear to move through the constellations. The exact positions of the planets and the zodiac constellations are slightly different every minute. These changes in position are the basis of astrology.

The stars in constellations look close together because they are very far from Earth, but most of the stars are even farther from each other than they are from Earth. The constellations have changed shape slightly since they were named thousands of years ago. After millions of years the shapes will be gone altogether, and new constellations will fill the sky in their place.

ALSO READ: ASTROLOGY, ASTRONOMY, MYTHOLOGY, NAVIGATION, STAR.

CONSTITUTION, UNITED STATES
Have you ever heard people in an argument speak of their "constitutional rights"? Or condemn the Supreme Court for ruling a law "unconstitutional"?

The Constitution is the basic law of the United States. Among the men who wrote it were Alexander Hamilton, James Madison, and Thomas Jefferson, helped by Benjamin Franklin. They were influenced by the political theories of their age and by their own political experience as citizens of colonies ruled by Britain. They all worked for the independence of the colonies before and during the American Revolution. These men believed that problems could be solved by reason. They had faith that society could be improved. They felt that progress should be expected.

The Constitution defines the Federal Government and describes the duties of its three main branches. The *Congress* has legislative power, with responsibility for making the laws of the country. The *President* has executive power to "preserve, protect, and defend the Constitution of the United States." The *Supreme Court* has judicial power, with authority to enforce the laws made by Congress. Each of

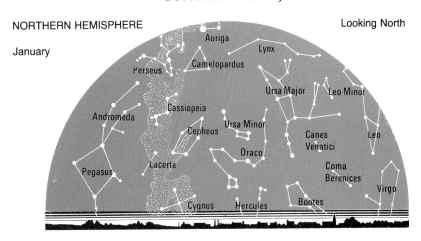

NORTHERN HEMISPHERE — January — Looking North

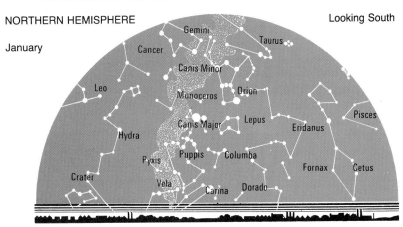

July

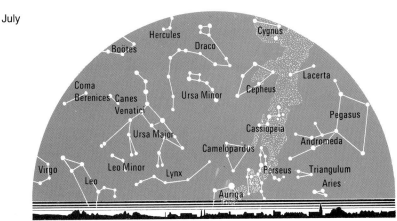

NORTHERN HEMISPHERE — January — Looking South

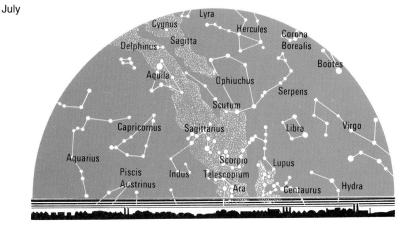

July

We the People of the United States, in order to form a more perfect Union, establish Justice, insure domestic Tranquility, provide for the common defence, promote the general Welfare, and secure the Blessings of Liberty to ourselves and our Posterity, do ordain and establish this Constitution for the United States of America.

Article I

Section 1. All legislative Powers herein granted shall be vested in a Congress of the United States, which shall consist of a Senate and House of Representatives.

Section 2. The House of Representatives shall be composed of Members chosen every second Year by the People of the several States, and the Electors in each State shall have Qualifications requisite for Electors of the most numerous Branch of the State Legislature.

▲ *The first few lines of the U.S. Constitution, one of the greatest documents ever written.*

The opening words of the United States Constitution are: "We, the people of the United States, in order to form a more perfect Union, establish justice, insure domestic tranquility, provide for the common defense, promote the general welfare, and secure the blessings of liberty to ourselves and our posterity, do ordain and establish this Constitution for the United States of America."

these branches checks and balances the power of the others.

The founding fathers did not want the government to have absolute power, as a king does. So they limited the powers of the central government and left some powers to the states.

In its first ten amendments (also called the *Bill of Rights*) the Constitution establishes the basic freedoms of Americans, such as freedom of speech, of the press, and of religion, and the freedom not to speak against oneself in court. The Bill of Rights is designed mainly to protect individual citizens against unlawful acts by their own government.

The Making of the Constitution
The Revolutionary War ended in 1781, and a peace treaty was signed with England in 1783. The 13 states, joined together loosely under the Articles of Confederation, soon began to squabble among themselves. Some states paid no attention to the laws and still openly opposed the rights of citizens. They disregarded jury trials, sentenced men to death without trials, closed down newspapers, and forcibly grabbed property. The leaders of the new country knew that a formal constitution must be written. But they probably did not know that they would create a document so effective and so timeless that it would function far into the 20th century and become a model for the governments of many other nations.

In May 1787, 55 delegates from 13 states gathered at Independence Hall in Philadelphia. They chose George Washington as president of the *Con-stitutional Convention*. The oldest of the delegates was 81-year-old Benjamin Franklin. James Madison took careful notes during the convention. His is the chief record we have of the delegates' debates and decisions.

The delegates to the Constitutional Convention soon divided into two groups. The "nationalists" wanted a strong central government with the power to declare war and make treaties, the power to trade with foreign nations, and the power to tax citizens. The "states'-righters" mistrusted strong national control and wished to make sure the rights of the states were respected. After a long summer of debate, the convention compromised. The "states'-righters" would have the protection they wanted in the establishment of a Senate composed of two representatives from each state, no matter how large or small in population. A larger legislative body, the House of Representatives, would also represent the people by states, but according to population. Together, these assemblies made up the United States Congress. A Supreme Court also was established. The President would be elected by the people, rather than born to the job like a king, and Congress could remove the President from office if necessary.

The delegates signed the Constitution of the United States of America on September 17, 1787. Each state then approved, or *ratified*, the Constitution.

Changing the Constitution On December 15, 1791, ten *amendments* (changes or additions) to the Constitution went into effect. These amendments, called the Bill of Rights, name and guarantee the rights of every citizen under the law. Other amendments were added as the United States grew. By 1986, there were 26 amendments.

Amendments may be made in two ways, according to the Constitution itself. A Constitutional Convention of delegates from every state may propose an amendment, but this method has been used only one time. A proposed amendment, called a *resolution,* may come from Congress. The resolution becomes law if two-thirds of the members of each house vote in favor of it, and if three-fourths of the state legislatures then ratify the amendment. The amendment may be ratified by special conventions in three-fourths of the states in place of legislative approval, but this has happened only once.

The Supreme Court is called the "guardian of the Constitution." Its duty is to interpret the laws and rights given in the Constitution or passed by Congress and signed by the President. The Supreme Court can rule a state law "unconstitutional," thus canceling it. The court can also declare an act of Congress illegal if the court does not think the act agrees with the meaning of the Constitution. This is known as the "power of judicial review."

ALSO READ: AMERICAN REVOLUTION; ARTICLES OF CONFEDERATION; BILL OF RIGHTS; CONGRESS, UNITED STATES; PRESIDENCY; SUPREME COURT; UNITED STATES GOVERNMENT.

CONSTRUCTION Everyone likes to watch a building being built. In cities, construction companies build fences around construction projects so that no one will be hurt. But watching the workers is so popular that most fences have windows in them, so that "sidewalk superintendents" can keep an eye on the progress of the work.

You can probably think of many kinds of buildings. Some, such as sports arenas and skyscrapers, are huge. Others, such as tool sheds and tree houses, are very small. But all buildings can be divided into a very few types, depending on their function, their structure, and the materials from which they are built.

Another word for *function* is *purpose.* Two important building functions are to protect people from the weather and to provide space for working and living. Some buildings, such as theaters, schools, libraries, and churches, have special functions. Some buildings have more than one function. Can you name the purposes of the buildings in a zoo? The function of a building has a lot to do with the size it will be and the materials it will be built from. Would you build a house for your family the same way that you would build an apartment house for many families? Would you build a school the same way as the house or the apartment building?

The *structure* of a building includes the parts of the building and the way they are put together. If a building is

A building permit gives a person the legal right to build a structure. It also gives community officials the right to inspect the structure to make sure that the builder has not violated the building code (**regulations**).

▼ *Methods of construction have changed greatly over the centuries, but the principles are still the same. Today, when building a house, people like the men below use smaller, lighter lumber, placed closer together, and nails, instead of the slower method of joinery and doweling.*

▲ *The famous Flatiron Building in New York was one of the first skyscrapers. It is 20 stories tall and was completed in 1902.*

▼ *Building skyscrapers is not easy. First, holes have to be dug in the ground and filled with concrete so that the skyscraper has solid foundations. Then, a high frame is built up from these foundations. Last, walls and floors are fixed to this frame.*

to be a large auditorium, its construction must allow for a broad, high room, to hold many people and to look spacious. Any kind of structure must be planned carefully, so that it does not conflict with the building's function. If a building cannot support itself and the weight of all the people and things to be put in it, its structure is poor. If a museum is to show airplanes, then it must have a door wide enough to get the planes into the building and hallways wide enough for the planes to be moved from one room to another.

Building Materials Materials are the basis of all buildings. There are three major kinds of materials. (1) Structural materials support the building, give it shape, form its protective "shell," and divide it into rooms. (2) Other materials protect the construction from weather or fire, or improve its appearance. (3) Different kinds of equipment supply heat, ventilation, light, and water.

The most important structural materials are wood, clay, stone, concrete, and steel. Each has special advantages and disadvantages. One or more of these materials is selected for a specific building depending on the advantages and disadvantages.

WOOD. Wood is an ancient building material, probably one of the first structural materials ever used. It is inexpensive, and it is easy to cut, shape, and fasten. Wood has three features that make it useful in construction. It does not break easily when it is bent—as do brick and stone. Wood is very strong—it can withstand a heavy load that presses down on it. And it's pliable—if a force bends the pieces of a wooden structure, the pieces "unbend" when the force is taken away. But wood must be protected by paint or other means. Unprotected wood can be eaten by insects, rotted by fungi, or ruined by wind and rain.

CLAY. Clay is used to make brick and tile. A wall of bricks, joined together by *mortar*, a kind of cement, can withstand very heavy weights. But such a wall is brittle—it cannot withstand forces that make it bend, unless it is very thick. Brick is cheap to make and easy to work with.

STONE. Stone is very strong and lasts a long time. It is an excellent building material, but it is expensive and difficult to handle. Stone must be cut from solid rock in a quarry. Many kinds of stone are shaped into blocks, trimmed to the desired size, and smoothed in order to fit tightly against other stones. Stone blocks are too heavy to move by hand, and a crane must be used to raise them into place. A stone wall must also be thick, or a strong bending force will make it collapse.

STEEL. Steel is a wonderful building material. It lasts nearly as long as stone, is very strong, and, like wood, has some pliability. Steel can be formed into any shape. However, it must be painted or it will rust. Steel is used to form the superstructure, or skeleton, of modern skyscrapers.

CONCRETE. Concrete is a mixture of cement, sand, and gravel that dries into a rocklike mass. Many ancient peoples used concrete to "glue" stones together. The Assyrians were probably the first people to do this, about 6,000 years ago. Modern engineers have found many uses for this substance. Along with steel, concrete is the most widely used structural material. Unlike stone, concrete does not have to be cut into blocks and fastened together. Wet concrete can be poured into wooden molds. When the concrete dries, it forms a solid structure the shape of the mold.

Concrete by itself withstands very great forces that push down on it. Like stone or brick, concrete is brittle. But *reinforced* concrete—concrete that has steel rods in it—takes on the pliability of steel. Reinforced concrete can withstand bending and stretching forces.

OTHER MATERIALS. Few buildings contain only structural parts. Most buildings have glass windows to let in light and let the people inside look out (or let the people outside look in). Buildings are usually insulated, to help keep the inside cool in summer and warm in winter. And most buildings have complicated heating, cooling, lighting, plumbing, and electrical systems. These systems use up miles of metal, plastic, and wood. Paint and wallpaper are also used in almost every building to decorate and protect the structural materials.

Building a Skyscraper Constructing a skyscraper or any other large building takes a long time. Many people with many different kinds of training take part. An architect and several different kinds of engineers design the building and the heating, plumbing, and other systems that any building includes. When all the plans and the hundreds of drawings are complete, the builder goes to work.

If a tall building were built on soft soil, the building would sink. So the building company's first job is to excavate (dig) a hole for the basements and to lay the foundation—the building supports. Bulldozers, steam shovels, and trucks appear at the building site. Following carefully planned marks, they dig a deep hole. Some skyscrapers have five or even more basements! Then, when the bottom of the hole is smoothed out, special machines lay the foundation. This can be done in two ways. A pile-driver, a kind of giant motorized hammer, can pound long steel poles, called *piles*, down through the soft soil to the bedrock beneath it. A newer, stronger method is to use a special digging machine that digs narrow holes down through the soil to the rock. Workers then pour concrete into the holes. The concrete hardens into very strong supports called *caissons*.

When the foundation is complete,

In Hong Kong, over half the 5 million people live above the tenth floor.

▼ *Constructing bridges involves many problems. Here the slim concrete piers that will support a new beam bridge over an alpine gorge are being prepared to receive the steel spans.*

▲ *On this construction site, the builders are creating the foundations and framework for a building using reinforced concrete piles.*

The world's tallest building, the Sears Tower in Chicago, Illinois is 1,454 feet (443 m) high and has 110 stories.

workers begin to erect the frame, the steel skeleton that supports the weight of the building. Cranes move each piece of steel into place, and workers fasten the pieces together. Riveting and welding were once used to join steel pieces, but bolts are quicker and easier to work with.

Some buildings have concrete frames. To erect such a frame, workers build wooden forms, put steel rods into them, and fill them with concrete. When the concrete sets, or hardens, the workers remove the wooden forms, and the frame is ready.

The next step is to construct the floors and the roof. Workers build a temporary wooden floor, then pour reinforced concrete onto it. When the concrete sets, the wooden floor is removed. Other workers then begin to put up the outside walls. The frame holds the weight of the building. The walls simply form a kind of shell that surrounds the building. Many skyscrapers have walls made mostly of glass. Sometimes thin stone, metal, or plastic slabs are used. The wall is hung on the frame in sections, much as curtains are hung on a window frame. The walls of frame buildings are called *curtain walls*.

The shell of the building is complete when the walls are up. But much work must still be done. Work-

ers install partitions that divide each floor into rooms. If it is part of the plan, these walls will be plastered. Still other workers put in the complicated systems that carry heat, water, and electric power all through the building. The elevators must be installed. The ceilings will probably be soundproofed and the floors covered with tile. Decorators and painters take over, and when they are through, the building is ready for use.

Building a House   Houses today are usually built in much the same way as they were hundreds of years ago, before construction machines were invented. A house does not need to stand on piles—it is not that heavy. And its frame does not have to be steel or concrete. It can be wood, which is much easier to work with. In fact, houses or other small buildings need not have frames at all. Special walls, called *bearing walls*, may replace the frame and support the weight of the building. A building may have bearing walls if its walls are brick, stone, or concrete. The lightness of the floors and roofs they support make them practical for houses. Before steel framing, some tall buildings had bearing walls more than 6 feet (1.8 m) thick.

One reason that houses cost so much money is that they are often built using slow, old-fashioned methods. Two new construction methods have come into use. *Prefabricated* and *modular construction* can provide good houses at lower cost. "Prefabricated" means "made ahead of time." The walls and roof of a prefabricated house are built in sections in a factory. Doors, windows, and electrical wiring are built into the sections. All the parts are loaded on a truck and driven to the place where the house is wanted. Workers connect the sections to a basement that is built before the sections arrive, attach the sections to one another, connect the house to gas, water, and electrical lines, and put on

CONTAGIOUS DISEASES

the roof. People may move into their house in only a few days.

Modular construction is also very quick and easy. Modules are sections that can easily be connected to one another. One module might be a living room, another might be a dining room and kitchen, and other modules might be bedrooms, recreation rooms, and garages. Modules are built in a factory, then hooked together where the house will stand. The people who buy a modular house can choose how many rooms they want and the arrangement of the rooms. A prefabricated house must be built exactly as it was designed. Both of these construction techniques will become more and more important because they offer good houses quickly at a low price.

ALSO READ: ARCHITECTURE, BUILDING MATERIAL, CAISSON, CARPENTRY, CONCRETE, EMPIRE STATE BUILDING, HOUSE, QUARRYING, STREETS AND ROADS, WOOD.

CONSUMER PROTECTION see SELLING.

CONTAGIOUS DISEASES Diseases that spread easily by close contact between one person and another are known as contagious diseases. An ordinary cold is a familiar example of such a disease. When one person gets a cold, people who are in close contact with him or her—at home, at school, or on public transportation—are also very likely to catch it. Cold germs travel on the droplets of moisture expelled when one sneezes and by making hand contact with someone having a cold.

The term "contagious" is used to set apart these diseases from noncontagious diseases. Noncontagious diseases are caused by agents that do not spread readily from one individual to another. Noncontagious diseases are

caused, for example, by organisms present in contaminated (impure) food or water, or as a result of being bitten by a disease-carrying insect or animal. To get malaria, a person must be bitten by a mosquito carrying the organism that causes this disease. Or a malaria organism must be directly passed on into the person's bloodstream by some other means. A person who is merely in contact with someone who has malaria will not get the disease because it is not contagious.

Another example of a noncontagious sickness is hay fever. Only a person sensitive to certain plant pollens in the air can get the runny nose and "stuffed head" feeling of hay fever. Hay fever will not spread to those who are near a hay-fever sufferer.

Mumps, measles, chicken pox, and other diseases people get when they are children are contagious. These usually happen when children first go to school or come together in groups in pre-school programs. Many contagious diseases can be prevented by vaccination. A good example is the successful prevention of smallpox, a highly contagious disease. It has been almost completely eliminated because of world-wide vaccination of children and adults. The last major outbreak of smallpox in the United States was in 1949, in the Rio Grande Valley on the Mexican Border.

Very occasionally a new contagious disease, such as *AIDS*, appears. Scientists have to study the disease and the way in which it is transmitted. Then they can try to develop a vaccine to eliminate it.

The World Health Organization (WHO), a United Nations agency, has extended the benefits of smallpox vaccination to underdeveloped countries throughout the world. In 1978, the WHO reported that the last known case of naturally occurring smallpox had been isolated in Somalia the previous year. Since then, some health

▲ *You can help stop any contagious disease you might have from spreading by using a handkerchief whenever you have to cough or sneeze.*

▲ *Contagious diseases can spread through people having germs on their hands while preparing food. So wash your hands first!*

▲ *If you are ill, your saliva (spit) probably contains a lot of harmful germs. Sharing a piece of food or a drink with a friend is always a bad idea.*

There are several points around the world where the continents nearly touch. Asia is 56 miles (90 km) away from America at the Bering Strait, which separates the Pacific and Arctic oceans. Europe and Africa are only 8 miles (13 km) apart at the Strait of Gibraltar. Europe is less than half a mile from Asia at the Bosporus strait in Turkey, and a bridge crosses the divide.

officials have declared the disease to be "conquered" or wiped out entirely. Since 1978 the only known cases of smallpox have arisen through accidents happening in research laboratories.

Contagious diseases such as diphtheria sometimes break out, however. But public health authorities and doctors make every effort to keep the disease from spreading. They may place infected people in *quarantine* (isolation) to keep them from passing on their diseases. People may be quarantined if they have been exposed to a person who has a contagious disease. The quarantine ends when the exposed person develops the disease or when so long a time has passed that it is clear that the person will not catch the disease. Public health regulations that quarantine people for certain diseases vary from state to state.

Steps to prevent spread of contagious diseases may be taken at a family or hospital level or may be applied internationally. Travelers who come from one country where serious contagious diseases have recently broken out have to be vaccinated before they can enter another country. Some travelers are even quarantined, in case they are carrying a disease.

In the United States, the Center for Disease Control helps keep an eye on contagious diseases and aids local authorities in preventing the spread of these diseases. The center sends experts into certain areas to track down sources of disease, to vaccinate as many people as possible, to educate them in ways of preventing disease, and to take other measures to keep contagious disease under control.

ALSO READ: CHILDHOOD DISEASES, DISEASE, FEVER, HEALTH, IMMUNITY, PUBLIC HEALTH.

CONTINENT The largest land areas of the Earth are called continents. They are nearly or completely surrounded by oceans. The continents take up less than one-quarter of the Earth's surface, but they total nine-tenths of the land area. (About seven-tenths of the Earth's surface is covered by water.) There are seven continents—Africa, Antarctica, Asia, Australia, Europe, North America, and South America.

Continents are vast masses of light rock floating on the heavier rock that makes up most of the Earth's crust. A continent is much longer and wider than it is deep. It is usually higher inland than near the edges. The highest points are called *continental divides*.

Scientists now believe that all the continents were one huge continent about 170 million years ago. This "supercontinent," called *Pangaea*, slowly broke up, and its pieces drifted apart and are still moving. Before Pangaea formed, about 280 million years ago, there were several continents, like today, but those continents were quite unlike the ones we now know.

Continental Shelves In most places, the edges of the continents slope gently downward into the oceans before making a sharper drop

Continent	Area	Highest Point	Lowest Point
Africa	11,850,000 square miles (30,691,350 sq. km)	Kilimanjaro, Tanzania, 19,565 feet (5,963 m)	Qattara Depression, Egypt, 440 feet (134 m) below sea level
Antarctica	5,500,000 square miles (14,245,000 sq. km)	Vinson Massif, 16,864 feet (5,140 m)	sea level
Asia	17,139,445 square miles (44,391,162 sq. km)	Mount Everest, Nepal-Tibet, 29,028 feet (8,848 m)	Dead Sea, Israel-Jordan, 1,296 feet (395 m) below sea level
Australia	2,974,600 square miles (7,704,179 sq. km)	Mount Kosciusko New South Wales, 7,316 feet (2,230 m)	Lake Eyre, South Australia, 36 feet (11 m) below sea level
Europe	4,000,000 square miles (10,400,000 sq. km)	Mount Elbrus, Soviet Union, 18,481 feet (5,633 m)	Caspian Sea, Soviet Union, 92 feet (27 m) below sea level
North America	9,124,000 square miles (23,631,050 sq. km)	Mount McKinley, Alaska, 20,320 feet (6,194 m)	Death Valley, California, 280 feet (85 m) below sea level
South America	6,894,000 square miles (17,855,380 sq. km)	Aconcagua, Argentina, 22,834 feet (6,960 m)	Salina Grande, Argentina, 131 feet (40 m) below sea level

to the ocean floor. The part of a continent under the ocean is called a *continental shelf*. The usual width of a continental shelf is about 40 miles (64 km), but there are many exceptions. The shelf is completely missing along the western coast of South America. And off the Arctic coasts of Europe and Russia, the shelf extends 750–800 miles (1,200–1,300 km), making the Arctic Ocean very shallow. Some continental shelves have higher parts that appear above the water as islands.

The edges of continental shelves are an average of 430 feet (130 m) beneath the surface of the ocean. Some may be as deep as 600 feet (180 m). The edge of the shelf drops sharply, forming a *continental slope* that leads to the bottom of the ocean floor.

ALSO READ: CONTINENTAL DIVIDE, CONTINENTAL DRIFT, GEOLOGY, ISLAND, PLATE TECTONICS.

CONTINENTAL CONGRESS

The Continental Congress was an organization representing the original 13 colonies. The First Continental Congress met in Philadelphia from September through October, 1774. Delegates from all the 13 colonies except Georgia drew up the *Declara-*

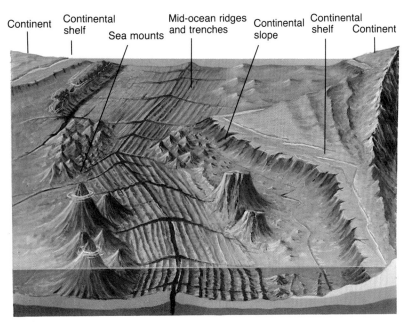

Continent | Continental shelf | Sea mounts | Mid-ocean ridges and trenches | Continental slope | Continental shelf | Continent

tion of Rights. They listed what they believed their rights as English colonists should be. They wanted representative government, the right to assemble, and trials before juries. Delegates to the Congress agreed that the colonies should not buy anything from Britain or sell anything there until their complaints were settled.

Fighting between colonists and British soldiers soon broke out in Massachusetts. The Second Continental Congress met in Philadelphia from May 1775 to early December 1776. Delegates from Georgia attended for the first time. The delegates organized a Continental Army to oppose the British and appointed George Washington, a delegate, as commander-in-chief. They also issued a declaration stating their reasons for taking up arms and made a final, but futile, attempt to persuade Britain to recognize their rights. Representatives were sent to foreign countries, notably to France, to obtain help for the colonists' cause.

After the outbreak of war, the Second Continental Congress urged the colonies to establish their own local governments, independent of Britain. Money was issued to carry on the war. On June 7, 1776, Richard Henry Lee of Virginia proposed that the 13

▲ *Continents do not really end at their seacoasts; the continental shelf, which extends under the seas, is also part of them. Where the water is about 600 feet (180 m) deep the continental shelf ends, and there is a steep slope down to the ocean depths. Here there is often an ocean trench, where one of the plates of our planet's crust is plunging under another. At mid-ocean ridges, rock is coming up from the mantle (the layer under the crust) to form new plates. It is because of both these processes that continents drift. A sea mount is a mountain deep in the ocean.*

▼ *The Pennsylvania State House (now called Independence Hall), Philadelphia. It was here that the Second Continental Congress met in May 1775.*

651

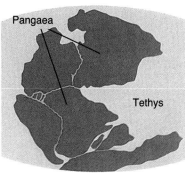

Pangaea

Tethys

200 million years ago

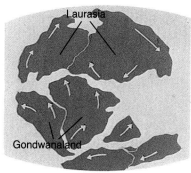

Laurasia

Gondwanaland

180 million years ago

65 million years ago

▲ *The map of the world has changed in the past because of continental drift, but this happens very slowly. As long ago as 65 million years, the continents were beginning to look like the ones we know today. See how North America and South America used to be separate. And can you guess what is the modern name for that triangular continent at the center-right?*

colonies be "free and independent states." Thomas Jefferson, John Adams, Alexander Hamilton, and others, helped by Benjamin Franklin, were asked to write a formal Declaration of Independence, which was approved by the Congress on July 4, 1776 at Independence Hall in Philadelphia. (The Fourth of July is today known as Independence Day in the United States.)

The Third Continental Congress met from late December 1776 to March 1781. It had to move from one city to another several times, to avoid the fighting. It took over direction of the war. The Congress agreed in 1777 on a plan to unite the 13 states into one nation. The plan was outlined in the Articles of Confederation, the nation's first constitution. This constitution was sent to the states and agreed to by 1781. By this plan, a new Congress of the Confederation replaced the Continental Congress. A more complete and stronger plan, the U.S. Constitution, was adopted in 1789.

ALSO READ: AMERICAN REVOLUTION; ARTICLES OF CONFEDERATION; CONSTITUTION, UNITED STATES; DECLARATION OF INDEPENDENCE.

CONTINENTAL DIVIDE If you had been a boy or girl in a wagon train heading west in pioneer days, at the Continental Divide your wagon would have been 7,550 feet (2,300 m) above sea level as you followed the Oregon Trail over the Rocky Mountains through South Pass. That might have meant high winds and snow, and possibly death.

The Divide is the imaginary line that runs north to south through North America, along the highest peaks of the Rocky Mountains. Rain falling west of it drains through rivers that flow toward the Pacific Ocean; rivers east of the Divide flow toward the Mississippi. The Divide is therefore called the continent's *watershed.*

The Divide of North America runs from Canada through Montana, Wyoming, Colorado, and New Mexico, then through Mexico. A lower divide runs across North America from east to west, separating those rivers that flow north to the Gulf of St. Lawrence, Hudson Bay, and the Arctic Ocean from those that flow south to the Mississippi and the Gulf of Mexico.

CONTINENTAL DRIFT If you look at a map of the world you will notice immediately that Africa seems as if it might fit snugly against South America. Over the centuries many people have suggested that the two continents were once joined together, but it was not until 1912 that someone put forward a serious display of evidence that continents do indeed "drift" around the surface of our planet. That man's name was Alfred Wegener.

Today continental drift is regarded as an established fact. The modern version of the theory is called *plate tectonics* because it is believed that the surface (crust) of the earth is made up of a number of rigid plates that float on the molten rock of the mantle beneath. It is these plates, rather than merely the continents that ride upon some of them, which "drift" relative to each other.

ALSO READ: CONTINENT, EARTH, PLATE TECTONICS.

CONVECTION see HEAT AND COLD.

CONVENT see MONASTERY.

COOK, CAPTAIN JAMES (1728–1779) James Cook, an English navigator and explorer, discovered Australia and the Hawaiian Islands on three famous voyages to the South Pacific. Cook was born in Yorkshire, England. He joined the British Navy and became an expert surveyor and astronomer. He helped map the St. Lawrence River and the coasts of Labrador and Newfoundland.

Cook set out in 1768 in the ship *Endeavour* on his first historic voyage to the Pacific, hoping to find "Terra Australis," a great continent believed to exist in the far south. On this voyage he visited Tahiti and New Zealand, and explored the east coast of Australia, claiming it for Britain.

In 1772, Captain Cook sailed again from England with two ships, *Resolution* and *Adventure*, on his longest voyage. He traveled about 70,000 miles (113,000 km) in three years, sailing across the Antarctic Circle for the first time in history, and discovering New Caledonia and the Cook Islands.

He set sail on his third expedition in 1776, in the ships *Resolution* and *Discovery*, looking for the Northwest Passage—a way to sail from the northern Atlantic Ocean to the northern Pacific Ocean. (It was not to be discovered until 1903–1906 by the Norwegian explorer, Roald Amundsen.) On this voyage Cook discovered the Hawaiian Islands in 1778. He sailed along and surveyed the west coast of North America from Oregon to the Arctic Ocean, through the Bering Strait. Cook then returned to the Hawaiian Islands, where he was killed in a fight with some islanders over a boat stolen from one of his vessels.

ALSO READ: AUSTRALIA, EXPLORATION, HAWAII.

COOKING No one knows how humanity discovered cooking. A famous English writer, Charles Lamb, once wrote a funny essay, "A Dissertation on Roast Pig." Lamb wrote about a Chinese man whose house burned down while his pig was inside it. The man happened to taste the cooked meat of the pig and discovered it tasted better than the raw meat he had always eaten. So to get more of the tasty cooked meat the man and his neighbors kept burning down houses with pigs inside. How do you think mankind *really* discovered cooking? However it was, cooking makes most foods taste better. It also kills harmful bacteria.

■ LEARN BY DOING

Learning to cook is fun. It is easy to cook when you learn the correct and safe way to do it. There are certain basic ways to prepare and cook food. The basic cooking methods include baking, frying, roasting,

▲ *Captain James Cook, English navigator.*

▼ *The traditional Thanksgiving Day meal: roast turkey, sweet corn, sweet potatoes, and corn bread.*

▲ *Cooking may be as little as heating a can of beans or as much as preparing a banquet. Here a French chef adds the finishing touches to a glorious display of cold cooked foods.*

boiling, broiling, stewing, poaching, and barbecuing. These methods are explained in the table. There are many kinds of utensils—such as pots and pans, measuring cups and spoons, knives, and bowls—that you use in cooking. Understanding how your family's stove works is also very important. Is it a gas stove or electric? How do you turn the heat off and on? Ask an adult to show you how to operate a stove safely.

A *recipe* lists the ingredients—what kinds of foods are needed—and gives the amount needed of each ingredient for a particular dish. A recipe also tells you, step by step, how to prepare the dish you've decided to cook. Below is a recipe for hamburgers. Perhaps you would like to try it. First check to see if you have in your kitchen the necessary ingredients and utensils. When you have everything, measure the ingredients carefully to get the exact amount the recipe calls for. You'll need to use special marked measuring spoons and cups that are exactly the right size.

SIMPLE HAMBURGERS
1 pound (450 g) ground beef or chuck
¾ teaspoon salt
¼ cup milk
1 tablespoon ice water

Lightly mix together in a bowl the meat, salt, milk, and water. With your hands, shape the meat mixture into four round patties about one inch (2.5 cm) thick. Be careful not to press the meat together too solidly, or the patty will be too heavy. Put the patties in a broiling pan. Broil them until they are browned on one side. Then use a spatula to turn them to brown on the other side. Cook both sides for three to five minutes, or until the hamburgers are done the way you like. If you cook them too long, however, they will taste very dry. Put the finished hamburgers on top of a paper towel on a plate so that the towel will absorb any excess grease. Remove the towel and serve the hamburgers either by themselves or inside hamburger buns.

Can you think of other ways to make hamburgers? You might like to add spices or herbs to give your hamburgers a special flavor? Try a teaspoon of thyme, ginger, curry, garlic or chili powder. But not all at once! Maybe you'd rather add bread crumbs or crushed cornflakes. How about some tomato catsup or mild mustard? Experiment by making some tiny hamburgers. On each hamburger sprinkle a bit of a different spice or herb, or add whatever you like.

After you cook the hamburgers, sample each one to see which kinds you like best. This would be fun to do with your friends, too. Half the fun of cooking is creating your own special dishes and being daring enough to cook something quite different from what you usually eat.

If you cook a whole meal, of course, you'll want to serve more than hamburgers. You'll want to have a well-balanced meal with meat or fish, a green or yellow vegetable, a starchy vegetable, fruit, milk, and dessert. Here is a recipe for potato salad, which you might want to serve with your hamburgers.

POTATO SALAD
4 medium-sized potatoes, washed
3 eggs

HOW A MICROWAVE OVEN WORKS

A microwave oven uses rays similar to radiowaves, to cook food. These rays penetrate the food, so that it cooks equally well on the inside as it does on the outside. In an ordinary oven, it takes time for the heat to reach the inside of the food. Microwaves are much quicker as they heat up the inside immediately. Some models have a conventional heating device to brown the food.

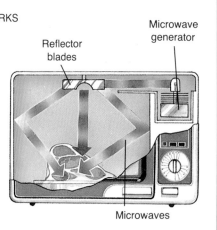

Reflector blades

Microwave generator

Microwaves

1 cup chopped celery
¼ cup chopped onion
¼ cup pickle relish
¼ teaspoon pepper
¼ cup mustard
½ cup mayonnaise
salt
paprika

Put the potatoes in a pot and cover them with water. Add one teaspoon of salt. Cover the pot and boil the potatoes over medium heat for 30 to 35 minutes, or until the potato skins start to break apart. The potatoes are cooked when you can easily push a fork into them. Drain off the hot water, but be careful that you don't get burned. Cover the potatoes with cold water to cool them while you cook the eggs. Cover the eggs with water in a saucepan and heat the water until it boils. Cook the eggs over very low heat for 20 minutes. Remove them from the hot water with a large spoon, and put them in cold water. Place the cooled potatoes on a wooden cutting board and carefully pull off the skins. Hold each potato with a fork while you peel it with a small knife. Ask an adult to show you how to cut the potatoes into small cubes. Put these into a large bowl. Next, ask an adult to help you carefully chop up the celery and onion on a cutting board. Now the eggs should be cool enough for you to peel and slice. Sprinkle the potatoes with ¼ teaspoon of salt. Add the eggs, celery, onion, pickle relish, mustard, pepper, and paprika to the potatoes. Toss all the ingredients together gently and cover the bowl. Chill it in the refrigerator for at least four to six hours. Add the mayonnaise just before you serve the salad.

GINGERBREAD FACES

1 box of gingerbread mix
⅓ cup raisins
maraschino cherries cut in half (if you wish)

COMMON TERMS USED IN COOKING

Process	Meaning	Examples of foods by this method
Baking	In the oven with little or no liquid.	Cookies, cakes, breads, meat loaf.
Barbecuing	On an open flame, usually built outdoors with charcoal.	Hamburgers, hot dogs, steaks.
Boiling	In bubbling hot liquid—at boiling point.	Potatoes, eggs, chicken.
Broiling	Under the oven's broiler.	Steaks, chicken, fish.
Frying	In hot fat or oil, usually over direct heat.	French fried potatoes, bacon, eggs.
Micro-waving	In a microwave oven.	Meats, vegetables, stews, fish, cakes.
Poaching	In simmering liquid that covers the food.	Eggs, fish.
Roasting	In the oven with little or no liquid, usually meat or fowl.	Beef, pork, turkey.
Simmering	In liquid, but under boiling point.	Vegetables.
Steaming	With steam from a boiling liquid.	Fish, plum pudding, brown bread.
Stewing	In liquid, but under boiling point, usually for a long period of time.	Tough cuts of meats.

Make the gingerbread according to the instructions on the box. As soon as you remove the cake pan from the oven, gently make lines with a knife on the top of it to mark off the squares.

Use the raisins to make a different face on each square. Make the eyes horizontal, vertical, or slanted. Give some faces large noses by using a big raisin. Give another one a pointed nose by poking the narrow end of the raisin into the cake. See how many different-shaped mouths you can create.

If you have the cherries, use them to make bright mouths and noses. Gingerbread is good to eat either warm or cold.

When you have learned how to make hamburgers, potato salad, and gingerbread faces, you will be able to cook a whole meal. ■

ALSO READ: BAKING AND BAKERIES, FOOD, NUTRITION, VEGETARIAN.

In the Middle Ages, meat was roasted on a spit in front of a huge fire. However, the meat needed to be turned so that it was cooked on all sides. In large house-holds such as castles, turning the spit was the job of a kitchen boy appropriately named a "turnspit." By the 1700's a small dog in a tread-mill above the fireplace took over the job. Eventually a clockwork system was invented to replace the dog.

▲ *James Fenimore Cooper, great U.S. writer of frontier adventures. His novel* The Last of the Mohicans *is internationally famous.*

President Coolidge was nicknamed "Silent Cal" because he spoke very little. A woman once told him she had made a bet that she could get him to say more than two words. "You lose," replied the President.

COOLIDGE, CALVIN (1872–1933)
President Warren G. Harding died in a San Francisco hotel on August 2, 1923. In the very early morning of August 3, Vice-President Calvin Coolidge was notified that he was now President. Coolidge was visiting his father's farm near Plymouth, Vermont. His father, a justice of the peace, administered the oath of office. Coolidge was re-elected President in the 1924 election.

As a boy, John Calvin Coolidge helped with the work on the farm in Vermont. He was graduated from Amherst College in Massachusetts. After serving in several lesser public offices, he became governor of Massachusetts in 1919. The Boston police went on strike while Coolidge was governor. With no police to stop them, criminals broke into stores and robbed people. Governor Coolidge called in the state militia to act as policemen. He said, "There is no right to strike against the public safety by anybody, anywhere, anytime." Leaders in the Republican Party liked the firm way that the governor handled the strike. They nominated Coolidge for Vice-President at the Republican Convention in 1920. Harding and Coolidge won the election.

Coolidge was a well-liked President, although he had a widespread reputation for saying very little. He was an upright New England Yankee. He believed in hard work and thrift. He even used to keep track of White House expenses. As President, he reduced the national debt by several billion dollars. He also lowered everyone's income taxes by seeing that the government spent less money. Coolidge was President during a time of great prosperity. He refused to sign many laws that would have given the government more control over business. He said, "When things are going all right, it is a good plan to let them alone."

The prosperity while Coolidge was President was followed by the Great Depression. The former President was saddened and bewildered by this disaster. He spent his last years in Northampton, Massachusetts, where he had once been mayor.

ALSO READ: DEPRESSION; ECONOMICS; HARDING, WARREN G.; PRESIDENCY.

COOPER, JAMES FENIMORE (1789–1851) The first important author seriously to use North American scenes and characters in his books was James Fenimore Cooper. His descriptions of North America's forests and prairies are not only beautiful but historically important. They are early descriptions of places where the pioneers lived. Cooper also showed the

---

CALVIN COOLIDGE
THIRTIETH PRESIDENT   AUGUST 3, 1923—MARCH 4, 1929

Born: July 4, 1872, Plymouth, Vermont
Parents: John Calvin and Victoria Josephine Moor Coolidge
Education: Amherst College
Religion: Congregationalist
Occupation: Lawyer
Political Party: Republican
State Represented: Massachusetts
Married: 1905 to Grace Anna Goodhue (1879–1957)
Children: 2 sons (1 of whom died at birth)
Died: January 5, 1933, Northampton, Massachusetts
Buried: Plymouth, Vermont

clash between the frontier and advancing civilization.

Cooper was born in New Jersey. When he was one year old, his father moved the family to Otsego Lake in New York, where he founded Cooperstown. The area was a wilderness, and many Indians lived nearby. Cooper later went to Yale University but was expelled. He then joined the U.S. Navy. Three years later, he left the Navy and was married.

Cooper wrote his first book, *Precaution*, after his wife dared him to write a better book than the English one he was reading. *Precaution* was a failure, but his next book, *The Spy*—a story of the Revolutionary War—was a success. Cooper's most famous works, the *Leatherstocking Tales*—written between 1823 and 1841—are *The Pioneers, The Last of the Mohicans, The Prairie, The Pathfinder,* and *The Deerslayer.* The stories' hero is a woodsman named Natty Bumppo, or Leatherstocking. The books are about pioneers and Indians in the American wilderness. All around Lake Otsego today are reminders of the main character of Leatherstocking Tales—Natty Bumppo's Cave, Leatherstocking Falls, and, at the mouth of the lake, just where the Susquehanna River begins, stands Council Rock, where Leatherstocking met his Indian friends. Cooper wrote a total of 50 books, including several sea adventures.

ALSO READ: LITERATURE, NOVEL, PIONEER LIFE.

COPERNICUS, NICOLAUS (1473–1543)

In the early 1500's, almost everyone believed that the sun, the planets, and all the other heavenly bodies revolved around (circled) the Earth. No one had questioned that "fact" for more than 1,000 years. But a Polish cleric and astronomer, Niklas Koppernigk, who took the Latin name Nicolaus Copernicus, had a different view of things. Copernicus's ideas caused a revolution in the thinking of astronomers.

Copernicus was trained not only in mathematics but also in medicine and church law. He spent most of his life serving as both a church official and a doctor in the town of Frauenburg, Poland. He also spent much time studying astronomy. He made observations of the positions of the sun, moon, planets, and stars. Copernicus was convinced from his studies that the Earth and the other planets really revolve around the sun. He realized that the sun and stars seem to be revolving around the Earth because the Earth itself is turning on its axis.

Copernicus wrote a book about his ideas. Because the ideas were so new, and because he was frightened of persecution, it took a long time to get the book published—13 years after he wrote it. He saw the first printed copy when he was on his deathbed.

ALSO READ: ASTRONOMY, SOLAR SYSTEM.

COPLAND, AARON (1900–1990)

Aaron Copland has helped develop a music that is clearly American, both in his own composing and in helping young composers.

Copland was born in Brooklyn, New York, and began piano lessons early. He was studying harmony and trying to write music even before he graduated from high school. He decided not to go to college, so that he would have more time for music. He studied musical composition in Paris, France, and began his career there.

His first large work, *Symphony for Organ and Orchestra,* was first performed in 1925 by the New York Symphony Orchestra. He has composed, taught music, and helped promote U.S. music ever since. His early compositions used jazz material. His ballet *Billy the Kid* contained cowboy songs, and Mexican folk music sparked the orchestral piece *El Salón*

▲ *Copernicus, who promoted the idea that Earth and the other planets go around the sun.*

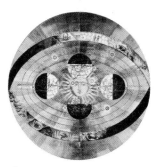

▲ *Copernicus' idea of the solar system. He thought the planets went around the sun in circles. Only later did Kepler show that the orbits were ellipses.*

▲ *U.S. composer Aaron Copland conducting a recording of one of his own works.*

México. Copland has written symphonies, operas, music for piano, scores for movies, and books about music.

The poet Carl Sandburg spoke Abraham Lincoln's words at the first performance of Copland's *Lincoln Portrait,* a work for orchestra and narrator. *Appalachian Spring,* music written for dancer Martha Graham, won a Pulitzer Prize.

ALSO READ: COMPOSER, MODERN DANCE, MODERN MUSIC, MUSIC.

COPYRIGHT see PATENTS AND COPYRIGHTS.

CORAL   If you are lucky, you may have found some coral on a beach. Maybe it looked and felt like white stone with an interesting shape or design. Possibly it was a lacy sea fan or a many-branched sea whip tinted green or lavender.

Coral *polyps* are tiny, soft animals that live in the ocean. They are called *anthozoans* or "flower-animals." They are simple living "cylinders" that spend their lives anchored in one place. They eat tiny particles of sea life, which they trap with their tentacles. Corals are coelenterates and are related to jellyfish.

Many kinds of coral polyps remove calcium from ocean water and produce a hard material called *corallite,* or calcium carbonate. This material

▲ *Coral is made up of the hard shells of millions of dead sea-creatures, called coral polyps. Coral looks soft and colorful, like a flower, but can cut you very badly if you pick it up carelessly.*

forms a cup around the soft polyp. When the polyp dies, the corallite remains behind, like a skeleton. We call this skeleton coral.

Many polyps living together in a colony form a single piece of coral. Over the years coral structures grow larger and larger. Their shapes depend on the kind of polyp that formed them. A *sea fan,* for example, is a community skeleton of polyps of just one variety of anthozoan. *Reef-building corals* make enormous underwater ridgelike formations, as new generations of polyps grow on coral left behind by dead polyps. In the warm waters of the Pacific Ocean, coral polyps have built up whole islands. In the warm waters at tropical resorts, such as those in the Caribbean Sea, there are often underwater "trails." Snorkelers and skin divers who follow the trails may observe coral and the many fish that seek the shelter of coral reefs.

Coral polyps reproduce in two ways. Small bumps called *buds* appear on the body of an adult polyp. The buds grow larger. Then they break off from the "parent," attach themselves to the colony, and begin to produce calcium carbonate. *Budding* increases the size of a coral colony. Polyps also lay eggs. The eggs hatch into free-swimming larvae that swim away from the colony, drop to the ocean bottom, and begin a new coral formation.

Not all coral animals form corallite.

HOW A CORAL REEF FORMS

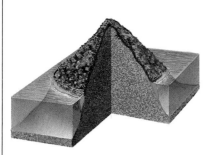

Coral growing in warm and shallow water has formed a reef around an island created by volcanic action.

The sea rises or the island sinks, but coral continues growing upward.

The island has vanished, but coral reefs remain, to form an atoll.

The *stinging coral* of tropical waters makes a spongy coating on rocks. Its polyps have stinging cells that can give painful rashes to swimmers.

ALSO READ: COELENTERATE, GREAT BARRIER REEF, ISLAND.

CORAL SEA The Coral Sea lies off the northeastern coast of Australia in the southern Pacific Ocean. It touches New Guinea to the north and the New Hebrides and Solomon Islands (Melanesia) to the east. Parts of it are very deep. Oceanographers have measured depths to 3 miles (5 km) in some parts.

The sea's name comes from the large number of coral atolls and reefs that dot the sea's expanse. One of the largest reefs in the world, the Great Barrier Reef, runs through the Coral Sea, extending more than 100 miles (160 km) outward from Australia and stretching about 1,250 miles (2,000 km) along the coast into the Gulf of Papua. This ancient reef is approximately 15,000 years old and consists of some 350 species of brightly colored corals. Many kinds of fish, such as grouper, snapper, barracuda, and shark, swim along the reef making it very popular with skin divers and snorkelers. Beautiful beaches washed by the warm Coral Sea waters run along the Australian coast. Two major Australian port cities, Brisbane and Townsville, also lie along that coast. Products such as wool, sugarcane, meat, grain, and minerals flow through these ports.

U.S. warships stopped a Japanese task force in these waters in May 1942 in a decisive World War II battle. U.S. forces were then able to begin their drive toward Japan. An aircraft carrier, the U.S.S. *Coral Sea*, built at the end of World War II, is named for this battle.

ALSO READ: AUSTRALIA, CORAL, GREAT BARRIER REEF.

CORM see BULB.

CORN The word "corn" means corn-on-the-cob, flavored with salt and butter, to most North Americans. Elsewhere the plant is called *maize*. To the British, "corn" means wheat, rye, oats, and barley. The plant we call corn is a cereal grass that grows on most continents. (The other five main cereal grasses are rice, wheat, oats, rye, and barley.)

American Indians learned to cultivate corn thousands of years before white men set foot in the New World. Corn became one of the Indians' most important foods. They showed it to Columbus. Friendly Indians taught the early English colonists how to plant, harvest, and cook several kinds of corn.

Corn plants grow from 2 feet to 20 feet (60 cm–6 m) high. The corn plant has a central stalk from which long leaves grow. At the top of the plant is the male flower (*tassel*), which produces millions of grains of pollen. Ears grow from the stalk where the leaves join it. Each ear is covered with a special kind of leaf, the *husk*. Inside the husk is the *corncob*. *Cornsilk*—long, thin, hairlike tubes—forms along each corncob. The silk is part of the female flowers. Pollen falls from the tassel and travels through the tubes to fertilize the flowers. Each flower develops into a kernel.

Almost all corn grown in the United States is *hybrid* corn, produced by using pollen from one kind of corn to pollinate another kind. The seeds that result from this special *cross-pollination* have features from both plants. By choosing the "parents" very carefully, experts can produce very useful new kinds of corn. Some hybrid corns, for example, have extra long roots, which help them grow in poor soil. Other hybrids may have longer, fatter ears than their parents. Still others have ears that

HELIOPORA BLUE CORAL

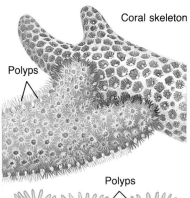

Coral skeleton

Polyps

Polyps

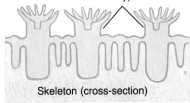

Skeleton (cross-section)

▲ *Corals are closely related to sea anemones. But sea anemones are usually large and unprotected, while corals are small and protect themselves with a chalky skeleton.*

The ears of corn we eat today were only an inch (2.5 cm) long in their wild form, hundreds of years ago. By the time Columbus reached the New World the Indians had developed corn into the size we know.

▲ *A corn plant. The little spikes at the top of the stalk make up the tassel. The tassel contains hundreds of small flowers that produce pollen. The pollen is taken by farmers, or blown by the wind, to the silk threads (shown below) of young ears of corn.*

▲ *The pollen fertilizes the corn flowers. Without pollination the kernels would not ripen.*

ripen all at the same time, so that machines can harvest the corn without wasting any ears.

Corn kernels provide us with large amounts of valuable carbohydrates, fats, and proteins. Sweet corn, which we often eat as corn-on-the-cob or as canned or frozen corn, is high in vitamin-A content. Corn is an important food for animals, too. Farmers use most of what they raise to feed their cattle, sheep, poultry, and especially hogs.

Corn is processed in different ways to be used in the foods we eat. Kernels are canned or frozen for vegetables. Cornmeal comes from ground kernels. Tamales, corn bread, and some cold cereals are made from cornmeal. Kernels are refined (separated into different parts) to obtain many products, called by-products. *Corn oil* comes from the central part of the kernel, or *germ*. Corn oil is used in salad dressing and margarine. Corn oil is also used in cooking—when frying such things as doughnuts or chicken. *Cornstarch*, a white powder, comes from the substances that surround the germ of each kernel. Cornstarch thickens gravies and sauces. *Corn syrup* is a liquid used in baking and in making candy.

But many by-products of corn are not eaten. Buttons and phonograph records can be made from cobs. Cornmeal is used in manufacturing adhesives and plywood. Many soaps and paints contain corn oil. Cornstarch is needed for making drugs, cosmetics, and explosives. Cornstarch is also used to stiffen fabrics and yarns. Husks are sometimes used as a filler material, and stalks may be used for making paper and wallboard.

The United States is the world's leading producer of corn. China ranks second. It is the world's third most important cereal crop after wheat and rice. Corn grows in areas that have summer temperatures in the 70's and 80's F (20's–30's C). At least 6–12 inches (15–30 cm) of rainfall are re-

quired during the growing season. Rich, well-drained soil is needed.

So much corn is grown in the U.S. Midwest that this region is known as the *corn belt*. States in this area include Nebraska, Kansas, Minnesota, South Dakota, Iowa, Missouri, Illinois, Indiana, Wisconsin, and Ohio.

ALSO READ: GRAIN; INDIANS, AMERICAN; PLANT BREEDING.

CORONADO, FRANCISCO

(1510–1554) Francisco Vásquez de Coronado, explorer of the American Southwest, was born in Salamanca, Spain. He went to Mexico in 1535, drawn—like other conquistadors—by tales of gold. He soon became governor of a Mexican province. Five years later, Coronado formed an expedition to seek the legendary Seven Cities of Cibola and to claim new lands for Spain. He led 300 Spanish soldiers and 1,000 Indians northward into what is now Arizona and New Mexico. They found only Zuñi Indian villages instead of the golden cities.

Part of the group turned westward, becoming the first Europeans to see the Grand Canyon. Coronado and the others crossed the Rio Grande and the Texas Plains. They were the first Europeans to see American buffalo (bison). Next, Coronado traveled north to look for Quivira, another "city of gold," but he found only more Indian villages in what is now Kansas.

Failure to find gold made Coronado unpopular with the Spanish government. His governor's post was taken away in 1544. He later received a small land grant for his services.

ALSO READ: ARIZONA; CIBOLA, SEVEN CITIES OF; CONQUISTADOR; EXPLORATION; NEW MEXICO.

CORONATION see KINGS AND QUEENS.

CORPORATION A corporation is an organization created by law and formed for the purpose of carrying on an activity. Most of the things that Americans buy and use every day are made by corporations in the United States or abroad. For example, your family's car may have been made by a U.S. corporation such as General Motors, Ford or Chrysler.

Corporations make and sell many kinds of goods and services. Gas and electricity are sold by corporations. Radio and television networks are owned by corporations. Public corporations are formed to govern towns, cities, and schools. The officials who run public corporations are elected by the voters of the area.

A business does not have to be large to be a corporation. Suppose ten people want to join together to make and sell shoes. They need a *capital* of 20,000 dollars to begin work. They *invest*, or put up, about 16,000 dollars. This is broken up into small parts, or *shares of stock*. To get the 4,000 dollars they still need, they sell shares to other people. The shareholders then own part of the company. To become a corporation, they must ask a state government for a *charter*, or permit, to *incorporate*. The letters "Inc." (for "Incorporated") are then written after the company's name. The shareholders elect a *board of directors* to manage the business. Each shareholder has as many votes as he or she has shares of stock. One owner can take the place of another by buying the shares of someone else who no longer wants to own shares. Every corporation must obey special laws. A Federal Government agency, the Securities and Exchange Commission, makes rules to govern the sale of stock by the corporation. These rules protect the stockholders.

A corporation is especially helpful in running a big business. For example, it would be difficult for 10 or 12 people to put up millions of dollars to build and run a railroad. But many thousands of people can invest small sums of money in a corporation to make up the large amount it needs. No matter how large a corporation is, under law it is treated in the same way as an individual person. This means that the directors of the corporation can sign contracts in its name, just as they would to borrow money for themselves. You can sue a corporation if it does something you think is wrong. But individual persons within a corporation cannot be sued for something done in the name of the corporation.

ALSO READ: STOCKS AND BONDS.

CORROSION All metals suffer on contact with the environment, usually because they are attacked by oxygen in the air and especially in the presence of moisture. This attack is called corrosion. The commonest example is *rust*. The surfaces of iron objects are attacked by both oxygen and water so that a flaky *oxide* of iron is formed. Soon the entire object may be rusted away. Other metals are more resistant, suffering merely *tarnishing*. Here, although the surface of the metal is attacked, the *oxidized* surface layer protects the metal beneath from further attack. Copper and silver are metals that tarnish readily.

Air pollution contributes greatly to corrosion, since many gases attack metals even more severely than oxygen. Sulfur dioxide, from domestic and industrial chimneys, is a very bad offender.

Corrosion costs the United States over $5 billion a year. Corrosion-resistant materials like stainless steel as well as paint, varnish, and electroplating can be used to prevent it.

CORTÉS, HERNANDO (1485–1547) In March 1519, Yucatán Indians of Mexico saw white-skinned

▲ *Rust is the most familiar form of corrosion. It happens because oxygen and water in the air attack iron to produce a flaky iron compound called iron oxide.*

▲ *Cortés* (center), *the Spanish conquistador who conquered Mexico, with Montezuma* (right), *the Mexican king.*

On February 10, 1519, Cortés set sail from Cuba with 508 soldiers, 100 sailors, and 16 horses. His men were armed with flintlock rifles and bows. Despite their small number, this poorly armed force conquered the Aztecs. They did it with military skill, cunning, and determination. Cortés ruled out any possibility of retreat by ordering all his ships to be destroyed.

men arriving in strange ships. Their leader was Captain Hernando Cortés. The goal of this conquistador was the conquest of Mexico.

Cortés was born in Medellín, Estremadura, Spain. He began studies in a university but soon left, preferring adventure. He sailed to the New World in 1504 and helped Diego Velásquez conquer Cuba. Velásquez heard about a rich empire in Mexico. He sent Cortés and about 600 men to the unknown country to find gold.

They established the settlement of Veracruz, then traveled inland to Tenochtitlán (later Mexico City). There they found a dazzling city and a highly developed culture. The natives looked at the Spaniards' ships, cannons, and especially their horses, and thought white-skinned gods had come to their land. Cortés took the ruler, Montezuma, prisoner and ruled the Aztecs through him. Malintzin, a native woman who was deeply in love with Cortés, aided his conquest by serving as interpreter and guide. Native tribes who feared the Aztecs also helped Cortés. The Aztecs attempted to defeat the Spanish at Otumba in 1521, but Cortés won the battle and Mexico became a Spanish colony.

The king of Spain named Cortés governor of Mexico. Cortés discovered the lower peninsula of California in 1536 and founded a settlement there. Gradually his cruelty—and his personal ambition—cost him the king's good will. He returned to Spain, where he was coldly received. He died a neglected man.

ALSO READ: AZTEC INDIANS, CONQUISTADOR, MEXICO.

▶ *An ancient painting showing Egyptian women wearing kohl around their eyes. Kohl is made from the powder of antimony, a poisonous metallic element, and is still used in some countries.*

COSMETICS Cosmetics are substances that people use to make their faces and bodies more attractive. Eyes are thought by many to be prettier when highlighted by makeup. Skin is softer when creams and lotions are used. Hair looks shiny and stays in place because of cosmetics. Men put lotion on their faces after they have shaved to make their skin feel fresh.

Cosmetics include those that can be seen, such as lipstick, face powder, eye makeup, and nail polish. Others, such as hand lotion or hair dressing, are rubbed in.

Most cosmetics are made from a base of fats and oils. These are mixed with water or alcohol and held together by vegetable gums. Colors and perfumes are added. So are other materials that keep the mixture from spoiling. Lipstick is made of castor oil and melted wax with coloring and scent added.

Hand lotions and "skin food" creams help skin that has been dried out by sun, wind, and water. Special oils are put into these creams. Turtle oil, avocado oil, cod-liver oil, and raisin-seed oil are often used. The color of the skin can be made lighter by using creams containing cucumber or lemon juice.

Cosmetics have been used since the beginning of recorded history. The

▲ *A model creates a striking effect using bold, vibrant colors that complement her modern hairstyle and jewelry.*

or beeswax, oil, and water. They washed their faces with buttermilk to remove freckles and colored their lips and cheeks with berry juice.

Until the 1900's, cosmetics were sold only in barbershops and drugstores. Today, many people want to look youthful and attractive, so the making of cosmetics has become a giant industry. Beauty preparations and nonallergenic cosmetics can be bought in department stores, supermarkets, beauty salons, and drugstores, from door-to-door salespersons, or through the mail. A government agency, the Food and Drug Administration, sets rules for ingredients in cosmetics. Since 1976, cosmetics labels must carry a list of all ingredients.

ALSO READ: FASHION, MAKEUP, PERFUME.

earliest uses were in religious ceremonies, in which incense and oils were mixed according to old recipes. This was the job of priests or slaves. Cosmetics have been found in ancient Egyptian tombs. The Egyptian queen Cleopatra was famous for her brightly painted face and strange perfume. She bathed in milk to keep her skin soft and beautiful. The Romans were fond of bleaches, dyes, and lotions. Their public baths and barbershops were well stocked with perfumes and oils. Roman women wore chalk and white lead on their faces. They stained their lips and cheeks red.

Until the Crusades, only the very rich in Europe had money to spend on cosmetics. Then returning Crusaders brought perfumes and cosmetics from the East, and the use of beautifiers spread. In the 1500's, Queen Elizabeth I rouged and painted her face. Mary, Queen of Scots, used wine for her beauty bath.

In the United States, pioneer women mixed their own face creams of lanolin (grease from sheep's wool)

COSTA RICA Christopher Columbus began his last voyage to the New World in 1502. He sailed along the Caribbean coast of a country where he saw Indians wearing golden ornaments and headdresses. He knew he had found another rich land. He named the country Costa Rica, which means "rich coast." (See the map with the article on CENTRAL AMERICA.)

Costa Rica is one of the smallest countries in Central America. It is about as large as New Hampshire and Vermont put together but has many more people.

Costa Rica's shores are washed by the Pacific Ocean on one side and the Caribbean Sea on the other. From hot coastal plains dotted with forests and banana plantations, the land rises sharply up to high, rugged mountains that include many volcanoes. In 1963, the volcano Irazu spilled volcanic ash over much of Costa Rica. The ash poisoned thousands of acres of farmland, killing many valuable crops.

Costa Rica is the only Central

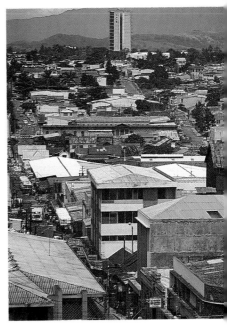

▲ *The capital of Costa Rica is San José, a fascinating city and a major tourist attraction.*

COSTA RICA

Capital City: San José (390,000 people).
Area: 19,600 square miles (50,700 sq. km).
Population: 2,980,000.
Government: Democratic republic.
Natural Resources: Coffee, bananas, lumber, gold, hematite, sulfur.
Export Products: Beef, sugar, fertilizers, coffee, bananas, manufactured goods.
Unit of Money: Colon.
Official Language: Spanish.

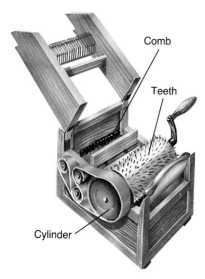

▲ *The cotton gin, invented by Eli Whitney in about 1793, plucked cotton fibers from the plants much more efficiently than could be done by hand. More cotton could therefore be produced.*

▶ *A cotton plant showing the feathery cotton bolls that open after the flowers of the plant have withered. The bolls are now mostly picked by machine.*

American country whose people are mostly of European descent. They call themselves "Ticos." More than 90 percent of the population can read and write. More than half of the people are farmers who raise coffee, bananas, cacao, sugarcane, and beans. Costa Rica was the first Central American country to raise coffee, which is its most valuable export. Most "Ticos" live in the fertile central highlands where days are warm and nights are chilly all year. Rich soil is Costa Rica's chief resource, but minerals, especially gold, are mined in mountains along the Pacific Coast.

San José, the capital and largest city, seems to tourists a charming part of the Old World, with iron grillwork balconies hanging over narrow cobbled streets and lovely gardens.

Costa Rica was a Spanish colony for about 300 years. It broke away from Spain in 1821. As in other Latin American countries, revolutions have upset the government from time to time, but Costa Rica has been a stable democratic republic for many years. Every election to date has been won by the party previously in opposition.

ALSO READ: CENTRAL AMERICA, COFFEE, SPANISH HISTORY.

COTTON One of the most widely used of all plant fibers is cotton, probably the first plant fiber to be used by human beings.

The cotton plant is a big-leaf shrub of the mallow family. It grows only within an area from 40 degrees north to 30 degrees south of the equator. (Look at this band on a globe or map.) Cotton seeds are planted in long rows in early spring. A good crop of cotton needs a large amount of fertilizer and must be kept free from weeds. Cutting out weeds with hoes was once called *cotton chopping*. This was one of the tasks given to slaves who worked on cotton plantations in the southern United States. Weeds are now controlled by chemicals.

Yellow blossoms appear on the plant when it is about three feet (90 cm) tall. The blossoms are followed by sticky green capsules, or *bolls*, that grow to the size of a small fist. During the fall, the capsules turn brown and burst open. Inside are many black seeds among the silky white cotton fibers.

Cotton-picking machines were first

used in the 1940's. Before this time, each boll had to be picked by hand. Wagonloads of bolls are carried to a machine called a *gin*, which separates the fibers, seeds, and husks. The fibers are packed into long bales. Each bale weighs about 500 pounds (225 kg). It is wrapped in burlap and bound with metal straps for shipment to spinning mills, where it is made into thread. From this thread a light, hard-wearing cloth is made, used for making garments, furnishings, and other products. Other products are made from the cottonseeds, fibers, and husks. These include cottonseed oil, margarine, fertilizers, cellulose fibers, cardboard, artificial leather, and medicines.

Planters began to grow cotton crops in America after 1620. The cotton gin was invented by Eli Whitney in 1793. The gin made the short-fibered upland cotton easier to process. Cotton was then grown all across the southern United States to California. Other types of cotton grown in the United States are Egyptian and Sea Island cotton. Both have very long fibers.

Cotton growing was severely hurt in the years following 1890 when the *boll weevil* from Mexico began attacking the crops. This insect's grubs ate the cotton plant's buds and made them fall off the plant. The boll weevil still exists today, but now it can be controlled. Some good came out of the boll weevil blight. Farmers turned from one-crop farming to growing several crops and to raising livestock. The new ways of farming, because they were better for the soil, were generally more profitable.

The world's major producers of cotton are the Soviet Union, the United States, China, India, Pakistan, and Brazil.

ALSO READ: CONSERVATION; SLAVERY; TEXTILE; WHITNEY, ELI.

COUGAR   see CAT, WILD.

COUNTERFEITING   On his way home from school, a boy found a dollar on the street. He tried to buy some ice cream with it, but the storekeeper refused to accept the dollar because it was a *counterfeit* bill—a worthless copy of a real bill.

"Copy" and "counterfeit" have different meanings. An ordinary copy is not made to cheat anyone. A counterfeit is used to cheat people by making them believe it is genuine, not a copy. Paintings, stamps, and labels for products have been counterfeited. But money has been counterfeited more than anything else.

Only a government is allowed to print and coin money. The government guarantees, or promises, that the money has value and may be used to pay for goods and services. Storekeepers and banks might be afraid to accept bills and coins if a great amount of counterfeit money were in circulation (use). People might then lose trust in the money and the government. This could even result in the closing of stores and other places of business. If that happened, the nation's economy could be hurt badly. The U.S. Secret Service—an agency of the Treasury Department—helps prevent this. Each year, the agency seizes millions of dollars in counterfeit money before it can get into circulation. It also prints booklets telling us how to recognize counterfeit money.

Look carefully at a dollar bill. It has many words, pictures, and designs on it. A counterfeiter would have to be a very good artist to copy it exactly. He would have to know how to make and use plates for printing. He would also have to match the colors of ink and use the special kind of paper on which U.S. dollars are printed. Counterfeiters can rarely make a perfect copy, and so they are usually caught.

ALSO READ: MONEY.

▲ *A cotton-picking machine harvests cotton bolls in Turkey.*

▼ *Part of a counterfeit bill* (left) *compared with part of a real one. The counterfeit money does not have the same detail as the real money. U.S. dollar bills are now being made with a special "security thread" woven into the paper.*

COUNTING   see NUMBER.

COUNTRY MUSIC   see POPULAR MUSIC.

The largest United States county is San Bernardino County, California, 20,102 square miles (52,060 sq. km). The smallest is New York, New York, 22 square miles (57 sq. km).

COUNTY   A county ("borough" in Alaska and "parish" in Louisiana) is a government unit smaller than a state but usually larger than a city or township. The 50 states are divided into more than 3,000 counties.

The word "county" comes from the French word *comte*, or "count." A French county was the estate of a count. The English originally called their counties "shires" but began to use the French word during the 1400's. England is divided into 45 counties. When English colonists came to America, they brought the word "county" and the idea of local government with them.

States do not all have the same number of counties. Delaware has 3, and Texas has 254. Counties are very important in the southern and western parts of the United States. But in New England, where towns are closer together, town and city governments have taken over many county-government jobs and functions.

Each state sets up its own counties, and state laws say what powers the county governments will have. Many counties collect taxes, build and maintain roads, and run schools, parks, hospitals, fire departments, courts, and jails.

State laws decide the form of county government. Many counties are run by a *county board*, an elected group of 2 to 100 people. Other counties are run by a *manager* and a nine-member *council*.

■ LEARN BY DOING

Ask your parents or teacher what form of government your county has. What powers does it have? Who are its leading members? You may be able to see how decisions are made if you attend a meeting of your county board or council. ■

ALSO READ: LOCAL GOVERNMENT, STATE GOVERNMENT.

COURT SYSTEM   "Oyez! Oyez!" calls the clerk of court. That means that the people in the courtroom should get ready, for the judge is arriving. The people in the spectators' benches usually stand when the judge enters. Standing up closest to the judge are the lawyers. They are allowed to be there because they have been "admitted to the bar." In old English courts, an actual bar separated the judge from the people. There is no such actual bar in today's courtrooms.

A court is a room in which a trial takes place. The word "court" can also mean the people who have the right to make the decision in a trial. Some courts have a judge who makes all the decisions. Some have both a judge and a *jury* (a group of people chosen from the citizens at large whose job is to reach a *verdict*, or decision, after hearing facts about both sides of a case). Other courts have a group of judges who take a vote to decide cases.

Most courts have court reporters who take down in shorthand or on a machine every word spoken while court is in session. This is important, particularly when witnesses are giving *testimony* (their knowledge of some of the facts of a case). Before witnesses testify, they must take an *oath*—swear that they will tell the truth. There are often interested people watching the trial proceedings. Nearly all trials are open to the public.

Two kinds of cases come before courts. In *criminal* cases, a person accused of a crime is *prosecuted*, or tried (taken before a court), to see if he or she did commit the crime. In *civil* cases, two people or groups of people come to court to settle a disagreement between them. One person or group (the *plaintiff*) has filed charges against (*sued*) the other (the *defendant*). The United States has two different court systems—the federal courts and the state courts.

The Federal Court System Federal courts make judgments in cases having to do with the U.S. Constitution or other federal law. They hear cases in which the United States is suing or prosecuting someone, or some group, or is being sued. They handle disputes between citizens of two different states and disputes involving foreign countries and U.S. citizens. Crimes that happen on ships at sea, called *admiralty cases*, are also brought into federal courts.

Federal courts are set up on three levels. The lowest federal courts are the *district courts*, where most federal cases are heard first. The United States is divided into more than 90 areas. In each area is a district court.

The *Court of Appeals* is the next highest in the federal court system. The Court of Appeals is divided into 11 circuits (areas). Together they cover all the states, territories, and possessions of the United States. Defendants who are not satisfied with the decision of a district court can *appeal* (take a case to) to the Court of Appeals.

The highest federal court is the *Supreme Court* in Washington, D.C. It reviews cases from the Court of Appeals and from the state supreme courts when questions of federal law are involved. Not every case can be taken to the Supreme Court. The *justices* (judges) of the Supreme Court agree to review only the cases they think involve important legal questions. The Supreme Court has the right to decide that any state or federal law is unconstitutional and must be taken off the books.

The federal system also provides courts for special kinds of cases. The *Court of Claims* handles money claims made against the Federal Government. The *Tax Court* handles cases involving federal tax laws. The *Customs Court* hears cases relating to payment of duties (taxes) on imported products. The *Court of Customs and Patent Appeals* reviews some of the cases of the Customs Court as well as decisions made by the Patent Office. The *Court of Military Appeals* reviews cases from the military courts of the U.S. Armed Forces. A military trial is called a *court-martial*.

The State Court System The state courts handle all cases relating to state laws. The court system of each state is organized differently. In small towns, the lowest courts are usually run by officials called *justices of the peace*. In larger towns or cities, the lowest courts are usually *police courts* or *magistrates' courts*. These courts have judges but no juries. Above them are the state (and sometimes county) *trial courts* with judges and juries. Cases from these courts may be taken to state appeals courts and then, if necessary, to the state's supreme court. States also have special courts for certain types of cases. *Juvenile courts* hear cases involving juveniles—people who are not yet 18 years old.

The Supreme Court of the United States consists of the chief justice and eight associate justices, all appointed by the President with the advice and consent of the Senate.

▼ *This impressive, Grecian-style building houses the Supreme Court—the highest federal court in the United States.*

667

Bill Pickett, a black cowboy on the famous 101 Ranch in Oklahoma, is credited with inventing the art of steer wrestling, or bulldogging.

Probate courts deal with inheritance cases. Special courts handle divorce trials. Many states set up special small claims courts for civil cases involving small amounts of money.

ALSO READ: LAW, LAWYERS AND JUDGES, PATENTS AND COPYRIGHTS, SUPREME COURT, TRIAL.

COUSTEAU, JACQUES-YVES

(born 1910) Have you ever swum underwater? You can hold your breath only for a minute or so. Then you have to come up for air. A diver wearing self-contained underwater-breathing apparatus (*scuba*) can stay underwater much longer and dive much deeper. This kind of breathing apparatus, also known as an *aqualung*, was invented by Jacques Cousteau.

In the 1930's the French Navy was testing new diving techniques. A deep-sea diver had to wear a clumsy suit with a metal helmet. He breathed through an air-tube stretching up to the surface. One of the French divers, Jacques Cousteau, wanted to be able to swim freely underwater. He and his team invented scuba diving, wearing air-bottles, face masks, and rubber flippers.

Cousteau proved that people could stay underwater for long periods. He built a seabed research base called Conshelf. He made TV films of underwater life and sailed the world's oceans in his ship, *Calypso*. He also helped develop the bathyscaphe, a deep-diving submersible.

ALSO READ: SCUBA DIVING.

COVERED WAGON see WESTWARD MOVEMENT.

COWBOY
A cowboy is a skilled horseman who helps care for cattle on a ranch. People everywhere in the world know about the cowboys of the North American West. Just as famous are the *gauchos*—the cowboys of

▲ *A time to halt on the mounted trail in Oregon. Mounted cowboys are still common on the cattle ranches.*

South America—and the *vaqueros*—the cowboys of Mexico. "Buckaroo," another word for "cowboy," comes from the Mexican word *vaquero*.

The life of a cowboy in the early days of the West was not always so adventurous and exciting as you might imagine from a Western movie or a television show. It was often dull and dreary. Even today, with all the modern inventions, cowboys must work long hours in all kinds of weather at difficult jobs.

Old-time cowboys had to spend many lonely weeks on the plains. Their food was bad. Their pay was low. They often faced danger. They always had to work very hard. But the job cowboys did was very important. They helped in the development of the modern United States. The people in the growing U.S. cities needed meat. This meat came from the cattle that the cowboys tended.

▼ *The cowboys of the ranches in Argentina are called* gauchos. *They ride their horses on the grasslands where the cattle roam.*

Cattle in the North American West grazed on open range, grassland not closed in by fences. The cattle could wander anywhere to find food. Cowboys patrolled the range to protect the cattle and to make sure the cattle did not wander too far. They rounded up strays that got lost. When the cattle ate all the grass or drank all the water on one part of the range, cowboys led them to grass or water somewhere else.

Roundup time came every spring and fall. The cowboys gathered all their cattle together in a big herd. A herd often included thousands of cattle. The cowboys counted the cattle and branded the calves. A *brand* is a mark burned on the side of an animal to show who owns it. Cowboys caught cattle and held them for branding with long ropes called *lariats* or *lassos*. Cowboys have often said that a strong rope and a good horse are the two things they need most.

A cattle drive began when the roundup and branding were finished. Cowboys took the herd to the nearest railhead, a town with a railroad station. The cattle drive was the most difficult of the cowboy's tasks. It meant guiding the huge herd of cattle hundreds of miles across open range from the ranch to the railhead. The cattle had to be protected and kept from straying, and there was always danger that the herd might be frightened into a *stampede*—a wild run. The cowboys had to work long hours each day for several weeks to make sure that the cattle made the trip safely. At the railhead, the owner sold his herd to cattle buyers from the East, and the cowboys received their pay for the drive. They often spent all their money celebrating the end of the cattle drive.

Many early cowboys who helped shape North America were blacks. It was unusual in those days for whites and blacks to work together as equals, but on the open range, with so much hard work to be done, any man who did his part was accepted. No one had time to worry about the color of his skin.

The modern West has no open ranges. All the land belonging to a ranch is now surrounded by fences. Cattle drives are no longer necessary. A railroad station is near every cattle ranch, and cattle are shipped to the station by truck. But cowboys still have plenty of work. Cattle must still be rounded up and branded. Modern cowboys still ride horses, but they also use helicopters, jeeps, motorcycles, and short-wave radios. Cowboys are proud of their skills. They have contests, called *rodeos*, with each other to see who is best at riding, roping, and other skills.

ALSO READ: CATTLE, RANCHING, RODEO, WESTWARD MOVEMENT.

COYOTE The coyote is a wild dog of North America. Coyotes have brown coats touched with black and gray sprinkles. They have pointed ears and noses and bushy tails. Coyotes also have strong voices, as anyone who has heard their evening "concert"—a series of howls and sharp barks—will tell you. Fully grown coyotes stand about 21 inches (53 cm) high at the shoulder and weigh about 30 pounds (14 kg). They can run a long time at 30 miles (48 km) an hour while chasing prey.

The original habitat of the coyote was the Great Plains of the United States. This animal often appeared in Plains Indian myths and legends as a clever trickster. The coyote roamed this area from the flatlands to the timberline (the height above which no trees grow) of mountains. The range of the coyote has expanded to new territory—from Costa Rica to Alaska, and east all the way into New England.

Coyote young, called pups, are born in the spring, in a *den* or small cave. The usual litter is five or six.

For a long time the coyote has been the symbol of all that is cowardly and sneaky in animals. When sheep first appeared on Western ranches, coyotes were such a danger that some states offered rewards for coyote scalps.

▲ *The coyote is found from Alaska to Central America.*

▲ *The water rail, a relative of the crane, is a common bird in Europe, Asia, and Africa. It is thin and about 11 inches (28 cm) from beak to tail. Birds like this are said to have brought about the expression, "skinny as a rail."*

▼ *A whooping crane chases off a rival that has invaded its territory. Its giant wingspread is about 90 inches (2.3 m). The whooping crane, the largest crane in North America, is very rare.*

The father helps rear the pups. He delivers food to the den entrance. By autumn the young have to find territories and food of their own.

Coyotes are carnivores (meat-eaters). People have always blamed coyotes for hunting sheep and cattle. But recent studies have shown that coyotes do more good than harm. They eat rabbits, gophers, rats, and other crop-destroying rodents. They are fast enough to catch jackrabbits, which eat the grass sheep need.

Coyotes that live near surburban areas and cities have sometimes bred with tame dogs to produce *coydogs*, which resemble both the wild coyote and the tame dog.

ALSO READ: DOG, MAMMAL, PRAIRIE.

CRANE Cranes are long-legged, long-necked birds. They are known for their loud cry that can be heard for miles and for the high-jumping dance they perform during their mating season. Cranes fly in large flocks, with their long necks pointing straight forward and their stiltlike legs pointing straight back. Many species are found throughout the world, but no cranes live in South America, Malaysia, or the small islands of the Pacific. Cranes are "old" birds. Fossils from France, Greece, and the United States show that birds like them were flying around about 60 million years ago.

Two kinds of cranes live in North America. One is the common *sandhill* crane. Its feathers are gray, and on its forehead is a bright red bald spot. Most sandhills live west of the Mississippi River. In winter they live in southern California, Mexico, and Central America. In summer they nest from Michigan west to Washington state, and as far south as Colorado. Many of these cranes spend the summer in Canada, where they nest as far north as Baffin Island. A few live in the marshes of Florida and southern Georgia.

The second North American member of this family is the *whooping crane*, whose voice sounds like a trumpet. Its feathers are white, except for a few black ones on the wing tips. Its face is bright red. Whooping cranes are large birds, over 5 feet (1.5 m) tall and with a wingspread of 90 inches (2.3 m) or more.

Whooping cranes summer in part of the Northwest Territories of Canada. They winter on the Texas coast, in the area now called the Aransas Wildlife Refuge. Whooping cranes were numerous in the 1800's, but fewer than 100 are living today, partly because people killed thousands of these birds for food. Whooping

▼ *One of the most handsome cranes, the crowned crane of southern Africa.*

cranes are in danger of dying out, so laws in North America have made it illegal to kill them.

Cranes are marsh or water birds. They eat mainly berries, fruits, roots, and fish. Sometimes they eat mice, insects, snakes, and snails.

Cranes have several close relatives in North America. These include the ducklike *coot*, an expert swimmer and diver, whose body is gray and black and whose tail is white; the *common* and *purple gallinules*, who usually feed at the edges of lakes; and several species of *rails*, all of whom fly poorly, but who run swiftly and silently through tall grass to escape enemies.

ALSO READ: BIRD, STORK.

CRANE, STEPHEN (1871–1900)
Stephen Crane was an American author. His most famous novel, *The Red Badge of Courage* (1895), describes the thoughts and experiences of a young Union soldier in the Civil War.

Crane was born in Newark, New Jersey. He studied at Lafayette College and Syracuse University, where he was a catcher on the baseball team. He then worked in New York City as a newspaper reporter. His first novel, *Maggie, a Girl of the Streets* (1893), tells the story of brutal life in the slums. Crane, along with other authors of the time, developed a way of writing called *naturalism*, using detailed realism and factual description, which he used to tell the reader his ideas about life. Crane thought that people were all victims of chance.

Crane became a foreign correspondent for several newspapers. He reported the war between the Greeks and Turks and, later, the Spanish-American War. He told about one of his own scary experiences in a short story, "The Open Boat"—the tale of a shipwrecked expedition to Cuba. This short story—and several others that Crane wrote—are important in the history of U.S. fiction. Crane showed later writers how to use the short-story form effectively.

Crane wrote two important books of poetry, *The Black Riders* and *War Is Kind*. He wrote in free verse and in a style used later by other poets. He developed tuberculosis during his travels and died in Germany at age 28.

ALSO READ: LITERATURE, NOVEL, POETRY, SHORT STORY.

CRATER see METEOR, VOLCANO.

CREE INDIANS A large tribe of Algonkian-speaking Indians, the Cree, once wandered freely through the woodlands of eastern and central Canada. A small number of Cree moved into the United States in the 1700's. They became buffalo hunters, like other Plains Indians. A Cree hunter could move either by land or by water to find food for his family. If animals were plentiful, he killed deer, caribou, moose, or rabbit. If animals grew scarce, he took to his canoe to fish.

The Cree knew their way around the rivers, and they willingly guided European explorers. According to white fur trappers who knew them, the Cree were generous, good-natured, and friendly. They were also good bargainers when it came to trading furs for pots and utensils. Cree men wore tight leather leggings up to the hip, short leather pants, and moccasins. Cree women wore knee-length garments made of skins, pulled in at the waist with a belt. They added detachable sleeves when the weather grew cold. Smallpox, introduced by the white settlers, killed a large number of Cree Indians. About 33,000 live today on reservations set up in Manitoba and several other Canadian provinces.

ALSO READ: ALGONKIAN; INDIANS, AMERICAN.

▲ *Stephen Crane, U.S. author and poet, introduced a new realism to fiction.*

▲ *A Cree woman from Quebec, Canada, carrying a bowl of fresh blueberries. The Cree Indians of the United States moved south from Canada.*

▲ *Cricket requires great concentration for both batsmen and fielders alike.*

King Edward IV of England declared cricket illegal in 1477 because his soldiers played the game instead of practicing archery. Nearly 300 years later, cricket was legally declared "an honorable sport."

CREEK INDIANS The Creek Indians included several tribes whose members spoke similar languages of the Muskogean family. The Creeks lived in about 50 permanent towns in the present-day states of Georgia, Alabama, and Florida.

Creek women raised corn, beans, squash, and pumpkins, and they learned from the Europeans to grow potatoes and melons. Creek men hunted deer, bear, beaver, and squirrel. The warriors made their own bows and arrows and blowguns, and they later used rifles. The tribes saved part of each harvest in public storerooms to protect themselves against poor crops. Each town provided passing travelers with free food. The leaders of all the towns met each year to discuss common problems.

In each town, four public buildings—two for leaders, one for warriors, and one for young people— were built around a public square. In the square was the *chunkey yard,* where young men played the ball game now called lacrosse or shot arrows at a pennant hung from the top of a pole. The wooden houses of the townspeople spread out from the square, and the tribal fields were beyond the houses.

One Creek tribe, the Red Sticks, fought against the United States in 1813 and 1814. Andrew Jackson led the army that defeated the Red Sticks, and all Creek tribes were forced to give up much of their land. Whites took the rest of their land in the 1830's, and the Creeks were marched to Indian Territory (now Oklahoma). Nearly half the people died on the trip. Today, about 20,000 Creeks live in northeastern Oklahoma.

ALSO READ: INDIANS, AMERICAN; JACKSON, ANDREW; LACROSSE; WAR OF 1812.

CRETE see GREECE.

CRICKET Cricket is a popular pastime in many nations, especially Great Britain and the Commonwealth. It is played mainly by men but is growing in popularity among women.

A cricket ball is slightly smaller than a baseball but weighs a little more. The wooden bat measures a maximum 38 inches (96.5 cm) long by 4¼ inches (10.8 cm) wide. About two-thirds of the length is the broad, flat *blade* (striking surface); the rest is a narrower, cylindrical handle.

A cricket team has 11 players. When one team is batting (each player has a turn to bat), one member of the other team *bowls* (somewhat like a baseball pitcher) while the other 10 field. An important fielder is the *wicket-keeper;* he stands behind the wicket at which the bowler aims (just like standing behind the plate in baseball). A cricket *innings* is complete when every person on the batting team has had a turn at bat, or when the captain of the batting team decides that his team has scored enough runs. Some matches (games) consist of one innings per team; others, notably *test matches* (played between countries over five days), have two innings per team.

A cricket match is played on a grassy field called a *pitch*. In the center of the pitch, 22 yards (20.1 m) apart, stand two *wickets*. Each wicket is 9 inches (23 cm) wide and consists of three upright *stumps* (sticks) 28 inches (71 cm) high. Two small sticks called *bails* rest on top of the stumps.

Two batsmen play at the same time. The one who faces the bowler is "on strike." Bowling is rather like throwing overhand, except that the bowler runs up and must keep his arm straight. He bowls from one wicket while the batsman on strike defends the other. Bowlers try either to knock the bails off the batsman's wicket or to make him strike the ball so that it is caught by a fielder before it touches the ground. In either case the batsman is out. Batsmen may also be out if they block the bowler's ball with their body, if they knock the bails off with their bat or a part of their body, or if they are run out (see below). Two umpires adjudicate (act as judge).

A run is made when the batsman hits the ball hard enough that he and the non-strike batsman can both run to their opposite wickets. A run may also be made if the bowler is guilty of some infringement (for example, bowls too wide of the stumps). A *bye* occurs when the batsman misses the ball, the wicket-keeper fails to stop it, and it goes far enough for the batsmen to have time to swap ends. A batsman scores four runs if he has hit the ball so that it goes over the pitch's *boundary*, six if it does so without first bouncing.

If the fielders throw in the ball so that the wickets are knocked over while a batsman is in the middle of making a run, that batsman is out (*run out*).

The team with the highest total of runs wins the game.

CRIME   If you play your radio so loudly that you disturb the other members of your family, you may be punished. You have broken a family rule and disturbed the peace of other people. A family makes rules to help all the people in the family live together.

In much the same way, a *society* (a large group of people who have many common interests and kinds of behavior) also makes rules, or *laws*, to help all the people live together. A person who breaks the laws—by stealing, for example—has committed a crime and may be punished for that action.

In ancient times, when the first part of the Bible was written, the *Mosaic Code*, also called the *Ten Commandments*, provided laws for people to follow. The Mosaic Code has survived as the basic concept of right and wrong for 4,000 years. Thou shalt not kill, thou shalt not steal—these laws still hold true in modern times.

Attitudes to crime do not always stay the same. Laws may be changed as society develops. The definition of crime also varies from country to country. In Muslim countries, a man can have several wives. But in the United States, having more than one wife or husband at a time is a crime called *bigamy*.

Some crimes have always been considered more serious than others. In the United States, serious crimes are called *felonies*. They are usually punished by imprisonment, but in some states certain felonies may be punished by death. Some of the most serious felonies are murder (intentionally killing a person), armed robbery (stealing with the use of a gun or other weapon), assault (attacking a person with the purpose of injuring him), and arson (intentionally setting a fire). The crime of *treason* (an act of betraying your country) is usually punished by life imprisonment, but during war it may be punished by death.

Other serious felonies are *forgery* (signing another person's name with intent to cheat), *counterfeiting* (printing fake money or other papers), and *embezzlement* (taking other people's money for your own use). *Rape* and other forms of sexual assault are also serious crimes, and they are becoming increasingly common.

Less serious crimes are called *misdemeanors*. Punishment for these offenses is a fine or imprisonment for less than one year. Minor traffic offenses and public drunkenness are sometimes misdemeanors.

In the United States, a person accused of a serious crime has certain rights guaranteed by the *Bill of Rights,* the first ten amendments to the Constitution. These rights include (1) the right to a fair trial; (2) the right to a trial by jury; (3) the right to a

▲ *A man with his feet in the stocks, a punishment used in olden times. People used to throw rotten fruit and vegetables, mud, and even stones at persons put in the stocks, so the punishment was no joke! It was handed down for misdemeanors (minor crimes), but sometimes people died in the stocks.*

The highest amount of damages ever sought was in a case in 1971 in which Mr. Walton Bader asked for $675,000,000,000,000 from General Motors for polluting the atmosphere in all 50 states. As that sum was then equal to ten times the U.S. national wealth, it is unlikely that Mr. Bader expected to get what he asked for.

▲ *The guillotine was first used for carrying out the death penalty in France in the 1790's during the French Revolution.*

▲ *A modern alternative to the guillotine is the San Quentin Gas Chamber, United States.*

lawyer, a person who has studied law and can represent the accused in court (if the accused is too poor to pay for a lawyer, the court appoints one for him); (4) the right to keep silent and not testify against oneself; and (5) the right not to be tried twice for the same crime, even if new evidence is later found.

A person is considered innocent under U.S. law unless proved guilty beyond a reasonable doubt. In a criminal case, the *prosecutor*, a lawyer who works for the government, must prove the guilt of the accused, who is called the *defendant*.

Reasons for Crime Crime is committed for many different reasons. Most people have desires they hope to satisfy. They may want to be loved, to be rich or to have a beautiful car. Sometimes a person's desires are so strong they become twisted. Such a person may commit crimes. Automobiles have caused crimes to multiply. They are symbols of wealth and are, therefore, very often stolen. They also make it much easier to escape from the scene of a crime.

"Organized crime," often called the "underworld," is a name for groups of criminals who run illegal operations, including selling dangerous drugs. Drugs have caused a frightening escalation of crime. Addicts are sometimes so desperate to pay for their drugs that they will commit any number of crimes to raise the money.

Many crimes are committed by the poor and uneducated. The poor are often unable to feel a part of our complicated society. Because of this frustration, they may go "outside the law" to satisfy their personal ends. Often their fellow poor suffer as the victims of their crimes. Society can help prevent crime by curing conditions known to cause it—by combating poverty, by improving schools in poor areas, by cleaning up the slums, and by providing decent housing and jobs for all people.

But some crimes are difficult to detect in a complicated society. Crime can be committed by companies who *defraud*, or cheat, the people who buy their goods. Factories belching smoke cause pollution that can kill people. Pharmaceutical companies, who publicly deplore the sale of illegal drugs to young people, distribute products that find their way into the illegal market. These people are indeed committing crimes that often go unnoticed.

Every citizen should be keenly aware of the law and one's rights under the law. Citizens should know how justice is administered in the community and nation. They should be aware of various criminal practices. Only in this way can they protect themselves and their society.

ALSO READ: BILL OF RIGHTS, CITIZENSHIP, COURT SYSTEM, JUVENILE DELINQUENCY, LAW.

CRIMEAN WAR About 500,000 soldiers were wounded or killed in the Crimean War, often called the "war of errors." But the war is best remembered for a famous nurse and for a foolish charge into battle by some gallant British cavalrymen.

The war started in 1854 because of some misunderstandings over control of land. Russia fought on one side against Great Britain, France, and Turkey. Sardinia later joined those against Russia. Most of the war was fought on the large peninsula of Crimea, which pokes into the Black Sea from the Russian mainland.

The nurse whom the war made famous was Florence Nightingale. She is said to have started modern nursing. She did such a good job of taking care of the wounded British soldiers that she became a national heroine in England.

The famous cavalry charge was at the Battle of Balaklava on October 25, 1854. A brigade of nearly 700 British cavalrymen obediently followed their leaders' unwise orders and charged straight into the fire of Russian cannon. Only 195 cavalrymen lived through this dreadful massacre. However, Russia lost the battle. Alfred, Lord Tennyson, an Englishman, wrote a poem, "The Charge of the Light Brigade," which made this event famous as an example of the British soldier's absolute devotion to duty.

Historians say that the generals on both sides in this war made many errors. These mistakes cost the lives of many soldiers. The war ended when Russia finally gave in. The four countries that took part in the start of the war finally signed a treaty in 1856 and agreed to respect each others' territories.

ALSO READ: NIGHTINGALE, FLORENCE; TENNYSON, ALFRED.

CROCKETT, DAVY (1786–1836)
"I'm half horse, half alligator," Davy Crockett once said. Davy is considered the father of the "tall tale."

David Crockett was born in Limestone, Tennessee. He fought under Andrew Jackson in the campaign against the Creek Indians during the War of 1812 and rose to the rank of colonel. He was elected to the Tennessee legislature in 1823. Three years later, he accepted a dare to run for Congress and, to his surprise, he was elected. He served three terms, becoming a beloved figure in Washinton, D.C., because of his backwoods costumes and "big brag" stories. He could "whip his weight in wildcats . . . shoot six cord of bear in a day . . . and jump higher, dive deeper, and come up dryer than anybody else." Popular songs and plays were written about him. *The Crockett Almanacks*, first published in 1835, gained worldwide fame.

Crockett lost the election of 1835 because of his opposition to President

Jackson's land and Indian policies. He went to Texas to aid the independence movement. At San Antonio, he volunteered to help defend the Alamo. He died on March 6, 1836, with 182 other defenders, when the fort fell to the Mexicans.

ALSO READ: ALAMO; JACKSON, ANDREW; WAR OF 1812.

CROMWELL, OLIVER (1599–1658)
Oliver Cromwell governed Britain from 1649 to 1658. These nine years were the only period in British history when the nation had no king or queen. Britain was proclaimed the Commonwealth.

Cromwell was elected to Parliament in 1628 and again in 1640. While in Parliament, he joined the Roundheads, who opposed King Charles I. Charles wanted no interference from Parliament (the people's elected representatives); he believed in the *divine right of kings*, that monarchs were responsible only to God, and that their subjects should therefore obey them without question.

In 1642, a civil war began between the Roundheads (who got their name because they cut their hair very short) and the Cavaliers (who supported the King). As lieutenant-general of the

▲ *Many soldiers lost their lives in the misery of the Crimean War. Here we see Scottish troops carrying their colors into battle.*

▲ *Davy Crockett, a hero of the U.S. frontier and subject of many a tall tale.*

▲ Oliver Cromwell, the ruler—"Protector"—of Great Britain during the Commonwealth.

▲ The banner of Oliver Cromwell.

army, Cromwell showed his military genius by building the Roundhead army into a great fighting force. He led the army in many victorious battles. After the war, Cromwell sat on the court that tried King Charles for treason, and was one of the signers of the King's death warrant. Supported by the Roundhead army, Cromwell became governor of Britain. He was made Lord Protector in 1653.

Cromwell granted religious freedom to the Puritans, Quakers, and Jews. He began as a great supporter of the people. But everyone was confused in the period after the civil war, and Cromwell met many problems. He had his own troubles with Parliament. For a time, he even locked up its meeting place. He was very cruel in putting down revolutions in Ireland and Scotland.

When Cromwell died, his son Richard (1626–1712) became Lord Protector. But where his father had been strong, Richard was weak. He had to resign after a few months, and the son of Charles I was crowned Charles II in 1660.

ALSO READ: CHARLES, KINGS OF ENGLAND; ENGLISH HISTORY; PARLIAMENT.

CROSS-SECTION see MECHANICAL DRAWING.

CROSSWORD PUZZLE Do you like to work puzzles? People in all parts of the world have enjoyed solving puzzles of various kinds for centuries. Among the most popular are crossword puzzles. They appear in daily and weekly newspapers, in magazines, and in books that have nothing but crossword puzzles in them. Special dictionaries have even been created to help the solver.

To work a crossword puzzle, a person must guess words from printed clues, and then put the letters of these words into a pattern of numbered squares.

To solve the crossword puzzle on this page, copy the pattern on a blank sheet of paper. Draw a large square on the paper and divide the square into 36 smaller squares by drawing 5 evenly spaced lines both across and down. Number the squares as shown—each number marks the beginning of a word—but be sure to leave room for the letters of the words. Shade in the dark squares, which help you see where words begin and end.

Now solve the puzzle on your own sheet. The completed puzzle is printed on the next page but don't peek until you have finished!

ALSO READ: WORD GAMES.

CROWN JEWELS Crown jewels are collections of pieces of jewelry worn or carried by rulers. These jewels have been passed down from one monarch to another for hundreds of years. It is impossible to state the worth of crown jewels in dollars, because of their historic and symbolic value. Some of the world's greatest gems are found in these collections.

The *crown* is the official sign of a ruler's power. There are two general styles. One is an open headband with designs and jewels set in. The other is the closed crown with arched pieces

Across
1 one of the seasons
5 3rd person singular of *to be*
6 sharp tool
7 Cincinnati team
10 the smallest unit of an element
12 instead
13 I and at least one other person
14 the European country whose capital is Stockholm

Down
1 gentlemen
2 to put into service
3 it supports a sail
4 formerly (abbr.)
8 challenge
9 the end of a prayer
11 to be in debt
12 exclamation of pain

of metal over the top of the head. Crown-jewel collections also may include *scepters*, ornate rods that rulers carry on special occasions, and *orbs*, jeweled spheres in which crosses are mounted.

Crowns differ from country to country and from age to age. Byzantine emperors wore either a closed crown or a high pyramid cap covered by pearls and jewels. The Iron Crown of Lombardy is said to contain a nail from the Cross on which Jesus was crucified. Napoleon carried this crown when he was made king of Italy in 1805.

St. Stephen's crown was used in coronations of Hungarian kings for 900 years. No king was considered legitimate unless crowned with it. In July 1945, a Hungarian Royal Crown Guard gave this jeweled crown and the coronation regalia (sword, scepter, orb, and gold embroidered robe) to the U.S. Seventh Army for safekeeping. He said he had removed the objects from their hiding places to keep them out of the hands of Soviet troops. The precious crown and regalia were kept in Fort Knox, Kentucky, until they were returned to the Hungarian people in January 1978.

The Austrian Imperial crown, dated 1602, is pure gold, set with diamonds. This crown, which sat on the heads of several rulers of the Hapsburg (Habsburg) family, is banded top and bottom with pearls. On top is a large sapphire.

The Scottish crown was originally a gold band set with large gems and pearls. In 1707, the Scots were afraid the English would take their crown jewels to England. They secretly hid them in Edinburgh Castle, in a chest with three locks. They put the chest in the crown room, which had two doors, one of oak and one of iron. Time went by, and the secret was forgotten. After 110 years, a group was chosen to hunt for the crown jewels. The chest was found, and Sir Walter Scott, a leading Scottish au-

thor and friend of the British royal family, was chosen to open it. Today the jewels are on display in Edinburgh.

England's Richard I, "the Lion-Hearted," had a crown so heavy that two earls had to hold it over his head. Edward II personally owned ten crowns—nine of gold and one of silver. Henry V wore his crown on top of his helmet at the Battle of Agincourt in 1415. While Oliver Cromwell ruled England, there was no king. At that time most of the crown jewels were broken down, melted, and sold. Later, some were bought again and reset.

In the 17th century, the royal goldsmith was put to work on a coronation crown for Charles II, called "St. Edward's Crown." The present Queen Elizabeth, Queen Victoria, and other monarchs used it for their coronations.

The British crown jewels include orbs, scepters, swords, bracelets, amulets (charms), and the royal spoon, as well as crowns. They are used on ceremonial occasions to indicate the ruler's various powers and responsibilities. Today, the crown jewels are owned not by the ruler but by the British people. They are displayed in the Tower of London for everyone to see. They are worn only on very special occasions. Ordinarily, the queen dresses like any of her subjects.

ALSO READ: KINGS AND QUEENS.

▲ *The crown of St. Stephen, part of the Hungarian royal regalia. According to tradition, it was given to Stephen (about 975–1038) by the Pope as a reward for having converted so many pagans to Christianity.*

▲ *The British Imperial State Crown is worn by the monarch of the United Kingdom on state occasions—for example, the annual speech to the British Parliament.*

¹S	²U	M	³M	⁴E	R
⁵I	S		⁶A	X	
⁷R	E	⁸D	S		⁹A
S		¹⁰A	T	¹¹O	M
	¹²O	R		¹³W	E
¹⁴S	W	E	D	E	N

Carrion crow

Rook

Hooded crow

▲ *The crow family,*
Corvidae, is a very large one,
containing many different types
of birds. Three of the more
common ones are shown here.

CROWS If you have ever traveled in the country, you have probably seen flocks of large, jet-black birds in fields or resting in tall trees. These birds are probably crows. Their loud, shrill "caw, caw" cry can be heard a long way as they warn each other of danger or tell of a new supply of food. Crows are found in all parts of the world except New Zealand. Birds of the crow family include rooks, ravens, jays, jackdaws, and magpies.

Although crows generally favor farmlands and woods, they have adapted to many different kinds of environments, including noisy, crowded cities. They are intelligent birds that can be tamed and can learn to imitate human sounds.

Crows eat almost anything—vegetables, fruits, insects, and small animals. One species, the fish crow, lives near the shore and eats small fish and shellfish.

Rooks are large crows with a whitish base to their bills. *Ravens* are even bigger and have a strong, large bill. There are some very famous ravens that live in the Tower of London, England. According to Greek myth, ravens used to be white. However, one day a raven told the god Apollo that the nymph Coronis was deceiving him. Apollo killed the nymph but hated the bird that had told him of her deceit so much he painted it black. *Jays* are smallish birds of the crow family. They have various colors. The Blue Jay is very well known. *Jackdaws* are also quite small. They are well known for stealing shiny objects such as coins and jewelry!

ALSO READ: BIRD.

CRUSADES Can you imagine thousands of people traveling together on a long journey? This took place between the late 1000's and the 1300's, when groups of people went to the Middle East. They were Christians fighting wars to win control of the Holy Land from the Muslims. Their journeys were called Crusades. The word comes from the Latin word meaning "cross." Almost all soldiers of the European armies sewed crosses on their clothing as a sign of their promise to win the Holy Land.

Palestine was important to Christians as the land of Jesus. To the Muslims, Palestine was the land where many of their prophets, like Abraham and Moses, had lived. The Muslims controlled the land and held rich trade routes there. These wars were bitter and bloody.

Wars between Christians and Muslims actually began long before the Crusades. Muslims conquered Italy, Sicily, and Spain, but by the time of the First Crusade they had been pushed from Italy and Sicily, and they were quickly losing Spain. Arab Muslims had also conquered Jerusalem in the 600's. They allowed Christians to visit the holy places. But after Turkish Muslims took Jerusalem in 1071 they did not allow Christian visitors. All of this helped to bring about the First Crusade.

The First Crusade (1095–1099) is said to have been led by a preacher, Peter the Hermit. He took bands of common people on this crusade. They headed for Constantinople (now Istanbul, Turkey), the capital of the Byzantine Empire. Most of these people starved or were killed by the Turks. But they were followed by armies of knights, mostly from France. They marched or took ships to Asia Minor. They met there in 1097 and started toward Jerusalem. On the way they fought many bloody battles, often robbing and destroying innocent villages along the way. They captured Jerusalem in 1099, and most of the crusaders returned home. Some stayed and formed a group of four states (the Latin States) on the eastern shore of the Mediterranean.

The Second Crusade (1147–1148) took place because not enough cru-

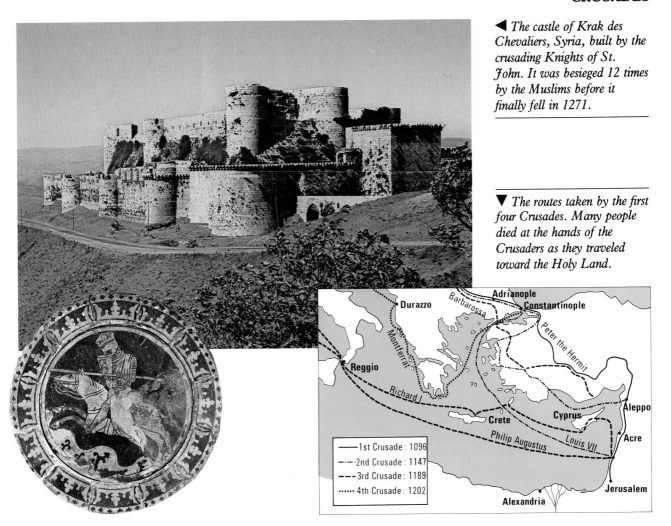

◀ The castle of Krak des Chevaliers, Syria, built by the crusading Knights of St. John. It was besieged 12 times by the Muslims before it finally fell in 1271.

▼ The routes taken by the first four Crusades. Many people died at the hands of the Crusaders as they traveled toward the Holy Land.

———1st Crusade: 1096
-·-·-2nd Crusade: 1147
- - - 3rd Crusade: 1189
········4th Crusade: 1202

▲ The crusading English King Richard I, from a 13th-century tile.

saders from the First Crusade stayed to defend the land they had taken. Less than 50 years later, the Turks took back one of the crusaders' four states. A Second Crusade was formed. King Louis VII of France led one army, and Emperor Conrad of Germany led another. But the two armies did not work together, and the Turks defeated them.

The Third Crusade (1189–1192) started because the Turks recaptured the city of Jerusalem in 1187. They also recaptured most of the Holy Land. Saladin was the Turkish leader. Several Europeans led the Third Crusade. But one of them, German Emperor Frederick I, also known as Frederick Barbarossa, died on his way to the Holy Land. An-

other, King Philip II of France, returned home soon after he arrived. This left King Richard I of England, called "the Lion-Hearted," to fight Saladin's army. Richard defeated Saladin in several battles, but he did not recapture Jerusalem. However, he did succeed in getting Saladin to allow Christians to visit the city on holy pilgrimages.

The Fourth Crusade (1201–1204) was not against the Muslims. Instead, it was an attempt to gain riches and trade. Merchants of Venice, Italy, made a bargain with French nobles. The Venetians supplied the ships to take the French to the Holy Land. The crusaders and the Venetians then got together and captured Constantinople. They removed the Byzantine emperor from his throne. Then they divided up the empire, thus starting its final decline.

▼ How a crusader knight looked when dressed for battle. Notice the huge sword. The swords of the Muslims were much lighter and more maneuverable.

679

The Children's Crusade (1212) was a bizarre episode in the crusades. It was made up of two armies of boys and girls, one from France, the other from Germany. These "soldiers" believed that only children could win the Holy Land for Christianity. Tragically, most of these 50,000 children never reached the Holy Land. Some died of hunger or cold. Others drowned. Many reached Palestine after being sold as slaves to Muslims.

There were four other crusades. None had much success. The failure of the Children's Crusade encouraged Pope Innocent III to begin *the Fifth Crusade* (1217–1221). This managed to capture a town at the mouth of the Nile River, but it was soon given back to the Muslims. *The Sixth Crusade* (1228–1229) was led by Emperor Frederick II of the Holy Roman Empire. He got the Muslims to turn over Jerusalem to the Christians without any fighting, but the Muslims took the city back again in 1244. King Louis IX of France led *the Seventh Crusade* (1248–1254). He was captured, then freed for a huge ransom. Louis sought revenge against the Muslims on *the Eighth Crusade* (1270), but he was old and sick. He died on the way to the Holy Land.

The Crusades brought many changes to Europe. The Europeans began to trade more with people living in the Middle East. They exchanged their textiles for new foods and spices they had found in the Middle East. Much Oriental philosophy drifted back to Europe. The increased trade and travel brought great curiosity about other unknown parts of the world. This led explorers to make great discoveries in the next centuries.

ALSO READ: BYZANTINE EMPIRE, HOLY ROMAN EMPIRE, PALESTINE.

▲ *Saladin, the great Turkish general who fought the armies of the Third Crusade. He recaptured many cities from the Christians.*

▶ *Six well-known types of crustaceans. Many crustaceans live in water, but many live on land, too.*

CRUSTACEAN If you mention "crustacean" to someone who likes seafood, he or she will probably think of lobsters, shrimps, or crabs. But these edible and important crustaceans are only a few of the world's 35,000 different kinds. Sandhoppers, woodlice, waterfleas, and barnacles are also crustaceans. Tiny crustaceans of many kinds are such an important source of food for fish and other water animals that much of the life of oceans, lakes, and streams would perish without them.

Crustaceans are *arthropods* of the class Crustacea. Insects are arthropods, too, and insects and crustaceans share some features. Like insects and other arthropods, crustaceans have jointed legs, bodies divided into sections or *segments*, and a tough outer covering, or shell, made of a material called *chitin*. Some crustaceans, such as lobsters, have very hard shells, while the shells of other crustaceans are fragile. Every crustacean hatches from an egg as a *larva*, which develops into a tiny adult. The adult grows until its shell is too tight, sheds it, and grows a larger one. This process, *molting*, happens several times before the animal is full grown.

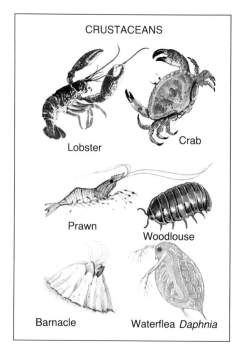

CRUSTACEANS

Lobster

Crab

Prawn

Woodlouse

Barnacle

Waterflea *Daphnia*

It takes an expert scientist to recognize some crustaceans. Many can be clearly seen only under a microscope. The larvae do not look at all like typical crustaceans.

Crustaceans live in many different places, in both salt and fresh water. Small ones live under the ice in Arctic water. Others survive heat up to 112° F (44° C) in hot springs. Tiny varieties even live in pockets of water caught in leaves of trees. But by far the greatest number live in the seas.

The Ten-legged Crustaceans The larger crustaceans are called *decapods,* meaning "ten-legged." True *lobsters,* the popular seafood, have four pairs of walking legs. The fifth (front) pair of legs is used for crushing prey and tearing it apart. Most lobsters come from the north Atlantic Ocean, and Maine is especially famous for the lobsters caught off its coast. *Rock lobsters,* also called "spiny lobsters" or "langoustes," belong to a different family. They have no pincers. Many of these are caught for food off the coasts of Florida, Africa, and the West Indies. The part we eat, usually called the "tail," is really the animal's abdomen.

Crayfish look like small lobsters, but they do not live in salt water. You can find them under rocks in streams or in mud tunnels on the banks. Crayfish are considered a delicacy in some parts of the United States.

Crabs are much like lobsters, but their tails, or abdomens, do not show. They are neatly tucked away under the animal's shell. Some crabs live in shallow coastal waters. Others are found deep in the ocean. The *rock,* or *cancer, crab* scurries about on land and has legs suited for running. *Blue crabs* are active swimmers, with back legs shaped like small paddles. The largest of all crustaceans is the *spider crab* of Japan, whose outstretched claws may span 11 feet (over 3 m). The *hermit crab* frequently goes "house-hunting." It has no shell of its own on its abdomen. So it "borrows" snail shells or even coconuts as houses, moving to bigger ones as it grows.

Many crabs are good to eat. The blue crab of the Atlantic is caught in enormous numbers by commercial fishermen. Soft-shell crabs, a favorite food, are crabs that have shed their outgrown shells. They are harvested before the new shell hardens. The *Alaska king crab,* also called the *Japanese crab,* is an important food crab, too. These "kings" weigh about 12 pounds (5 kg) apiece. *Horseshoe crabs,* often found washed onto Atlantic beaches, are not really crabs at all, but "living fossils" whose way of life has probably not changed for 175 million years. They are most closely related to spiders and scorpions.

Shrimps and *prawns* are decapods with fragile shells; prawns are a variety of large shrimp. All are good swimmers, equipped with several sets of paddlelike legs. Many kinds of shrimps live in both fresh and salt water. One kind has been found three miles (5 km) deep in the ocean. The ones most often caught for food in the United States belong to the *Pennaeus* genus. They come from the sandy bottom of the Gulf of Mexico. *Mantis shrimp* live in mud burrows and wait for small fish. They slash their prey with hidden jaw blades that act like jackknives.

Barnacles Near the ocean shore, large numbers of *acorn barnacles* sometimes settle on rocks. Each limy shell contains a tiny crustacean. *Gooseneck barnacles* attach themselves to objects such as wharves and ship bottoms. They frequently have to be removed from ships. Other barnacles fasten themselves to sea animals such as whales and turtles.

Barnacles have two distinct stages in their life histories. They hatch from eggs as tiny, free-swimming animals. They later attach themselves by their heads to solid objects, and a

▲ *A North American lobster. You can see the main parts of a crustacean—jointed legs, segmented body, and a hard outer shell.*

▼ *Barnacles on a rock. Barnacles start life as free-swimming animals but later attach themselves to solid objects.*

Edible crab

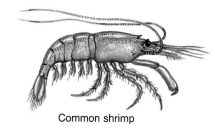

Common shrimp

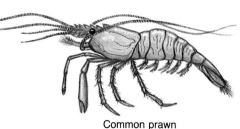

Common prawn

▲ *Three common crustaceans that you might see when you are at the seashore. Or perhaps you've eaten them?*

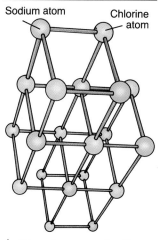

Sodium atom   Chlorine atom

▲ *How the atoms of sodium and chlorine bond together in a crystal of table salt. Of course, in any crystal large enough for you to see, there would be many more atoms than shown here. However, the overall arrangement of the atoms is still the same.*

hard shell forms around them. The shell is always made up of five plates of limy material, although barnacle shells come in many shapes. The animals remain in place for the rest of their lives.

The Tiny Crustaceans The word "zooplankton" is used to describe communities of extremely small, drifting animals in the sea. Often zooplankton communities are so vast they color the water for miles. Crustaceans make up a large part of this moving cloud of sea life. The most abundant of them—and perhaps the most abundant animal in the world—are called *copepods*. They look like shrimp about the size of a rice grain. They swim with jerky movements and feed on algae. Millions of them are eaten by other sea animals. One kind of cold-water, red-colored copepod, known as *krill*, is the main food of herring and baleen whales. Scientists believe that in the future krill will become an important food for humans, too. Krill and other kinds of crustaceans, at sea and in fresh water, are very important to the underwater balance of nature.

■ LEARN BY DOING
You can easily study the life history of some crustaceans. Brine shrimp can be raised in an aquarium. Buy the shrimp in a pet store and get instructions on how to raise them. Or keep land-living crustaceans, such as "sow bugs" and "pill bugs"—which are not insects—in a terrarium. Feed them a dead caterpillar or earthworm once in a while. ■

ALSO READ: AQUARIUM, CENTIPEDES AND MILLIPEDES, INSECT, MARINE LIFE, MOLTING, PLANKTON, SHELL.

CRYOGENICS You may be familiar with the balloons you can buy that float as if by magic in the air above you. They can do this because they

are filled with a gas called *helium*. But if you cool helium to the very low temperature of about −452° F (−269° C) it becomes a liquid. Scientists have discovered that this is a very odd liquid indeed. For example, it is so "runny" that if you were to put it in a cup it would flow up and over the side of the cup! This is called *superfluidity*.

Cryogenics is the study of what happens to things at very low temperatures such as this. Such temperatures are often close to what is called *absolute zero*, the coldest temperature there can possibly be. It is −459.69° F (−273.16° C), although scientists usually describe it as 0 K, where "K" stands for "Kelvin." (Kelvins are the same "size" as Celsius degrees, so that 0° C, the freezing point of water, equals 273.16 K.)

Some materials behave very oddly at low temperatures. The light gas hydrogen, for example, when cooled almost to absolute zero, becomes a solid that is very like a metal. Many substances display *superconductivity*: if you made a loop out of them and started an electric current in that loop, the electric current would keep flowing around the loop forever!

Some day, scientists hope to achieve superconductivity at room temperature.

ALSO READ: SUPERCONDUCTIVITY.

CRYSTAL A snowflake, a grain of salt, and a diamond are alike in one way. All are crystals. A crystal is a form of matter in which the atoms or molecules are arranged in very regular patterns. Each substance has its own pattern.

The Unit Crystal Look at some grains of table salt (sodium chloride) with a magnifying glass. Note that each is a tiny cube. (Some may not be cubes because they have been broken, or two or more grains may be stuck together. And other substances, such as iodine, are added to some salt. These other substances do not form cube-shaped crystals.) Each cube is a crystal of salt.

Suppose you had a knife with which you could split a grain of salt as many times as you wished. If you split the grain again and again, you would finally have several million cubes. Each would have edges about one twenty-five-millionth of an inch (1 ten-millionth of a centimeter) long. Each cube would have the sodium and chlorine atoms arranged as in the drawing opposite. Each cube has 14 chlorine atoms and 13 sodium atoms—one between each pair of chlorine atoms. You cannot split this cube any smaller and still have this arrangement of atoms. That is why this tiny cube is called a *unit crystal*.

The shape of a unit crystal decides the shape of the larger crystal, which is made up of great numbers of unit crystals. Because a unit crystal of sodium chloride is a cube, a grain of salt is also a cube-shaped crystal.

Solutions and Crystals When certain solid substances are put into liquids and moved about, the solid disappears. We say the solid *dissolves* in the liquid. The liquid and the dissolved solid together make up a *solution*. Salt crystals dissolve in water, making a salt solution. When you have dissolved so much solid in a certain amount of a liquid that the liquid can hold no more, you have made a *saturated* solution. Most crystals form in saturated solutions.

■ **LEARN BY DOING**
Put one quarter inch (6 mm) of water into a wide-mouthed glass jar.

▲ *These crystals of calcite have formed a weirdly pretty piece of rock. Calcite is a very common mineral.*

Place the jar into a pot one-fourth full of water. Heat the pot until the water in it just simmers, but does not boil rapidly. Slowly stir table salt into the water in the jar until no more salt will dissolve. (You should have an adult with you when you do this.)

Take the pot away from the heat. Use a potholder or towel to remove the jar from the pot. Let the jar become cool enough to touch. Using absorbent cotton, swab some of the salt solution on a piece of glass. Put the glass in a box or a drawer, where no air currents will blow on it. After an hour, put the glass on a dark-colored surface. With a magnifying glass, examine the salt crystals that have formed on the glass.

Repeat this experiment using Epsom salts instead of table salt. ■

ALSO READ: ATOM, CHEMISTRY, ELEMENT, METAL, MINERAL.

▲ *Some of the shapes a snowflake may have. These crystals of water have different shapes depending on the exact circumstances in which they formed. It is said that no two snowflakes are ever alike!*

▼ *Some of the basic shapes of natural unit crystals.*

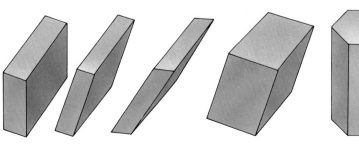

▲ *Havana, the capital city of Cuba, is famous for its cigars.*

CUBA Cuba is an island nation in the West Indies, lying about 90 miles (145 km) south of Key West, Florida. It consists of one large island, Cuba, and many smaller ones. Its coastline is fringed with beautiful sandy beaches, coral reefs, and *cays* (low islands). Cuba is almost the same size as Pennsylvania. Cubans call their country the "Pearl of the Antilles" because of its West Indian island beauty. (See the map with the article on WEST INDIES.)

Southeast Cuba has rolling hills, but much of the island consists of lush, flat plains. The climate is warm and sunny all year, and very dry in some seasons. The temperature often reaches 75° F (24° C) even in midwinter.

Sugarcane growing is the biggest industry, and even city workers help during sugarcane harvest. Coffee, rice, beans, and tobacco are also important crops. Cigars made in Havana, Cuba's capital, are famous.

The majority of Cubans are white and of Spanish (or European) descent. Others are blacks with African ancestry and *mulattoes* (persons of mixed black and white ancestry). Cuba also has some persons of Asian descent.

American Indians lived in Cuba long before the white man came. But they died during the 1500's from overwork as Spanish slaves and from diseases the Europeans brought with them. Today, almost all Cubans speak Spanish. Some English is also spoken, especially in the large cities, such as Havana and Santiago de Cuba. A few blacks speak a West African language called *Yoruba*.

Columbus discovered Cuba on his first trip to the Americas, in 1492. A Spanish colony was firmly established by 1511. During the next 200 years, Cuba became a center for illegal trade with pirates. England controlled the island for a short time, and then traded it back to Spain for Florida. Cubans grew wealthy from sugar and the slave trade. In time, Spanish rule became unpopular, and political unrest disturbed the island. After the Spanish-American War of 1898, Cuba was freed from Spanish control. The United States ruled the country until 1902, when the island became independent.

Fidel Castro led a revolution in the 1950's. Fulgencio Batista, the dictator who ruled Cuba at that time, fled the country in 1959, and Castro took power. The United States and Cuba had several disagreements and ended diplomatic relations in 1961. In April of that year, a group of anti-Castro Cubans supported by the United States landed at a place called the Bay of Pigs to try to overthrow Castro. But his army was well organized. The fighting was over in three days.

Cuba became a Communist state under Castro, who turned to the Soviet Union for military aid and protection. The Soviets built missile bases on the island. On October 22, 1962, President Kennedy demanded that the Soviets remove all missiles or

CUBA

Capital City: Havana (2,100,000 people).
Area: 44,292 square miles (114,524 sq. km).
Population: 10,600,000.
Government: Communist republic.
Natural Resources: Many metals and minerals.
Export Products: Shellfish, citrus fruit, tobacco.
Unit of Money: Peso.
Official Language: Spanish.

risk war with the United States. He also ordered a naval blockade of Cuba. Soviet Premier Nikita Khrushchev agreed to remove the missiles, and Kennedy lifted the blockade.

Castro has kept Cuba free from Russian domination. He has aided revolutionary groups in Latin America and Africa. Many Cubans have emigrated to the United States and other places since Castro came into power.

ALSO READ: CASTRO, FIDEL; KENNEDY, JOHN FITZGERALD; SPANISH-AMERICAN WAR; WEST INDIES.

CULTURE If you tried to eat your dinner by kneeling at the table instead of sitting in a chair, and if you dug your fork into the large bowls of food at the center of the table instead of putting a portion of food on your plate, your parents would probably tell you that you were being very rude. But you could do these things—and eat with chopsticks instead of a knife, fork, and spoon—if you lived in Japan. You would have good table manners, according to Japanese culture.

Culture is how a particular group of people behave. From earliest times, people have lived together in groups. A group might be very small, a few families living together in a village. Or it might be as large as a vast nation. The group develops a language, a government, laws, religious beliefs, and a particular type of art. The word "culture" means all these things together.

A cultured person is one who has learned the way of life of his or her culture. The way we speak, our manners, our ideas of good art and good literature, the songs we sing, the clothes we wear, even the games we play—all are parts of culture.

Cultures change all the time. So do their languages. Everyone now knows what a microcomputer is—you may

even have one of your own—but only a few years ago the word did not exist. Ideas about dress change, too. Ask your parents or your teacher what students wore to school 20 years ago. Does it sound as though clothing was the same then as now?

People "belong" to more than one culture. A large culture is made up of several smaller ones. The United States is part of *Western culture*, the culture based mostly on ancient Greece and Rome that developed in Europe. Judeo-Christian religious beliefs have become an important part of Western culture.

People in the United States also belong to North American culture. And even this is made up of other cultures. If you live on a farm in the Midwest, you have many different habits from a person who lives in a large Eastern city. But in some ways cultures are becoming more and more alike. For example, in almost every capital city in the world you can now see the same makes of automobile and the same restaurant chains.

The culture of a group is passed on—parents teach it to their children. But one culture can "borrow" from another. Although Western culture came mainly from the ancient civilizations of Greece and Rome, now parts of other cultures are being borrowed, too. If you enjoy country mu-

▲ *These firewalkers in Hong Kong feel little or no pain as they tread on the red-hot coals. Firewalking is one small part of their Eastern culture.*

▼ *Japanese culture requires obedience to strict rules for eating and social occasions.*

▲ *Marie and Pierre Curie, the famous French scientists who did so much to aid our understanding of radioactivity. The child with them is their daughter Irène, who also became a famous scientist.*

▼ *Although curling began in Scotland, it is now played in the U.S., Canada, and throughout Scandinavia. Curling was a spectator sport in the 1988 winter Olympic games also.*

sic, you may think the banjo is a North American instrument. But it is an instrument borrowed from African culture. In the same way, pieces of the cultures of China, Japan, and other countries have become part of our culture. And some aspects of our culture came from the Indians. However, many parts of U.S. culture are original to it. For example, the automobile and the airplane were not borrowed from another culture. Can you think of any other examples of "invented" culture?

ALSO READ: ANTHROPOLOGY, CIVILIZATION, CUSTOMS, SOCIOLOGY.

CURIE FAMILY Marie and Pierre Curie are famous for their work on radioactivity. Their daughters Irène and Ève, and their son-in-law Frédéric, also became well known.

Marie Sklodowska Curie (1867–1934) was born in Warsaw, Poland. She traveled to Paris, France, to study chemistry and physics. There she met Pierre Curie (1859–1906), a brilliant French scientist. Marie and Pierre were married in 1895. The next year, a French scientist named Antoine Henri Becquerel discovered the radioactivity of uranium ore, or *pitchblende*. Marie and Pierre began to experiment with radioactivity even though they had little money for research. They soon realized the ore was more radioactive than pure uranium, so they guessed that another material must be causing the "extra" radioactivity. They set out to find this material, and they discovered two new radioactive elements—*polonium* and *radium*. Marie and Pierre were able to extract tiny amounts of these elements from several tons of pitchblende by working hard and long.

The Curies, together with Becquerel, shared the Nobel Prize for physics in 1903. Marie was the first woman to receive this award. She received a second one for chemistry in

1911—the first person ever to win two Nobel prizes.

Irène Joliot-Curie (1897–1956) was her mother's assistant in the Radiation Institute in Paris and the third member of the Curie family to win a Nobel Prize. She and her husband, Jean Frédéric Joliot-Curie (1900–1958; original surname Joliot), made discoveries that helped later scientists produce radioactive forms of elements that are not normally radioactive. The Joliot-Curies won the Nobel Prize for chemistry in 1935. Like Marie, the Joliot-Curies both died of cancer, probably because of the radioactivity with which they all worked. (Pierre was killed in a street accident.) Ève Curie (born 1904) is a musician and author. Her most famous book is *Madam Curie*, a biography of her mother.

ALSO READ: ELEMENT, RADIOACTIVITY, URANIUM.

CURLING The game of curling probably began in Scotland or Holland in the early 1500's. The game is similar to bowling but is played on frozen lakes or indoor ice rinks. Curling is popular today in Canada, Scandinavia and is played in some parts of the United States.

Curling players slide heavy, rounded stones, with metal handles attached, on an ice court toward a round target. The ice court is 146 feet (44.5 m) long and 14 feet (4.25 m) wide. The object of the game is to slide the stones as close as possible to the center of a target, a three-ringed bull's-eye on the ice. The target's center is called the *tee* or *button*. Two four-person teams, called *rinks*, compete in a curling match. The rink that gets the greatest number of stones nearest the tee wins.

The rink captain, called the *skip*, tells his or her rinkmates where and how hard to slide their stones. Each rink has eight stones. Each player uses two of these, as he or she takes turns curling against a player from the opposing rink. When all the stones of both rinks have been played, this is called an *end* (inning), and scores are totaled. Ten ends usually make a game.

Curling stones are made of real stone. Each stone usually weighs 38 pounds (17 kg), but they can weigh as little as 35 (16 kg) or as much as 50 (23 kg). The stone is about 36 inches (90 cm) around. The top and bottom of the stone are flat and slightly scooped out. A handle is attached through a hole that is drilled through the stone from top to bottom.

To slide a stone, a player holds it by its handle and tries to give it a slight twist as he or she slides it forward. The twist makes the stone spin, or *curl*, as it slides, which gives the game its name. Each rink tries to aim its stones to knock its opponents' stones out of the target boundaries. The players all carry brooms with them to sweep frost from the ice ahead of a rinkmate's sliding stone.

ALSO READ: BOWLING, GAMES, SPORTS.

CURRENT see OCEAN.

CUSTER, GEORGE (1839–1876) George Armstrong Custer was a blond-haired army officer and Indian fighter. Historians do not agree whether he was a hero. He died in the battle of the Little Big Horn.

Custer was born in New Rumley, Ohio. He dreamed of becoming a soldier and graduated from West Point in 1861. In the Civil War he fought as a cavalry officer at Bull Run, Gettysburg, and Richmond. He became the youngest general in the Union Army.

Settlers swarmed westward after the war, killing the buffalo and driving the Plains Indians from their homes. The Indians fought back. The army began to force them onto reser-

vations. Custer, who held the rank of lieutenant colonel, commanded the famous Seventh Cavalry in many attacks—often brutal ones—on the Sioux and Cheyenne tribes.

In 1876 he led a column of soldiers in search of Sioux who had left their Black Hills reservation to hunt buffalo. He found them at the Little Big Horn River in Montana. He was supposed to wait for reinforcements, but he attacked on June 25, before other troops could arrive. About 2,500 braves, led by chiefs Sitting Bull and Crazy Horse, surrounded "Yellow Hair," as the Indians called him, and his soldiers. Custer and all his men were killed.

There were arguments after the defeat. Some thought Custer was a fool who disobeyed orders. Others honored his memory. The argument may never be settled.

ALSO READ: INDIANS, AMERICAN; INDIAN WARS.

CUSTOMS Why do many people shake hands when they meet? Why do Japanese bow to each other in greeting? They are following customs. Customs are ways of acting and living—learned and followed by a great many people—that have come down from generation to generation. Customs often change as time goes by and the lives of people change.

How does a custom start? Many develop because people find them the easiest, most convenient way to do things. For example, it is a custom to close schools during the summer. This practice was begun so that children could help with the harvest. Some customs begin because some people believe certain ways of behaving are proper and good. Other customs come from religious beliefs.

Some are taken more seriously than others. Some have become laws of the land. These are sometimes called *mores*, the Latin word for "customs."

▲ *George Custer, the famous U.S. Army officer who lost his life, and those of several hundred of his soldiers, in a battle with the Sioux Indians.*

▲ *It is the custom in some Muslim countries for women to wear veils over their faces whenever they are in the presence of men other than their husbands, fathers, or brothers.*

▲ *A fortified castle built in the 12th century near Limassol on the southern coast of Cyprus. Cyprus has been an important military base for thousands of years because of its location along the main ship routes in the Mediterranean Sea.*

Many written laws have come from mores, and persons who break these laws are punished. For example, people in most countries drive their cars on the right-hand side of the road. They can be arrested, or have accidents, if they drive on the left side. In some African tribes and in several Muslim countries, it is considered proper for a man to have more than one wife at a time, but this practice of polygamy is against the law in the United States.

Some customs are short-lived and can really be called *fashions*. Such fashions may include ways of dressing, length of hair (short or long), and beards. The custom of shaking hands when you meet someone may have begun in the dangerous days of knighthood. When one knight met another, they would shake hands to prove they were not carrying hidden weapons.

People even practice a few customs that were originally *superstitions*. Superstitions are unscientific beliefs that certain actions will cause good luck, happiness, bad luck, death, pain, or other events. For example, you've probably been told it is rude to point at people. People of ancient times believed pointing at someone was a way of killing that person by magic.

ALSO READ: BURIAL CUSTOMS, CLOTHING, CULTURE, FASHION, HABIT, HAIR STYLE, MANNERS.

CYBERNETICS see COMPUTER.

CYCLONE see WEATHER.

CYPRUS The rocky coast of Cyprus rises out of the eastern Mediterranean. (See the map with the article on EUROPE.) Parts of the island are covered by cedar forests. Two mountain chains cross Cyprus from east to west. Between them lies a fertile plain. Small villages dot the countryside, surrounded by wheat fields and groves of oranges and lemons. Farmers also grow bananas, grapes, and olives.

Most Cypriots are of Greek or Turkish origin. Cyprus was ruled by Egypt, Greece, and the Roman Empire at different times during its early history. A legend tells that Greek heroes founded settlements on the island of Cyprus 5,000 years ago. The Turks conquered the island in the 1500's. They ruled there for 300 years. Cyprus came under British rule in 1878. Britain gave the island independence in 1960.

The Cypriots then raised the white flag—a symbol of peace—of their new republic. But an old quarrel divides the 550,000 Greek Cypriots from the 150,000 Turkish Cypriots. Greek Cypriots believe that the Turks are intruders. Many want Cyprus to be united with Greece.

Since 1964, serious fighting has erupted between the Turkish and Greek Cypriots. The United Nations has sent various peacekeeping forces

CYPRUS

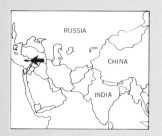

Capital City: Nicosia (160,000 people).
Area: 3,578 square miles (9,251 sq. km).
Population: 701,000.
Government: Republic.
Natural Resources: Marble, clay, asbestos, chromite, iron pyrites, copper.
Export Products: Grapes, citrus fruits, potatoes, wine, clothing, shoes.
Unit of Money: Pound.
Official Language: Greek, Turkish.

to work out a solution and to establish a unified government. Archbishop Makarios tried unsuccessfully as President to end the fighting. In 1975 the Turks set up their own government in the north, but it has yet to be internationally recognized. After Makarios's death in 1977, Spyros Kiprianou as President continued to seek peace. Today, Cyprus is still a divided nation.

ALSO READ: GREECE, MEDITERRANEAN SEA, TURKEY.

CZAR see RUSSIAN HISTORY.

CZECHOSLOVAKIA Czechoslovakia is a former Communist country in central Europe. It is about the size of Pennsylvania and has no seacoast. Czechoslovak goods reach foreign markets on barges that steam up and down the Danube River. (See the map with the article on EUROPE.) Prague, the capital, is a beautiful city over 1,000 years old.

Czechoslovakia is divided into three main regions. *Bohemia*, in the west, is a land of hills and forests. Many of these hills are topped by quaint old castles that might have come out of a fairy tale. *Moravia*, in the center, is an area of valleys and gentle, rolling plains. *Slovakia*, in the east, is a rough mountainous area.

Czechoslovakia is the homeland of two different peoples—the Czechs and the Slovaks—each with their own official language. The Czechs live in Bohemia and Moravia, and the Slovaks live in Slovakia.

The Czechs and the Slovaks both belong to the Slavic family of peoples. Like members of most families, they sometimes disagree with each other. They insist on using their own languages, and they prefer their own special clothing and foods. Czechs, for example, prefer potato dumplings fried, but Slovaks prefer them boiled. Czechs and Slovaks each insist that their own way of making potato dumplings is the best in the world!

Slovakia and Moravia have many farms where potatoes, grain, sugar beets, and vegetables are grown. Czechoslovak farmers also raise pigs and cattle. The many factories of Bohemia produce steel, glass, automobiles, firearms, beer, and shoes. Wine is of growing importance.

The Czechs and the Slovaks were ruled by other nations, including the Austrian Empire, for a long time. They joined together and formed their own nation in 1918. But Germany under Hitler gained control of the country 21 years later. After World War II, Czechoslovakia was dominated by the Soviet Union. In 1968 a freer style of Communism sprang up, but the Russian army invaded and crushed it. In 1989, the Czechs threw off Communism and held free elections to choose a Socialist government.

ALSO READ: DANUBE RIVER, EUROPE.

▲ Blowing glass in a factory in Czechoslovakia. Czechoslovakia's most valuable products are manufactured goods.

St. Wenceslaus was a good man who lived in the city of Prague in the 900's. He is known as the patron saint of Bohemia, now part of Czechoslovakia.

CZECHOSLOVAKIA

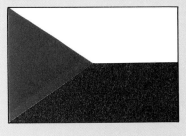

Capital City: Prague (1,220,000 people).
Area: 45,453 square miles (127,869 sq. km).
Population: 15,900,000.
Government: Federal socialist republic.
Natural Resources: Coal, lignite, magnesite, uranium, iron ore, copper, zinc.
Export Products: Machinery, manufactured goods, fuels, minerals, metals, meat.
Unit of Money: Koruna.
Official Language: Czech, Slovak.

▲ *The spirit of Dada is still seen in modern art. This is* Dalmatian Lamp, *a work of 1972 by the U.S. artist Karen Breschi.*

DADAISM In 1914, World War I broke out. Many artists had already been disgusted by the society they lived in and its lack of interest in new forms of art. Now they had to join the armies of their countries, whether they liked it or not. In 1915 a few artists met and decided to start a series of "anti-art" activities—to ridicule art and confuse art lovers rather than to create art.

The name they gave to their new movement, Dada, tells us how their minds worked. They stabbed at a dictionary with a penknife and hit the word *dada*—the French for "hobbyhorse"—and decided they liked its sound.

The public was indeed confused. One Dadaist, Kurt Schwitters, made compositions out of rubbish. The public was invited to a show of Dadaist "art" where visitors were given hatchets and invited to destroy an exhibit. The Dadaists gave absurd lectures and entertainments, such as a dance where the performers were dressed in stovepipes. The public was outraged—a thing that greatly pleased the Dadaists.

Though Dadaism was mainly European, there was some in the United States too. Modern art was unpopular in the United States, but Alfred Stieglitz, a New York photographer, ran a gallery where it was shown. Dadaists, including some Europeans, gathered there.

Out of the apparent madness of

▼ *A work of Dadaist art by one of the founders of Dadaism, Marcel Duchamp. This is called* Three Standard Stoppages.

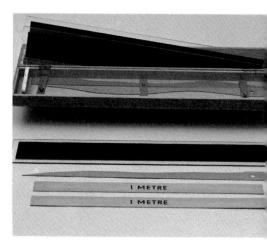

Dada came some valuable artistic techniques. Germans invented photographic collage, in which bits of photographs are glued together to give a vivid impression of something, such as a city. Dada publications used type in new and daring ways. Dada's use of machine forms—symbolizing modern life—anticipated the use of advertising art, comic-strip drawing, and other familiar things used by the Pop artists in the 1960's.

In 1918 a Dada political movement began in Germany to denounce the military authorities. The war ended in November 1918, though, and the Dadaists returned to the creation of art. After 1922, what was left of Dadaism was absorbed by Surrealism.

ALSO READ: SURREALISM.

DAEDALUS
One of the ancient Greek myths is about a famed builder, inventor, and sculptor named Daedalus.

One of his students, his nephew Talos, was so brilliant that Daedalus became jealous and killed him. Daedalus then had to escape from Athens. He fled to the island of Crete. King Minos, ruler of Crete, asked Daedalus to build the Labyrinth (a winding maze of passageways) to imprison the Minotaur, a horrible monster who was half man and half bull.

King Minos later became angry at Daedalus and imprisoned him and his son Icarus in the Labyrinth. Daedalus decided to escape. He made wings from feathers and wax for himself and Icarus. They soared together into the sky. Icarus foolishly flew too near the sun. The heat of the sun melted his wings, and he fell into the sea (now called the Icarian Sea) and drowned. Daedalus flew on in grief. He finally landed safely on the island of Sicily, where he lived peacefully.

ALSO READ: MAZE, MYTHOLOGY.

DAIRY FARMING
The industry that processes and sells products such as milk, cheese, and butter is called dairying. The animals that produce milk are raised and tended on dairy farms. In some countries goats, sheep, reindeer, camels, or water buffalo are the milk producers. But much of our milk comes from cows.

A modern dairy farm with 30 or more cows may have about 200 acres (800 sq. km) of land. Some of the land is needed for growing corn, soybeans, and other plants for making cattle-feed. The cows must also have spacious pastures where they can graze and exercise. A dairy farm usually has a large, two-story barn. The ground floor has stalls where the cows are milked and where they are sheltered during the cold months. The second floor has lofts piled with hay and bins full of grain. Nearby is a silo—a tall, windowless tower for storing cattle-feed made of chopped cornstalks and other grasses. This feed is saved for the wintertime, when the cows have no grass to eat.

Milking the Cows A cow's body begins to produce milk a short time before the birth of a calf. The calf normally feeds on its mother's milk for several months after birth. When it is old enough to eat solid food, its mother stops giving milk. In order to

▲ Dairy cattle chewing their cud in a pasture. In the background is the barn where the cows are milked. Next to the barn is the silo, where cattle feed is stored.

More people in the world drink goat's milk than cow's milk.

▲ *Today's modern farm machinery means that cows can be milked quickly and efficiently.*

▼ *How butter is made. Cream is churned vigorously so that its fatty droplets come together to form butter. The liquid left over is called buttermilk. Salt and colorings are often added to the butter.*

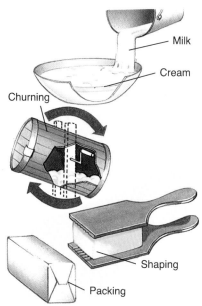

Milk

Cream

Churning

Shaping

Packing

get the cow's milk, the dairy farmer must take the calf from its mother after only a few days. The farmer teaches the calf to drink milk from a pail, using a rubber nipple. A regularly milked cow will then keep producing milk for many years.

Most cows are milked at least twice a day. If they are not milked regularly, their *udders* (milk glands) become painful. Special milking machines are used. The machine fits onto the four *teats* (nipples) of the cow's udder. Four suction cups draw the milk from the teats.

Many large dairy farms have a special room called a *milking parlor*, which has stalls on a raised platform. The cow walks up a ramp and into one of the stalls. Feed is automatically placed in the trough before her, and the milking machine is attached to her teats. As she munches her food, the machine milks her and pumps the milk into a central tank. When the milking is finished, the stall is unlocked and the cow walks out.

Milk can spoil easily, so it must be refrigerated as soon as it comes from the cow. Most dairy farms deliver milk daily to a dairy plant for processing and distributing. The milk can be carried long distances without spoiling in a refrigerated truck or railroad car.

ALSO READ: CATTLE, DAIRY PRODUCTS.

DAIRY PRODUCTS Milk is one of our most important foods. It is the basic product of the dairy industry and the raw material used to make all other dairy products. Milk is the liquid produced by all female mammals to feed their young. Cow's milk is the main kind of milk drunk in the United States.

Milk is an excellent food. It is easy to digest, tastes good, and has many nutrients important to growth. Milk is made of water, proteins, fats, sugars, and various minerals. It contains vitamin A, vitamin B_2 (riboflavin), and calcium, a mineral important to the growth and health of bone.

Making dairy products is a big and complicated business. The milk you drink goes through many processes in the complex machines of the modern dairy plant before you buy it at the supermarket. Milk is *pasteurized*, heated to kill harmful bacteria. Most milk is *homogenized*, that is, fat particles are made much smaller and dispersed through the liquid part of the milk.

When milk is not homogenized, fat quickly rises to the top, where it forms cream, which is used for fine baking and flavoring. And butter results when cream is churned (stirred rapidly). When cream is removed from unhomogenized milk, skim milk is left. Skim milk contains all of milk's nutrients except vitamin A, which is in the cream. Skim milk has less fat than whole milk, so it is good for people who are trying to lose weight or who have heart ailments.

Concentrated milk products include evaporated milk, condensed milk, and dry (powdered) milk. All are made by heating pasteurized milk to remove water from it. About half of milk's water is removed to make evaporated milk, which is almost always canned. Condensed milk is made the same way, but sugar is added first. Condensed milk keeps a very long time because the sugar prevents bacteria from turning the milk sour. Almost all the water is removed to make dry (powdered) milk. It is as nourishing as fresh milk when the water is replaced. Dry milk can also be kept a very long time without spoiling. It is light in weight, so it can easily be shipped over long distances.

Several other products are made when other substances are added to milk or cream. Different types of harmless bacteria are added to turn milk sour. Sour milk is used to make cheese, sour cream, yogurt, and buttermilk. When sugar and some other ingredients, such as egg whites or gelatin, are mixed with cream, milkfat, or butterfat and the mixture is frozen, the result is ice cream.

ALSO READ: CATTLE; CHEESE; DAIRY FARMING; ICE CREAM; NUTRITION; PASTEUR, LOUIS.

DAKOTA INDIANS see SIOUX INDIANS.

DALI, SALVADOR see SURREALISM.

DALLAS With over a million people, Dallas, Texas, is the seventh largest city in the United States. It is nicknamed "Big D." It is a wealthy place and claims to have more Cadillacs per person than any other city outside oil-rich Arab countries! It is a major business, financial, and industrial center, producing such things as electronics and electrical equipment and parts for aircraft and missiles. Dallas is also famed for its fashion industry. Its many educational institutions include the Southern Methodist University, which opened in 1915.

Dallas was founded in 1841 by a trader, John Neely Bryan, who built a cabin on the Trinity River. People argue about the origin of the city's name. Some believe that it was named

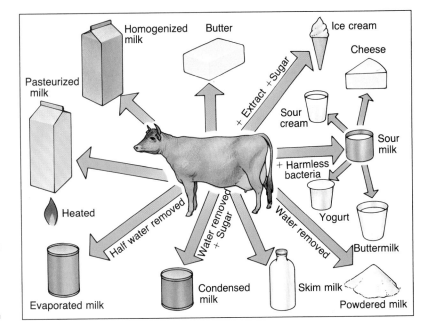

▲ *This diagram illustrates the many different kinds of dairy produce that come from a cow.*

for one of Bryan's friends. Others think that it was named for a U.S. Vice-President, George Mifflin Dallas (1792–1864). The city grew rapidly after the arrival of railroads in the early 1870's. Industries developed and Dallas has stayed in the forefront of industrial technology ever since. State Fair Park, site of the Texas State Fair every October, attracts tourists with its museums and Cotton Bowl football stadium. Other attractions include the famous and expensive Neiman-Marcus store and the Reunion Tower, which offers fine views of Dallas. But the city's most photographed building is the Texas Book Depository, from which President John F. Kennedy was shot on November 22, 1963. Nearby stands the John F. Kennedy Memorial, 30 feet (9 m) high.

ALSO READ: TEXAS.

DAM A dam is a structure built to hold back the water of a river or stream. A dam may block the flow of a river so that the water is stored for

◀ *Dallas, in Texas, is one of the richest and fastest growing cities in the United States.*

DAM

▶ *Four different types of dams. (1) Gravity dams are concrete or stone structures heavy enough to hold back the weight of the water they contain. (2) Arch dams are built across rivers that flow through narrow canyons. Their curved flanks deflect the immense pressure of the water they contain against the canyon walls. (3) Buttress dams are relatively thin-walled gravity dams, strengthened at regular intervals by buttress supports. (4) Earth embankment or earth-fill dams are made by heaping earth and rock into a rough triangular shape across a river's course. These dams are often made with a core of clay and a covering of masonry or concrete.*

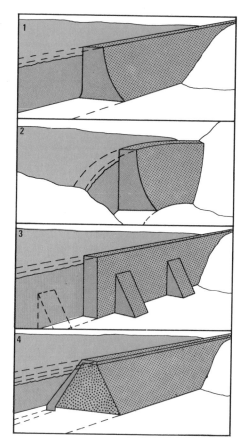

▲ *The Hoover Dam on the Colorado River, named for President Herbert Hoover.*

irrigating crops in dry seasons. The stored water may be used to produce electricity (*hydroelectricity*). A dam built on a shallow river often makes the water behind the dam deep enough for large ships to sail on it. Part of the Panama Canal was formed by damming the Chagres River to make Gatun Lake, which is deep enough for oceangoing vessels to steam across. Other dams are built mainly to control flooding.

More than 40 dams have been built in the valley of the Tennessee River. The dams are built and operated by the Tennessee Valley Authority (TVA), a U.S. government agency. The dams provide flood control, electric power, navigable waters, and

lakes for swimming, fishing, and boating by holding back water or channeling it in certain directions.

Kinds of Dams The materials most often used to make dams are concrete, stone, and earth.

The *gravity dam*—usually built of rock or concrete—is wider at the bottom than at the top. A gravity dam's shape and great weight keep it in place against the tremendous pushing force of the water that it holds back. Some gravity dams are solid. Others are hollow and are reinforced by walls called buttresses.

Single-arch dams are usually constructed in narrow gorges or canyons. The arch curves so that the sides are farther downstream than the center. This arrangement transfers the force of the water to the side of the canyon. Wider rivers may be blocked by a *multiple-arch dam*. Thick, solid concrete towers between arches give the dam strength. Gravity and arch dams are built of either concrete or masonry (large stones held together by mortar). The stones may be cut to fit together like bricks.

Earth-fill dams are made of a mixture of sand, clay, and silt. Water can seep through an earth dam, so most have a waterproof inner section of steel or concrete that runs the whole length of the dam. In small earth-fill

▼ *An earth-fill dam that has been nearly finished. Notice the small dam a little upriver. This has been built to divert the water around the site while the big dam is being built.*

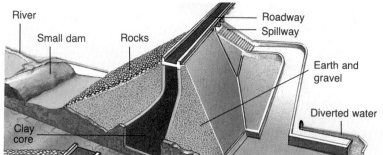

River
Small dam
Rocks
Clay core
Roadway
Spillway
Earth and gravel
Diverted water

HIGHEST DAMS			
Name of Dam	Construction Material	Height	Year Completed
Rogun, U.S.S.R.	Earth	1,099 feet (335 m)	1985
Nurek, U.S.S.R.	Earth	984 feet (300 m)	1979
Grande Dixence, Switzerland	Concrete	935 feet (285 m)	1962
Chicoasan, Mexico	Earth	863 feet (263 m)	1982
Valont, Italy*	Concrete	860 feet (262 m)	1961
Sayano-Shushenskaya, U.S.S.R.	Concrete	794 feet (242 m)	1982
Mica, Canada	Earth	787 feet (240 m)	1972

* Valont Dam, damaged by a landslide in 1963, no longer operates.

LARGEST DAMS			
Name of Dam	Construction Material	Volume	Year Completed
Tarbela, Pakistan	Earth, rock	5,024,924 cubic feet (142,290 m³)	1975
Fort Peck, Missouri	Earth	3,392,150 cubic feet (96,055 m³)	1940
Guri, U.S.S.R.	Earth, rock	3,107,690 cubic feet (88,000 m³)	1985
Oahe, Missouri	Earth	2,484,140 cubic feet (70,343 m³)	1963
Mangla, Pakistan	Earth	2,318,584 cubic feet (65,655 m³)	1967

Some tailing dams (mine-waste piles) are larger, but have constantly changing sizes. Biggest is probably New Cornelia Tailings, Arizona, at 7,398,000 cubic feet (209,488 m³), completed 1973.

dams the inner section may be soft. The earth piled on either side of the inner section gives it strength. The upstream side of an earth dam is usually covered by a thick coating of waterproof material.

Spillways and Gates Although built to block a river, a dam must allow water to pass downstream. This is done by means of spillways and gates.

A *spillway* is a section of the top of the dam that is lower than the rest. When the stored water rises close to the top of the dam, it flows over the spillway and downstream.

Instead of a spillway, a dam may have one or more *gates* that can be opened and closed by machinery. Water flows downstream through the open gates. The gates can be closed when rain is heavy, so the country-side downstream is not flooded. The extra water can be allowed to flow slowly downstream after the rain is over.

When certain rivers are dammed up, some migratory fish, like the salmon, cannot reach their spawning grounds. To keep such fish from becoming extinct, *fish ladders* are built beside the dams which fish can swim up.

About 3,000 large dams have been built in the United States. Remains of dams more than 6,000 years old have been found along the Tigris and Euphrates rivers in Iraq. The ancient Romans built many good dams in Europe and Africa, and some are still in use.

ALSO READ: ABU SIMBEL, FLOOD, HYDROELECTRICITY, IRRIGATION, PANAMA CANAL, WATER SUPPLY.

DAMOCLES Damocles belonged to the court of Dionysius the Elder, ruler of Syracuse, Sicily, in the 300's B.C. Damocles once mistakenly flattered Dionysius, telling him how lucky he was to be wealthy and happy, so the king decided to teach Damocles a lesson. Dionysius invited Damocles to a great feast, where he was given everything he wanted. During the feast, Damocles looked up and saw a sharp sword held by a single hair hanging over his own head. Dionysius was showing Damocles that even a powerful person cannot always feel safe and content. The term "sword of Damocles" means "a disaster to come," or "a threat of disaster."

DANCE Dance is probably the oldest of the arts. Early people may have shown how they felt by moving their bodies in ways that expressed this feeling. Maybe they jumped, waved their arms, clapped their hands, and stamped their feet. They may have danced to tell a story. They used expressive movements to cele-

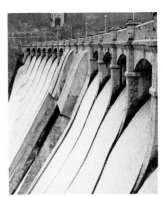

▲ *A buttress dam. Notice how the concrete buttresses support the dam against the force of the water behind.*

▲ *An Indian miniature of Krishna, a Hindu god, performing a dance to music played by three women. Indian religious dances have changed little in centuries.*

▼ *The Hollywood musical of the 1930's can be traced back to the music-hall tradition of Britain and to the operetta (short, comic opera).*

brate the important moments in life—marriage, birth, death, and the beginning of war all had their dance patterns. The patterns gradually came to be considered magic. People imitated animals, hoping to be lucky in the hunt. People danced before planting or harvesting to ensure good crops. People danced to arouse emotion and build strength before going into battle. *Ritual* or religious dance grew from belief in the power of regular motion.

As people developed cities, dance changed. Religious dance was no longer for all the people but was done by men or women connected with a temple. Some of the temple dances of the Hindus in India today are much the same as they were 2,000 years ago. Ancient Egyptian dance is known only through wall paintings. We know little about dance in Biblical times, except that the Bible mentions that people danced. King David danced for joy to celebrate a victory. In ancient Greece, sculpture and paintings on pottery show dancers.

As rulers became powerful and wealthy, a kind of dance developed simply for their entertainment. Each land developed different kinds of ceremonial dance. This dancing, neither part of religion nor folk dancing for pleasure, was the beginning of dance as a form of art.

Dance as an Art   Ballet and modern dance are the two main kinds of dance art. Ballet dates back several centuries, having grown out of dances done in European courts. It is based on traditional rules, uses dancing on the toes and other special movements, and often tells a story. A ballet is done with music, stage settings, and costumes. Ballet sometimes has an important place in the opera.

Modern dance has grown out of traditional ballet. It is a freer kind of movement. Isadora Duncan helped show the way to this new kind of dance by using her body in free expression, moving naturally and gracefully. There is music in modern dance, as in the ballet. It may be made by machines ("electronic") instead of by traditional musical instruments. Sometimes modern dance tells a story and uses costumes and settings. But modern dances may simply express some idea or emotion, or just exhibit beautiful patterns of movement with no meaning at all.

In recent decades, musical stage shows such as *Oklahoma*, *West Side Story*, and *Chorus Line* have presented skillful, well-planned dancing that is part of the story. Movies and television have made much use of this form of the dance art.

Planning Dances   As the writer uses words and the composer combines sounds, so the *choreographer* makes up a dance, whether ballet or modern. Choreographers decide which dance steps will best tell the story, which music to use, and what costumes the dancers will wear. They then teach each new dance to the performers.

Choreographers in the past always kept the patterns of their dances (the *choreography*) in their heads. From time to time, someone has tried to write down dances so they can be repeated later. Two systems of dance

▼ *A May festivity at Aston-on-Clun, England. These people are dancing around a maypole.*

▲ *The dance these African dancers are performing dates from the distant past. Many African dances are a part of magic or religion.*

notation, or dance writing, are now in use. Both employ a kind of shorthand.

Folk Dancing   Although some types of dancing are for art, most people dance for *recreation*, for fun. In the Middle Ages in Europe, folk dancing was done by the ordinary people, the peasants. They danced for fun at holiday gatherings. Most folk dances were and are done by groups of people. Sometimes folk dances are called *ethnic* (cultural, or racial) dances because different groups or races of people each developed their own dances.

Square dancing is an example of folk dancing. English country dancing, Spanish classical dancing, and Mexican folk dancing are others. Some folk-dance groups, like the Ballet Folklorico of Mexico, have professional dancers.

Citizens of many countries today treasure their traditional dances as signs of national unity. The hula dancers of Hawaii, for example, can tell the history of their islands through their movements.

Ballroom Dancing   The noblemen and their ladies in the courts and castles of European countries danced the minuet, the gavotte, and the pavan. In time a new kind of dancing called ballroom dancing evolved from these dances. Many people, both rich and poor, took up ballroom dancing. The polka and the waltz were two kinds of early ballroom dancing.

Lively, catchy ragtime music became very popular in the late 19th century. Ragtime and other forms of music developed into jazz, and new dances were made up to fit this new music. The foxtrot became an important new dance and is still enjoyed by some people today. The Charleston was a very fast jazz dance enjoyed by many Americans in the 1920's. Dances from Africa and from South American countries (such as the tango, rumba, and samba, from Argentina, Brazil, and Cuba) also became popular in the 1930's and 1940's.

Ballroom dancing is done by couples. A man and woman face each other and do certain steps together in time to music. Dance steps are usually based on a walking step, but patterns are different for different dances. The basic waltz and foxtrot are two popular ballroom dances.

Rock 'n' Roll Dancing   With the popularity of rock 'n' roll music in the 1950's and 1960's, a dance called the *twist* was created. It was based on *jitterbugging*, the fast and energetic dance of the 1940's. Other dances, *fad* dances, quickly became very popular for a short time. Today's rock 'n' roll dancing has no fixed movements, but this may change in times to come. Couples who dance to rock 'n' roll music dance more or less independently of each other.

▲ *Competitions in ballroom dancing are often held: a couple must move together well, keep in good time with the music and be graceful if they are to succeed.*

697

Other Kinds of Dancing   Ice skating or roller skating to dance music, alone or with a partner, is another kind of dancing that is fun. Folk dancing is also enjoyed by many people. Square dancing, which was popular with the pioneers in the early days of the U.S. West, is still enjoyed by many Americans.

For further information on:
Composers for the Dance, *see* BERNSTEIN, LEONARD; COPLAND, AARON; MENDELSSOHN, FELIX; STRAVINSKY, IGOR; TCHAIKOVSKY, PETER.
Dancers, *see* DUNCAN, ISADORA; FONTEYN, MARGOT; NIJINSKY, VASLAV; PAVLOVA, ANNA.
Kinds of Dance, *see* BALLET, FOLK DANCING, MODERN DANCE, MUSICAL COMEDY, OPERA, SQUARE DANCING.

▲ *A modern dance by the Nikolais Dance Theater. Modern dance is rather like ballet, but the shapes of the dancers' bodies are emphasized.*

DANTE ALIGHIERI (1265–1321)
Dante's *Divine Comedy* is one of the most important and beautiful poems in the world. Dante is often said to have started Italian literature, because he was the first important poet to write in that language (writers before him used Latin). And his poem was imitated by many later poets. Dante also developed a form of poetry used by later poets.

Dante was born in Florence, Italy. He probably studied philosophy and religion. He became a politician. When his opponents took power, he was exiled from Florence in 1302. He traveled from place to place before spending his last years in the Italian city of Ravenna.

The *Divine Comedy* is the make-believe story of Dante's trip through Hell, Purgatory, and Paradise. He meets many famous people from history, from mythology, and from his own time. Virgil, the famous Roman poet, takes him through Hell and Purgatory. A beautiful young lady, Beatrice, guides him through Para-

dise, where he searches for God. The Beatrice of the poem was Beatrice Portinari, who lived in Florence. Dante saw Beatrice only twice, once when he was 9 and again when he was 18, but he remembered her all his life and thought of her as a saint. She was his inspiration for the *Divine Comedy*. The love poems of his other very famous work, *The New Life*, also are addressed to her.

ALSO READ: POETRY, VIRGIL.

DANUBE RIVER   The lilting melody of the famous "Blue Danube Waltz" was inspired by one of the great rivers of the world. The Danube River rises in the Black Forest in southern West Germany and flows 1,750 miles (2,818 km) eastward to the Black Sea. It touches seven countries—West Germany, Austria, Czechoslovakia, Hungary, Bulgaria, Yugoslavia, and Romania. The river forms the border between several of these countries. The capitals of three countries lie along the banks of the Danube—Vienna, Austria; Budapest, Hungary; and Belgrade, Yugoslavia. (See the map with the article on EUROPE.)

The Danube carries a great deal of silt (mud) in its waters. Over 80 million tons of silt are deposited in the Danube's delta every year. Constant dredging is needed to keep the river navigable, but still the Danube's delta is growing into the Black Sea by 80 to 100 feet (24 to 30 m) each year.

The Danube is the second longest river in Europe (only the Volga River is longer). It has always been an avenue of migration, conquest, and trade. It is still a busy river today. Tugs tow large barges carrying coal, oil, and iron ore. If you were a crewman on such a barge, a tug might tow you from the Black Sea upstream to Regensburg, West Germany—a journey of 1,200 miles (1,932 km). Early in your journey, you would pass through a narrow gorge called the Iron Gate, where Romania and Yugoslavia built a large hydroelectric power plant. You would see many sights, such as farmers cultivating vineyards in Yugoslavia; the city of Budapest—split into two parts, Buda and Pest, by the river; and great castles along the river in Austria.

DARTS Darts is an old English game that has become popular in many countries, especially the United States. The game is played by throwing darts, small arrows with sharp metal points and guiding feathers at the other end. They are thrown at a board, usually made of cork or bristle. The board is divided into 20 segments, like the slices of a cake. Each segment has a different number. A dart thrown into the narrow ring running around the outside of the segments counts double. The ring around the middle of the segments counts triple. There are also central circles that count 25 and 50.

Several different darts games can be played, but the most popular is that in which each player starts with 301 and reduces it to zero by subtracting each score as he or she throws. Each player takes alternate turns with three darts and must begin and end his score with a double.

There are now many international darts tournaments.

ALSO READ: GAMES.

DARWIN, CHARLES (1809–1882) Charles Darwin wrote a book, *Origin of Species*, first published in England in 1859. Darwin's ideas brought about a revolution in the science of biology, in how we think of ourselves, and in our ideas about the history of Earth.

Many people of Darwin's time thought that Earth—and all forms of life on it—were created less than 6,000 years ago. They thought each species (kind) of animal and plant was created exactly as they knew it. Some scientists did not accept this belief. They thought that plants and animals had slowly changed and developed, or evolved, over thousands of years. But they had no proof for their ideas.

Darwin was born in Shrewsbury, England. He went to Edinburgh and Cambridge universities. His father wanted him to be a minister, but Darwin was more interested in studying nature. He became the naturalist on the five-year voyage of the H.M.S. *Beagle* when he was 22. As the ship explored the Pacific Ocean, Darwin discovered a peculiar fact. Although the finches of the Galápagos Islands (off the coast of Ecuador) were much like other finches, they differed in several small ways. What could this mean?

▲ *Barges and small boats carry passengers and cargo up and down the Danube River. Here the river flows past Vienna, the capital of Austria. Many writers and composers have been inspired by the Danube's great beauty. Have you heard Johann Strauss's waltz-tune, "The Blue Danube"?*

▼ *A dart board is 8 feet (2.5 m) from the thrower.*

North American

English

▲ *Heads of finches from different islands in the Galápagos Archipelago. Darwin first hit upon the theory of evolution by natural selection when he noticed these minor differences.*

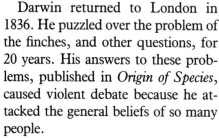

▲ *Charles Darwin, who with Alfred Russel Wallace created the theory of evolution by natural selection.*

▲ *Benjamin Oliver Davis, Sr., the first black general in the U.S. Army.*

Darwin returned to London in 1836. He puzzled over the problem of the finches, and other questions, for 20 years. His answers to these problems, published in *Origin of Species*, caused violent debate because he attacked the general beliefs of so many people.

He published *The Descent of Man* in 1871. This new book made the argument even more bitter, because in it he said that human beings have the same ancestors as chimpanzees and other apes. People of Darwin's time were furious because they believed that humankind was not related to any other animal. But scientists now generally accept this idea.

ALSO READ: EVOLUTION; GENETICS; PLANT BREEDING; PROTECTIVE COLORING; WALLACE, ALFRED RUSSEL.

DATA PROTECTION Businesses and government agencies store a great deal of information on computers, in what are known as *data bases*. Most of this information is private. But many of these data bases can be reached through telephone lines. Unscrupulous computer operators, known as *hackers*, find ways of breaking into these data bases and gaining access to the information.

A great deal of government information could be of value to an enemy of the United States. Companies keep valuable secrets that could interest their business rivals. So to protect data, Congress has passed a law making it a criminal offense to gain access to Federal government or business computers without authorization.

Several state legislatures have declared information stored in computer data bases property and therefore liable to the laws governing theft.

ALSO READ: COMPUTER.

DAVIS, BENJAMIN OLIVER (1877–1970) Benjamin Davis was born in Washington, D.C. He fought as a volunteer first lieutenant in the Spanish-American War in 1898. He enlisted as a private after the war, and he won a competitive examination and became the first black officer in the Regular Army in 1901. President Theodore Roosevelt personally signed the second lieutenant's commission, with the comment, "So, he's a Negro. Bully for him. He's *qualified* for the place." Benjamin Davis became the Army's first black general in 1940. He retired, after a distinguished career, in 1948.

ALSO READ: ARMY; DAVIS, BENJAMIN OLIVER, JR.

DAVIS, BENJAMIN OLIVER, JR. (born 1912) Born in Washington, D.C., Davis decided early in life to become a military officer like his father before him. In high school he was a top student, a fine athlete, and president of his class.

He won an appointment to West Point Military Academy in 1932. He was the only black in a class of 383 cadets. No black had graduated from West Point in 50 years. His fellow cadets practically ignored him for four years. But he refused to quit, and he graduated with honors in 1936.

Lieutenant Davis became a pilot upon graduation and led a fighter group during World War II. He held the rank of lieutenant general—the second highest rank in the U.S. military and the highest ever held by a black—when he retired in 1970. He earned 39 medals for heroism and outstanding service to his country.

ALSO READ: AIR FORCE; DAVIS, BENJAMIN OLIVER.

DAVIS, JEFFERSON (1808–1889) When the Southern states seceded (broke away) from the Union and formed the Confederacy, they chose Jefferson Davis as their president. Davis is one of history's "unknown" men. Most accounts of the Civil War tell very little about this man.

Jefferson Davis was born in Fairview, Kentucky, not far from the birthplace of Abraham Lincoln. His father was a veteran of the American Revolution. Davis's family moved to Mississippi soon after he was born. He attended West Point Military Academy. Lieutenant Davis fought in the Black Hawk Indian war in 1832. He then resigned from the Army and married Sarah Taylor, the daughter of Zachary Taylor, who would later serve as the twelfth U.S. President. Sarah died three months after the marriage, and Davis devoted all his time to his plantation. He organized a model democracy for the 30 slaves he owned.

Davis was elected a U.S. representative in 1845. He also married Varina Howell, daughter of a rich planter, in that year. He then fought as a colonel in the Mexican War. He served as a senator and as secretary of war under President Franklin Pierce.

Davis returned to the Senate in 1857. Arguments about slavery grew more heated, and Davis spoke more and more strongly for slavery and for states' rights. He sincerely believed

that slavery was necessary in the South—that the whole South would collapse if slavery were stopped too quickly. He also believed that slaves had to learn to be citizens and that they were not ready to be free.

Mississippi seceded from the Union in December 1860, and Davis resigned from the Senate. In February 1861, the Confederate convention chose him as president. Davis's leadership of the Southern states was often criticized by other Southerners who believed that he did not raise enough money to fight the war or that he made poor military decisions. But Davis was able to make the Confederacy so strong that it could withstand the Union—which had more men, more materials, and more money—for four years.

After the war, the United States charged Davis with treason. He was held in prison for two years but was released without trial. He gained the respect of many people, from both North and South, while he was imprisoned. When he was released, he returned to Mississippi, where he spent the rest of his life. He wrote a book, *The Rise and Fall of the Confederate Government*, about his experiences.

ALSO READ: CIVIL WAR, CONFEDERATE STATES OF AMERICA, INDIAN WARS, MEXICAN WAR, SLAVERY.

DAVY, SIR HUMPHRY see ELEMENT.

DAY AND NIGHT People once believed that day and night happened because the sun moved around the Earth. Today we know this is not true. Day and night occur because the Earth is turning, spinning like a huge top. It turns around its *axis*. The two ends of the Earth's axis are the North and South Poles. The Earth makes one complete spin every 24 hours. As

▲ *Benjamin Oliver Davis, Jr., the first black general in the U.S. Air Force.*

▲ *Jefferson Davis, president of the Confederacy during the Civil War.*

▲ *Using a flashlight and a rubber ball or a globe, you can see why we have day and night.*

Four or five million years ago a day lasted only 22 hours. Our days are two hours longer now because Earth's rotation is very gradually slowing down.

it turns, half of the Earth faces toward the sun. There it is day. On the other half of the Earth, facing away from the sun, it is night.

■ LEARN BY DOING

To see how night and day happen, get a rubber ball, a knitting needle, and a flashlight. (Alternatively you can use a globe as in the illustration.) Stick the knitting needle through the middle of the ball and mark an X on one side of the ball with ink. Imagine that the ball is the Earth. The needle is the Earth's axis. The flashlight is the sun. Shine the flashlight on the ball. The front of the ball is lighted (day). The back of the ball is dark (night). The sides get just a little light (dawn or twilight). Now turn the needle slowly, so that the ball turns. The X moves through the light and back into the dark. Imagine that the X on the ball is the place where you live on the Earth. As the Earth spins, you move from the dark to the sunlight and day begins. During the day, you move through the sunlight. When you have spun away from the sun, night begins again. ■

The axis of the Earth is tilted slightly. The North Pole tilts toward the sun in the summer and away from the sun in the winter. This makes summer days longer and hotter and winter days shorter and colder.

ALSO READ: SEASON, SOLAR SYSTEM, SUN, TIME.

DAY OF THE WEEK Have you ever wondered where the names for the days of the week came from? The names—and the reasons for the names—are different in different languages. In English, the names of three days—Sunday, Monday, and Saturday—come from the ancient Romans. They named all seven days after the sun, the moon, and the planets they knew. The names for the planets were also the names of their gods. Sunday was the sun's day. Monday was the moon's day. The other five days were named after Mars, Mercury, Jupiter, Venus, and Saturn in that order. Some languages, such as French, still have versions of these ancient Roman names for the days. In French these days are: *mardi* (Tuesday), *mercredi* (Wednesday), *jeudi* (Thursday), *vendredi* (Friday), and *samedi* (Saturday).

In English, the other four days do not have Roman names. The Anglo-Saxons, a Germanic people who settled in England about 1,500 years ago, made some changes. The Anglo-Saxons dropped the Roman names for four days and named these days after their own gods. Mars's day became Tuesday, after Tiw, their god of war. Mercury's day became Wednesday, after Woden, leader of their gods. Jupiter's day was changed to Thursday, after Thor, the god of thunder. And Venus's day became Friday, named after Frigga, Woden's wife and queen of the gods.

ALSO READ: GODS AND GODDESSES.

DEAD SEA Imagine water in which you can't sink, even if you can't swim. Imagine water so salty that it burns your eyes and leaves white crystals on your body when it dries. That is what the water is like in the Dead Sea.

Despite its name, the Dead Sea is

neither dead nor a sea. It is a lake, 1,320 feet (402 m) below sea level, located at the bottom of the deepest valley in the world. Although there is no life in its deep waters, the lake supports a few kinds of simple plants and a few fish near the shore. The Dead Sea forms part of the border between Israel and Jordan, both of which extract salt, potash, and bromine from the water.

The Jordan River flows into the Dead Sea. Like all river water, the water of the Jordan contains dissolved salts and minerals. Most other lakes have an outlet through which water can pass. When water flows out of a lake through an outlet, it carries its salts along. The Dead Sea does not have an outlet. Water can leave the Dead Sea only when it is evaporated by the sun. Evaporated water leaves its salts behind. This explains what makes the Dead Sea so salty.

Salt water has more buoyancy than fresh water. The saltier the water, the greater its buoyancy. The Dead Sea—the saltiest body of water in the world—is more buoyant than any other body of water.

■ LEARN BY DOING

Cut a piece of potato about the size of a large marble. The potato will sink in a large glass filled with water. Stir salt into the water, one teaspoonful at a time, until the potato rises and floats on the surface of the water. Next pour off half of the salty water. Add clear water slowly. What does the potato do? How does this help you to understand the Dead Sea? ■

ALSO READ: BUOYANCY, GREAT SALT LAKE, LAKE.

DEAD SEA SCROLLS In 1947 a Bedouin shepherd boy was looking for a lost goat in the hills near the Dead Sea east of Jerusalem. He wandered into a cave, found some jars, and opened one. He was disappointed when all he saw were pieces of parchment and papyrus covered with writing. But to the world they marked the first discovery of the ancient writings called the Dead Sea Scrolls. Many more manuscripts were found in nearby caves in the Qumran Valley in the late 1940's and early 1950's. They had been preserved because the atmosphere of the region is so dry.

Several complete scrolls and thousands of smaller pieces were discovered. The handwritten scrolls were translated and found to be the oldest known copies of the Old Testament books of the Bible. At least sections of all of the books except *Esther* are included. They are written in ancient Hebrew and Aramaic, the language Christ spoke, and are 1,000 years older than any other known Bible texts. The scrolls were probably written between 200 B.C. and A.D. 68.

The scrolls may have been part of a library that belonged to a Jewish religious group, possibly the Essenes. In 1951 archeologists in the area dug up a *scriptorium*, a writing room, in which were tables and even inkwells. This may have been where the scrolls were written. Other bits and pieces of writings have been found, in addition to the books of the Bible.

Finding the Dead Sea Scrolls has been of great value to students of ancient people, especially to Bible scholars. Some of the Dead Sea Scrolls are on display in The Shrine of

▲ *The Dead Sea, which lies between Israel and Jordan, is nine times as salty as the ocean. Swimmers float much higher in the Dead Sea because it is so salty.*

The Dead Sea has dropped about 30 feet (9 m) in recent years from increased use of the waters of the Jordan River for irrigation. To keep the sea from drying up eventually, Israel has proposed to build a 68-mile (110 km) canal and tunnel link to bring water from the Mediterranean Sea to the Dead Sea.

◄ *A portion of one of the Dead Sea Scrolls, the oldest known copies of the Old Testament.*

▲ *Sand dunes in Death Valley, which is known also for its unique rock formations, briny pools, salt flats, and beautiful canyons.*

▲ *Eugene Debs, U.S. labor leader and socialist.*

the Book, at the Israel Museum in Jerusalem. Others belong to Jordan.

ALSO READ: BIBLE, BOOK.

DEAF, EDUCATION OF THE
see SPECIAL EDUCATION.

DEAFNESS see HEARING.

DEATH VALLEY The hottest, driest, and lowest place in the United States is Death Valley. It lies mostly in southern California, but a small part sticks into Nevada. Death Valley lies between two mountain ranges, the Panamint Range west of the valley and the Amargosa Range to the east. About 500 square miles (1,300 sq. km) of the valley are below sea level, including the lowest spot in the Western Hemisphere—282 feet (86 m) below sea level. Over three dozen kinds of animals, including foxes, rabbits, and bobcats, live there, as well as over 200 kinds of birds. A few plants grow there, including the mesquite, creosote bush, and desert holly. The desert and surrounding area make up Death Valley National Monument.

In summer, Death Valley has temperatures that commonly reach 120° F (49° C). On July 10, 1913, the temperature there reached 134° F (56.7° C), the highest temperature ever recorded in the United States. At night, the valley can become very cold. Less than 2 inches (5 cm) of rain fall annually in Death Valley. Many persons enjoy the warm winter sunshine of the area, which has become a popular winter-resort spot.

Death Valley was named by survivors of a group of prospectors who crossed the valley in 1849. Other names in the area are just as sinister—Funeral Mountains, Deadman Pass, Desolation Canyon, Poison Spring, and Rattlesnake Gulch.

Early prospectors came to Death Valley looking for gold, silver, lead, and borax. A few mines paid off handsomely, but most produced little. Today, ghost towns stand quietly in the desert.

ALSO READ: DESERT.

DEBS, EUGENE V. (1855–1926) Eugene Victor Debs was one of the great pioneers of the U.S. labor movement. Born in Terre Haute, Indiana, he worked at various jobs before becoming a locomotive fireman for a railroad. He served as secretary and treasurer for the Brotherhood of Locomotive Firemen, a labor union, from 1880 to 1893. He was elected to the Indiana Legislature from 1884 to 1893. He saw a need for a union for all railroad workers, and in 1893 he organized the American Railway Union (ARU). The ARU supported a strike of Pullman-car workers the next year, and the whole union went on strike. President Cleveland sent in federal troops to break the strike. Debs was sent to prison for six months.

While in jail, he became deeply interested in the political system called *socialism*. He formed the Social Democratic Party of America in 1898. He ran for President as a socialist in 1900, 1904, 1908, 1912, and 1920. His 1920 campaign was the most successful. He ran it from prison, where he had been sent for making speeches against World War I. He was freed in 1921 after serving three years. He won respect for his strong devotion to his beliefs, even among those who did not agree with him.

ALSO READ: LABOR UNION, SOCIALISM.

DEBUSSY, CLAUDE (1862–1918) A French composer rebelled against the musical traditions of his time. He was Claude Achille Debussy, who developed a new style of music, called

Impressionism, which tried to create certain moods. His work helped shape modern music.

Debussy was born near Paris, France. An aunt encouraged him to learn piano, and he passed entrance examinations to study at the Paris Conservatory (music school) when he was 11. When he was 22, he won a prize (*Prix de Rome*) that allowed him to study in Rome for two years.

Debussy returned to Paris and became part of a group of young French poets and painters who were seeking new ways of writing and painting. These artists influenced each other, and a poem by Symbolist poet Stéphane Mallarmé inspired Debussy to compose *Prelude to the Afternoon of a Faun* for orchestra. This famous piece is a *tone poem,* a "poem" for an orchestra. The music has a supple rhythm that creates the mood of the story suggested in the title. It was followed by his one opera, *Pelléas and Mélisande.*

You can easily see why Debussy's music is called impressionistic. Listen to his piano composition *Clair de Lune* ("Moonlight"). What picture do you get from the delicate melody and the light, graceful harmony?

ALSO READ: COMPOSER, IMPRESSIONISM, MODERN MUSIC.

DECEMBER December is the twelfth and last month of the year. December has 31 days. *Decem* means "ten" in Latin. December got its name because, in early Roman times, it was the tenth month. However, Julius Caesar changed the old calendar and added two new months to a new one. This made December the twelfth month.

Winter begins in December in the middle latitudes of the Northern Hemisphere. The first day of winter, December 21 or 22, is called the *winter solstice,* the shortest day of the year. In the middle latitudes of the

SPECIAL EVENTS IN DECEMBER

2 ● President Monroe proclaimed the Monroe Doctrine in a message to Congress (1823).
 ● First nuclear chain reaction produced at University of Chicago (1942).

3 ● First heart transplant performed in South Africa by Doctor Christiaan Barnard (1967).
 ● Boeing 747 jumbo jetliner made its public preview flight from Seattle to New York City (1969).
 ● President Bush and President Gorbachev announced the end of the Cold War (1989).

5 ● President Martin Van Buren was born (1782).
 ● Walt Disney, cartoon moviemaker, born (1901).
 ● Prohibition ended in the United States (1933).

6 ● Feast of St. Nicholas celebrated in much of Europe. The tradition of Santa Claus comes from this festival.
 ● Calvin Coolidge made the first presidential radio message (1923).

7 ● Japan attacked the United States at Pearl Harbor (1941).

8 ● The United States declared war on Japan (1941).

9 ● Joel Chandler Harris, American author of the Uncle Remus stories, was born (1848).

10 ● Emily Dickinson, American poet, was born (1830).
 ● Spain ceded the Philippines to the United States (1898).

11 ● King Edward VIII of England abdicated his throne (1936).
 ● Germany and Italy declared war on the United States (1941).

12 ● Marconi received the first radio signal sent over the Atlantic Ocean, from England to Newfoundland (1901).

13 ● St. Lucia's Day, festival of light. In Sweden, the eldest daughter wears a crown of lighted candles at this winter celebration.

14 ● President George Washington died (1799).
 ● Roald Amundsen, explorer, arrived at South Pole (1911).

15 ● Royal and Ancient Society of Polar Bears General Assembly in Hammerfest, Norway. Arctic explorers meet to tell tall stories about their deeds.
 ● Ludwig van Beethoven, German composer, was born (1770).

16 ● The Boston Tea Party took place. Colonists resisting the tea tax threw a shipment of tea overboard in Boston Harbor (1773).

17 ● Orville Wright made the first heavier-than-air flight at Kitty Hawk, North Carolina (1903).

20 ● France sold Louisiana to the United States (1803).

21 ● Forefather's Day, a New England holiday, honoring the landing of the Pilgrims at Plymouth in 1620.
 ● Apollo 8 became the first manned mission to orbit the moon (1968).

23 ● Feast of the Radishes. (People and animals, carved out of radishes, are sold on the streets of Oaxaca, Mexico.)

24 ● Festival of Christmas Lanterns, a procession of colorful and gigantic lanterns in the Philippines.

25 ● Christmas Day, celebrating Christ's birthday.

26 ● St. Stephen's Day, a national holiday in England, commonly called Boxing Day (because of the tradition of giving Christmas boxes).

28 ● President Woodrow Wilson was born (1856).

29 ● President Andrew Johnson was born (1808).

31 ● New Year's Eve.

▲ *December's flower is the daffodil or narcissus. It is a golden yellow flower native to Northern Europe.*

It has been said that the most important invention of all time was the invention of the decimal number system. The man who invented the system was a Dutch mathematician born 400 years ago. His name was Simon Stevin or Stevinus. His great idea was the decimal point—numbers before the point should be whole numbers, those after it should be fractions.

Southern Hemisphere, summer begins at that time.

December's great holiday in many parts of the world is Christmas. Christian peoples celebrate the birth of Christ on this day, December 25. The eight-day Jewish Feast of Lights, Hanukkah, usually comes in December. The last night of the month is New Year's Eve (or Hogmanay), an evening when people stay up until midnight to welcome in the new year. December's birthstones now are the zircon and turquoise. Narcissus is the flower of the month. The holly, poinsettia, and mistletoe, used for Christmas decorations, are also associated with December.

ALSO READ: CAESAR, JULIUS; CALENDAR; CHRISTMAS; HANUKKAH; HOLIDAY; MONTH; NEW YEAR'S DAY; SEASON; WINTER.

DECIDUOUS TREE   see TREE.

DECIMAL NUMBER   The number system we use is called the decimal number system. The word "decimal" comes from the Latin word for "ten." Our number system is based on ten and numbers produced by multiplying ten by itself a given number of times, such as 100, 1,000, 10,000. We have only ten symbols for whole numbers—*1, 2, 3, 4, 5, 6, 7, 8, 9,* and *0.* These symbols are called numerals. Depending on their place in a number they can stand for groups of ones, tens, hundreds, thousands, and so on. In this way we can tell that the number 1,259 means 1 group of 1,000, plus 2 groups of 100, plus 5 groups of 10, plus 9 units.

Fractions in the decimal system are called decimal fractions. (Read the section on fractions in the article on NUMBER. Be sure you understand what "numerator" and "denominator" mean.) A decimal fraction is one whose denominator is 10, 100, 1,000, and so forth. To tell exactly what

number goes in the denominator, a *decimal point* is used.

The following are all decimal numbers that are part fractions and part whole numbers. The decimal points are in red:

   12 . 3   1 . 17   46 . 395

The number to the left of the decimal point is a whole number. The number to the right of the decimal point is a fraction. To form the fraction, place the entire number to the right of the decimal point in the numerator. In the denominator, put a 1 with as many zeroes (0's) after it as there are numbers to the right of the decimal point. For example:

$$0 . 3 = \frac{3}{10}$$

$$0 . 17 = \frac{17}{100}$$

$$0 . 395 = \frac{395}{1,000}$$

The entire decimal number is the whole number to the left of the decimal point *plus* the fraction to the right of the decimal point.

12 . 3 = 12 + 3/10 = 12 and three-tenths

1 . 17 = 1 + 17/100 = one and 17 one-hundreths

46 . 395 = 46 + 395/1,000 = 46 and 395 one-thousandths

Decimal fractions are used because they are much easier to work with than ordinary fractions. They can be added, subtracted, multiplied, and divided using the same methods as for whole numbers. For this reason, many money systems and measuring systems use a decimal system. Dollars and cents are an example. The decimal number $2.43 means "two dollars and 43 one-hundredths of a dollar."

The *metric system* of measuring is a decimal system now used by most countries.

ALSO READ: MEASUREMENT, METRIC SYSTEM, NUMBER.

DECLARATION OF INDEPEN-DENCE

"All men are created equal." So states the Declaration of Independence, written in 1776. This historic document declared the 13 American colonies free from Great Britain.

In May 1775, delegates from all the colonies met in Philadelphia at the Second Continental Congress to talk about their problems with Britain. Some delegates hoped to come to an agreement with Britain without war. Other delegates argued that Americans would never have their full rights unless they declared their independence. One delegate, Richard Henry Lee of Virginia, introduced a declaration in June 1776, stating that the colonies "are, and of a right ought to be, free and independent states." The delegates voted for Lee's statement on July 2, 1776. Meanwhile, they asked Thomas Jefferson to write a formal declaration. John Adams, Robert Livingston, Roger Sherman, and Benjamin Franklin helped Jefferson write the final draft.

On July 4, 1776, delegates from 12 colonies formally accepted Jefferson's draft of the Declaration of Independence (New York temporarily abstained). Fifty-six delegates from all 13 colonies signed it on August 2, 1776. News of the adoption of the Declaration soon spread. Americans then knew they had to fight to win their freedom, because they had dared to declare themselves independent.

The Declaration has two main parts. One paragraph tells of the rights of all people. It says that God creates all men equal. All persons have certain rights that no government can take away. Among these rights are the right to live, to be free, and to do those things that are meaningful, so long as no one is harmed. Every person, no matter who he or she is, should be treated as a human being. Government must be set up to protect these rights. The people have a right to change a government if it does not serve them. The second part of the Declaration explains how the British king had taken away the colonists' rights. The document ends with a declaration that the colonies are free from the king's rule.

This historic document has aroused people in other countries to make their governments more democratic. Many countries have been made independent since it was signed. The original parchment copy of the Declaration of Independence can be seen in the National Archives building in Washington, D.C., where it is displayed with the U.S. Constitution.

ALSO READ: ADAMS, JOHN; AMERICAN COLONIES; AMERICAN REVOLUTION; CONTINENTAL CONGRESS; FRANKLIN, BENJAMIN; JEFFERSON, THOMAS.

▲ The Declaration of Independence, signed by patriots in Independence Hall, Philadelphia, in 1776.

▶ *Some of the forms of deep-sea fishes can be very strange indeed! Many have organs that light up to attract prey.*

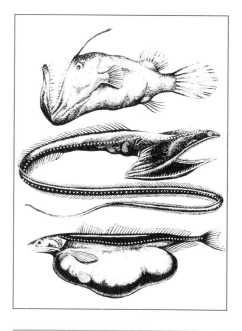

A small shrimp-like creature has been sighted at the fantastic depth of 32,118 feet (9,790 m) in the Philippine trench.

DEEP-SEA LIFE The deeper you go in the sea the darker it gets and the stranger the animals become. In the deepest parts of the ocean, below about 3,300 feet (1,000 m), it is completely dark and many of the fishes and other animals carry their own lights about with them. These lights help the animals to find food and to recognize their mates.

There are no plants in the depths and the animals are all either flesh-eaters or scavengers feeding on the debris sinking down from higher levels. Very little food actually gets down to the deepest parts and not a lot of animals can live there. Those that do manage to survive are all rather small, but they include some formidable predators. Most of the fishes, for example, have enormous mouths compared with the rest of the body. They don't find food very often and they must be able to tackle anything they meet—even if it is as large or even larger than themselves. Many also have their jaws full of needlelike teeth, which ensure that the prey never escapes. Among the best examples of these deep-sea predators are the *gulpers*, which appear to be little more than a mouth with a long tail. The tail has a luminous lure at the end, and when a victim approaches

the "bait" it is lassoed by the whiplike tail. *Angler-fishes* commonly have luminous lures hanging just above their enormous mouths. *Pachystomius*, a slender fish living just above the level of total darkness, uses a red searchlight to pick out its prey. The light streams out from near its eyes and, as most other fishes cannot see red light, the predator can approach them unseen.

Other creatures of the deep sea include various prawns and numerous squids. The latter are often beautifully colored and carry lots of luminous spots.

DEER Deer make up one of the best known mammal families. They are native to North and South America, Europe, Asia, and Africa. They have been introduced in Hawaii, Australia, and New Zealand, and they have made homes in these places.

Deer belong to the mammal group called *ungulates* (hoofed mammals). Deer range in size from about 20 pounds (9 kg) to more than 1,800 pounds (800 kg). They live in cold regions, in hot regions, in forests, on grassy plains, on deserts, on mountains, and on flat plateaus. But they all have certain features in common. They are all *herbivores* (plant eaters), and they all feed by browsing, or grazing. They eat leaves, twigs, bark, grasses, and lichens. They also eat buds, berries, and other fruit. The males of most species are called *bucks*

▼ *Two male red deer fighting to control a territory. Sometimes the tough antlers of two warring deer become completely interlocked. The deer cannot separate and finally die of starvation.*

▲ The white-tailed deer of North America have tails with a white underside. When the startled animal runs, raising its tail, the white warns the other deer.

and the females *does*. The male red deer of Europe and Asia may be called a *stag* or a *hart*, and the female deer may be called a *hind*. A male moose or caribou is a *bull*, and a female a *cow*. Most deer young are called *fawns*, but a baby wapiti, moose, or caribou is a *calf*.

Deer are the only animals with *antlers*. Males of almost all species have them, and so do female caribou and reindeer. Antlers are made of bone. They grow from two bony bumps, called *pedicles*, on the forehead. Antlers are shed and replaced every year.

Kinds of Deer *Whitetail deer*, or Virginia deer, are found in greater numbers and in more places than other deer. They live in forests from the East Coast to the Rocky Mountains, and from southern Canada to northern South America.

A whitetail doe often gives birth to twin fawns in spring or summer. The tiny fawn has a light-brown coat spotted with white patches. This coloring looks very much like patches of sunlight on the forest floor, and it helps

to hide a fawn from its enemies. The fawn grows so quickly that it is about the size of its mother by fall. Its coat slowly changes to the heavy, gray-brown winter coat. The next summer, the young deer will have a coat of light reddish brown.

A full-grown whitetail weighs 50 to 300 pounds (23–135 kg). The buck is always larger than the doe. The antlers of a really big buck may be 6 feet (1.8 m) above the ground.

The *mule deer* is the whitetail's close relative. Mule deer are found from the Great Plains to the west coast of North America, from Canada to Mexico. They have large eyes, exceptionally big ears (from which they get their name), and rounded white tails tipped with black.

The North American *blacktail* is smaller than the mule deer, and its ears are short and broad. Lewis and Clark, the famous explorers, were the first white men to see this deer, and they gave it its misleading name. Blacktails' tails are bushy and black, but the undersides are bright white. Blacktails range from around San Diego, California, to the vicinity of Sitka, Alaska.

The largest member of the deer family is the *Alaska moose*. Bulls weigh 1,500 pounds (680 kg) or more and have an antler spread of 6 feet

◄ Reindeer are large deer that live in cold climates. They are used to pull sleighs and for other heavy work.

▼ Moose wading through the water where they browse on lilies and leaves. The largest living deer, moose live in the coniferous forests of Europe and Asia (where they are called elk), as well as North America.

1   2   3   4

▲ *Four stages in the growth of a red deer's antlers. (1) Knobs grow on bones on top of the head. (2) Small antlers are covered in a soft skin called velvet. (3) Blood vessels under the velvet carry foods to the growing antlers. (4) The blood supply to the antlers stops, and the velvet is rubbed off before the start of the breeding season.*

▼ *The sika deer, a small native of eastern Asia that has been introduced to many European woodlands.*

(1.8 m) or more. Cows are somewhat smaller. One to three calves are born in late spring.

Moose can be found in only 12 states. Hunters killed so many moose that the animals have almost disappeared from the United States. Moose are protected by law in the United States and Canada. Moose also live in the northern forests of Europe and Asia, where they are called *elk*.

The *wapiti*, or *American elk*, once lived from the eastern forests to the west coast of North America. But as settlers spread across the country, the elk quickly died out. By the late 1800's, elk were plentiful only in Yellowstone National Park. Then, starting just after 1900, men from the National Park Service, part of the U.S. Department of the Interior, began to trap small groups of elk from the Yellowstone herds. The captured elk were given to state game departments to restore elk to their former homes. Elk herds live in 39 states today.

Caribou live in Alaska and Canada on tundras and spruce forests. Herds travel great distances in search of slow-growing lichen (reindeer moss), on which they feed. Unlike other female deer, caribou cows have antlers. Bulls shed their large, many-branched antlers during November and December. Cows and young bulls shed their much smaller horns in May or June.

The caribou's first cousin is the European and Asian *reindeer*. Reindeer are slightly smaller than caribou, and they are the only deer that have

been domesticated. The Lapps and other northern Europeans keep herds for meat, milk, and clothing. They are used to pull sleds.

The world's smallest deer is the *pudu* of Chile and Bolivia. Full-grown males are only 15 inches (38 cm) tall and weigh 20 pounds (9 kg). The *Chinese water deer* is also 20 pounds (9 kg) full-grown, with long, curved tusks.

ALSO READ: ANTELOPE, ARCTIC, HOOFED ANIMALS, HORNS AND ANTLERS, LEWIS AND CLARK EXPEDITION, TUNDRA.

DEFENSE see AIR FORCE, ARMY, MARINE CORPS, NAVY.

DEFOE, DANIEL (1660–1731) Daniel Defoe, an English writer, created the popular story of *Robinson Crusoe* (1719). The novel tells the story of a shipwrecked sailor who builds himself a home, raises goats, and wins a trusted friend named Friday. This exciting tale is based on the life of Alexander Selkirk (1676–1721), a Scottish sailor marooned on a Pacific island for over four years.

Defoe was born in London, England. His father was a butcher named Foe. Daniel added "De" to his name to make it more fashionable. He wrote mostly about politics and religion, which sometimes got him into trouble. He spent some time in prison. Defoe then became a newspaper writer. He also acted as a secret agent for people who were trying to bring Scotland and England together.

Defoe wrote an amazing amount of material—more than 500 books. *Moll Flanders* (1722), another famous Defoe book, tells the adventures of a misguided young lady who is determined to get ahead in the world. Many people think *A Journal of the Plague Year* (1722) is Defoe's best book. The disease called bubonic plague struck London in 1665, killing more than 70,000 people. Defoe's book pretends to be the diary of a man living in London at the time. All of these books show why Defoe is thought to be the first great realistic novelist in English fiction.

ALSO READ: NOVEL.

DE FOREST, LEE see RADIO BROADCASTING.

DEGAS, EDGAR (1834–1917) As you look at the painting of the prima ballerina dancing in her white costume, can't you almost hear the applause of the audience? Like a fairy queen she floats across the stage, while other members of the ballet company watch from backstage as she performs. Wouldn't you like to be in the audience?

This was the kind of rich life led by the painter of *Prima Ballerina*, Edgar Degas, the greatest of all painters of the dance. He was born in Paris to wealthy parents, and grew up enjoying the arts. Unlike most artists, he came from a family that had no objection to his becoming an artist. They fitted out a studio for him when he decided, at 18, that he wanted to paint. As a native Parisian, he was right on the scene when that city became more and more an art center of the 1800's. He was one of the circle of young painters called the Impressionists, who created a stir in art circles with their way of painting an impression of a scene in changing light and shade.

He first began to paint theatrical scenes in the 1860's. He painted café singers, circus artists, and horse races. But mostly he painted ballet dancers—at rehearsal, in the dressing room, on stage, practicing at the bar. He liked to paint from unusual angles, as in the picture here. You feel as if you are sitting in the first balcony, just above the ballerina. Note the lack of detail in the dancer's face, as if she were moving. You are allowed only a fleeting glimpse of her.

Although he painted dozens of people, Degas did not get along with others and lived alone. When his eyesight failed, he switched from oils to pastels. He turned to sculpture when he was nearly blind.

ALSO READ: CASSATT, MARY; IMPRESSIONISM.

DE GAULLE, CHARLES (1890–1970) Charles André Joseph Marie de Gaulle was the best-known French soldier and leader from 1940 to 1969. He gave France, a defeated nation in 1940, new pride. He led that country back to a leading position among Europe's nations.

De Gaulle was born near Lille, France. He graduated with honors in 1911 from St. Cyr, the famous French military school. During

▲ *Daniel Defoe, author of some very famous books including* Robinson Crusoe.

▲ *Edgar Degas, the great French painter of ballet scenes. This sketch was done by another famous French artist, Edouard Manet.*

◀ Prima Ballerina, *a painting by Edgar Degas.*

▲ *Charles de Gaulle, the great French general and statesman. He led the Free French opposition to the German occupation of France during World War II. Later he became French President.*

▼ *The Birkenhead rolling mills, built during the 1820's, are located in the Hagley Yards near Wilmington, Delaware. This famous museum area houses 21 old mills.*

World War I, he was wounded four times and captured by the Germans. He was a strong believer in mechanized warfare during the 1930's. In World War II, when France surrendered to Germany on June 22, 1940, de Gaulle, then a general, escaped to London, England. He refused to accept the surrender, saying that France had lost a battle, not a war. From his base in England he led and inspired the Free French army of patriots.

After the war, de Gaulle headed the French government. But he resigned in January 1946, because he felt his country's new constitution did not give him enough power. He was called back from retirement as French President in 1958 to deal with the crisis in Algeria. De Gaulle began a number of programs, such as increasing taxes and modernizing industry, to make France a power in the modern world and to restore what he called France's *gloire* ("glory"). He signed a treaty with an old enemy, West Germany, in January 1963. He was a strong opponent of Britain's membership of the European Economic Community. When his plans for changing the French constitution were defeated in April 1969 after a referendum, he resigned. Today, French politics are still very much influenced by the Gaullist movement.

ALSO READ: FRENCH HISTORY, WORLD WAR II.

DELAWARE Lord De La Warr was governor of Virginia in the early years of that colony. But his name, spelled differently, was given to the state of Delaware.

In the summer of 1610, Captain Samuel Argall sailed north from Virginia along the Atlantic Coast. Over 100 miles up the coast, he came to a bay. On the northern side was a cape, a point of land. He named it for his governor. (The cape, which is in New Jersey, was renamed Cape May.) De La Warr's name, spelled Delaware, was later used for the bay, too. It was then given to the long river that pours into the bay. The land west of the lower river and the bay also came to be called Delaware. That land became the state of Delaware.

The Land The only state smaller than Delaware is Rhode Island. Delaware has few natural resources, but the state has one great advantage. It has a fine location. Delaware lies between the North and the South. It is as far north as parts of Pennsylvania and New Jersey. It is as far south as parts of Maryland and Virginia. Delaware lies close to some of the largest industrial cities in the United States including New York, Philadelphia, Baltimore, and Washington, D.C.

The state has good water transportation. Oceangoing ships sail up the Delaware River to Wilmington. The river is connected with the Chesapeake Bay by the Chesapeake and Delaware Canal. This canal cuts through the northern end of a long peninsula (an "arm" of land that is almost surrounded by water). West of the peninsula is the Chesapeake Bay. East of it are the lower Delaware River, the Delaware Bay, and the Atlantic Ocean.

The peninsula is part of the Atlantic Coastal Plain. Most of Delaware, therefore, is in the plain. For this reason, most of Delaware is low and

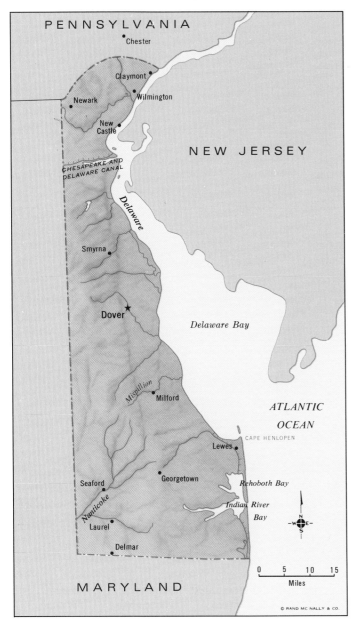

DELAWARE

Capital: Dover (26,000 people).

Area: 2,157 square miles (5,377 sq. km).

Rank: 49th

Population: 665,000
Rank: 47th

Statehood: December 7, 1787 (First of the 13 original states to ratify the Constitution)

Principal river: Delaware (390 miles/628 km)

Highest Point: 442 feet (135 m), near Centerville, New Castle County

Largest City: Wilmington (71,000 people)

Motto: "Liberty and Independence"

Song: "Our Delaware"

Famous People: Valerie Bertinelli, Pierre Samuel du Pont

▲ *The Grand Opera House, Wilmington, Delaware.*

STATE EMBLEMS

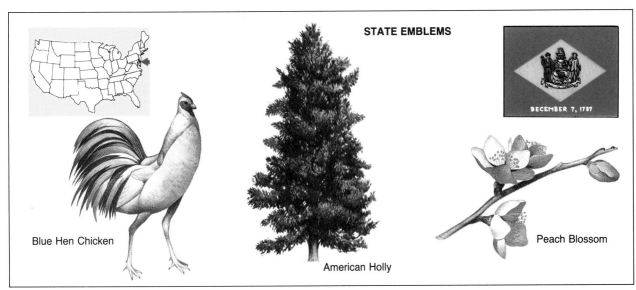

Blue Hen Chicken

American Holly

Peach Blossom

▲ *Delaware Memorial Bridge is a superbly graceful piece of modern architecture.*

In 1800 Delaware's population was 64,000. By 1900 it had risen to 185,000. By the 1980 census the figure had risen to 594,338.

rather flat. Some parts have so little slope that water does not drain well from them, and these parts are often swampy. The northernmost part of Delaware is not in the coastal plain. It is in a hilly region called the Piedmont.

Delaware in winter seems just the in-between state that it is. It is not so cold as New England, to the north. But it is colder than the Deep South. The Delaware summer is hot and humid. People flock to the beaches, where ocean winds bring relief from the heat.

History   Three European flags have flown in Delaware. The Dutch flag came first. It flew from the ship *Half Moon*. Its captain, Henry Hudson, was English but had been hired by the Dutch. Hudson sailed into Delaware Bay in 1609, the year before Samuel Argall reached it. The Dutch built a settlement at the entrance to the bay in 1631. It stood where the fishing port of Lewes is now. The settlement was named *Swaanedael* or "Place of Swans." (The swans were probably wild geese.) The Indians here got on well with the Dutch—at first. But a quarrel led to bloodshed, and the Indians killed almost everyone in the settlement.

Swedes and Finns were the first Europeans to build a lasting settlement in Delaware. Peter Minuit brought them from Europe in 1638. He was Dutch, but he was serving the 12-year-old Swedish queen, Christina. Minuit's two ships sailed up the Delaware River to the place where Wilmington stands today. There the settlers built a log fort. They named it Fort Christina. Soldiers from the Dutch colony of New Netherland captured Fort Christina and the Swedish settlement in 1655. But the victory did the Dutch little good. Less than ten years later the English seized New Netherland and renamed it New York. At the same time, the English took the Delaware territory from the Dutch.

Most of the Atlantic coast was then English, but the English colonies quarreled with each other about their boundaries. Pirates often sailed into Delaware Bay and raided towns along the shore. But in spite of such troubles, the Delaware colonists did well. Farmers raised good crops. Merchants grew rich through trade.

In 1776, Delaware became one of the 13 original United States. With its sister states, it fought Great Britain during the American Revolution. The First Delaware Regiment took as its nickname the "Blue Hen's Chickens." Rooster fighting was a sport in those days. And people believed that the bravest fighting roosters were those hatched from the eggs of blue hens. Sometimes Delaware is called the "Blue Hen State." Delaware is also called "The First State." This is because Delaware was the first state to accept the Constitution in 1787.

Working in Delaware   Manufacturing is Delaware's biggest business. The chemical industry is the most profitable. Canning and other food preparation come next. Most factories are in and around Wilmington, Delaware's largest city. Soon after 1800, mills for weaving cloth were opened in this area. So was the state's first gunpowder mill. It was started by Eleuthère Irénée du Pont de Nemours, who had fled from France during the French Revolution. The company he founded is known today as E. I. du Pont de Nemours and Company, or Du Pont. It is a huge company, with factories in many parts of the United States. It makes chemicals, dyes, paints, rubber, and synthetic fabrics, as well as explosives. Some buildings of the early powder mill are not far away on Brandywine Creek.

Delaware agriculture earns much less money than manufacturing. But it is important. Chickens, corn, and soybeans are the principal products.

Tourists bring millions of dollars to

the state every year. Some people visit the beaches. Others tour historic spots. One such spot in Wilmington is called the Rocks. This stone wharf on the Christina River is natural, not man-made. The Swedes and Finns landed there in 1638. The Old Swedes Church, built in 1698, is nearby. Before 1777, New Castle was the capital of Delaware. It has some beautiful old houses. Other points of interest are the Hagley Museum, with exhibits of early industries, and the Winterthur Museum, noted for its colonial furniture.

ALSO READ: STATE GOVERNMENT, STATE SYMBOLS.

DELPHI see GREECE, ANCIENT.

DELTA see RIVER.

▲ *Speakers' Corner, beside Hyde Park, London, England. Here anyone can come to express his or her opinions to the crowd. This is the British right of free speech in action. Democracies regard free speech as one of the fundamental rights of their citizens.*

DEMOCRACY A political system in which people have the supreme voice in deciding how their government should work is called a democracy. In modern democracies citizens elect, or choose by the process of voting, certain people to represent them. In some democratic countries, a head of government is also elected. U.S. citizens elect a President and Vice President, as well as senators and representatives who are members of Congress. They often vote for leaders of state and local governments, too. The government must consult the people, or their elected representatives, before taking any action or making any laws.

"Democracy" comes from a Greek word meaning "rule of the people." Democracies existed in Greece and Rome, but they were different from democracies existing today. They were *direct democracies* in which all *citizens* could speak and vote on all the issues. But in those ancient democracies, the word "citizen" only applied to men who owned property (land). Men who did not own property, women, slaves, and most people who were born in another country were not citizens, so they could not vote. Democracies have changed, mostly because modern democracies are much larger than the democracies of ancient Greece and Rome. Can you imagine a meeting of all the citizens of the United States? Can you imagine how long it would take for everyone to suggest ideas about a proposed new law? The United States is an *indirect democracy* or *republic*. Citizens vote to choose representatives who run the government.

Another change has taken place, too. Laws have been passed to protect the rights of many citizens. Not only men who own land can vote, but all citizens (other than children), regardless of their race, sex, or religious beliefs.

People living in a democracy have the right of individual freedom. They can choose their own careers and run

Kronborg Castle, near the Danish port of Helsingör (Elsinore) was the setting for Shakespeare's play Hamlet. *The play is performed in the castle each summer.*

their own businesses. All citizens are equal, and laws are supposed to be enforced the same way for all people. All citizens who meet certain qualifications, who are old enough and have lived in a certain place long enough, have the right to vote. Everyone can attend school.

Many philosophers, including John Locke and Thomas Jefferson, have written on what they thought a democracy ought to be. Some of Jefferson's ideas are included in the Declaration of Independence. It states: ". . . that all men are created equal, that they are endowed by their Creator with certain unalienable Rights, that among these are Life, Liberty and the pursuit of Happiness."

The Bill of Rights, the first ten amendments to the Constitution, promises other rights for all Americans—such as the freedom of speech and the freedom of the press. These rights allow people to hear, read, and discuss new ideas. These rights make it possible for people to help their elected representatives and leaders make their country a better place to live. These rights even protect people in the United States from a central government that has too much power.

Some countries use most or all of the democratic principles, such as legislatures and elections. Other countries use the word "democratic" in the official name of the country but do not have free elections or other evidence of rule by the people. One

example is the German Democratic Republic, which is commonly called East Germany.

ALSO READ: BILL OF RIGHTS, DECLARATION OF INDEPENDENCE, ELECTION.

DENG XIAOPING see TENG HSIAO-P'ING.

DENMARK Denmark is a prosperous country, with one of the world's highest standards of living. It is famous for its butter, cheese, ham, bacon, and pastry. Beautifully designed Danish furniture and silverware are also well known around the world. The Danes are today a peaceful people who enjoy life. However, 1,000 years ago, the Danes were warlike Viking sea-raiders who were feared throughout much of Europe because of their plundering ways.

Denmark is almost entirely surrounded by water. It consists of a mainland and more than 400 islands. The mainland is part of the Jutland Peninsula in northwestern Europe. (See the map with the article on EUROPE.) Most of the Danish islands are close to the mainland. But the rocky Faeroe Islands lie 800 miles (1,290 km) away in the northern part of the Atlantic Ocean, north of the British Isles. Greenland, a huge island near the North American continent, is a self-governing Danish country.

The surrounding sea gives Denmark a pleasant climate, even though

DENMARK

Capital City: Copenhagen (640,000 people).
Area: 17,430 square miles (45,069 sq. km).
Population: 5,160,000.
Government: Constitutional monarchy.
Natural Resources: Crude oil, natural gas, limestone, salt.
Export Products: Meat, meat products, fish, dairy products, metal goods, machinery, ships.
Unit of Money: Krone.
Official Language: Danish.

it is a northern country. The average temperature in winter is about 32° F (0° C), and in summer about 60° F (15° C).

One of the largest islands close to the mainland is Zealand (*Sjaelland* in Danish). It is separated from Sweden by a channel called the Oresund. Denmark's capital, Copenhagen, is on Zealand. The city was founded 800 years ago and is one of Europe's oldest seaports. It has a world-famous amusement park, called the Tivoli Gardens. Another well-known landmark is the statue of the Little Mermaid in Copenhagen's harbor. It was built in honor of Hans Christian Andersen. You may have read his famous story about a mermaid who fell in love with a human prince.

Denmark is poor in natural resources. Raw materials needed by factories must be bought from other countries. But Danish soil is very fertile, and Denmark's farms are among the most prosperous in Europe. Fishing, shipping, and manufacturing are important industries.

Denmark has been a constitutional monarchy for nearly 140 years. It is governed under a new constitution adopted in 1953. The monarch, or king, chooses the prime minister, who is the real head of government. Queen Margrethe II, who succeeded to the throne in 1972, is only the second queen Denmark has had. The members of the one-chamber legislature are elected by the Danish people in democratic elections. The government provides insurance for illness, accidents, old age, and unemployment. Denmark is a member of the European Community.

ALSO READ: ANDERSEN, HANS CHRISTIAN; EUROPE; EUROPEAN COMMUNITY; GREENLAND; SCANDINAVIA; SCANDINAVIAN LANGUAGES.

DENSITY see BUOYANCY, MATTER.

▲ *The beautiful city of Copenhagen, capital of Denmark, is one of Europe's oldest seaports.*

DENTISTRY Did you ever stop to think what a good friend your dentist is? A *dentist* is a doctor who takes care of the teeth and mouth. Dentists try to prevent tooth decay, or *caries*. The dentist shows you the best way to brush your teeth and reminds you not to eat too much candy. The dentist or a helper, the *dental hygienist*, also cleans your teeth in a special way to remove any materials your toothbrush and dental floss cannot. A fluoride solution may be applied to your teeth to help prevent decay. If you do what the dentist tells you, you will be doing all you can to grow up with healthy teeth. But, if you ignore what the dentist tells you, you will probably have a lot of difficulty with painful toothache and, as you grow older, lose a lot of your teeth.

When you visit the dentist, you sit in a special chair. It can be raised or lowered so that the dentist can work comfortably. The dentist turns on a large overhead light and asks you to "open wide." The dentist uses sterilized tools to examine the mouth and to care for tooth decay and other problems. Sometimes dentists take X-ray pictures to find decay or problems they might not see otherwise.

In earlier times, when a person had a toothache, the tooth was pulled.

George Washington had several pairs of false teeth made for him. Historians have identified three pairs he once owned. The Smithsonian Institution now has one pair of our first President's false teeth.

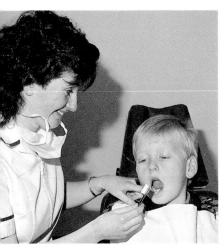

▲ *You should visit your dentist twice a year. The dentist can often help by treating tooth decay, but it's up to you to clean your teeth after meals.*

▼ *Crowds gather outside the New York Stock Exchange in October 1929, as the Wall Street Crash suddenly starts. Thousands of people who owned stocks and shares lost all their money. The Crash was the start of the Great Depression.*

People with gum disease often lost many teeth. There was no way to take care of decayed teeth and diseased gums as dentists do today. Then early dentists learned that a tooth could sometimes be repaired instead of pulled. They first used wax and gums to fill cavities and, by the Middle Ages, began using gold and lead to fill them. Silver amalgam, porcelain, and other synthetics (man-made substances) are generally used today. Until the mid-1800's, a person learned dentistry by working for a dentist. The first dental school in the United States was established in Baltimore, Maryland, in 1841. Today most students who want to study dentistry attend college for four years before enrolling in a four-year dental program. These students take many of the same courses as medical students, learning about the body and various aspects of illness. They are taught how to prevent and treat oral (mouth) diseases. People who graduate from dental school must pass a state examination before they can begin work.

Many dentists have helpers in their offices. Some are dental assistants, and some are dental hygienists. Each is educated to do special tasks to help the dentist with the patients.

Certain dentists specialize in various types of dentistry. Some take care of patients with diseases of the gums and the bones that support the teeth. This is known as *periodontics*. *Pedodontists* are dentists for children only. *Orthodontists* make sure that the teeth are correctly aligned and that they come together properly when the mouth is closed. The correct alignment of teeth is necessary to chew food properly and to prevent the teeth from being destroyed. Orthodontists make plaster impressions of the teeth and design corrective wire bands. These bands, fitted firmly on or around the teeth and attached to specially designed wires, bring the teeth into the correct position.

Some dentists, called *prosthodontists*, make artificial teeth to replace teeth that must be pulled. Sometimes they make only a one-tooth bridge. *Partial dentures* replace several missing teeth. *Full dentures* contain all of the teeth belonging in one or both jaws. Other dentists, known as *oral surgeons*, correct deformities, injuries, and diseases of the mouth by operating. Oral surgeons also work with other dentists and physicians, for instance in caring for persons injured in automobile accidents.

ALSO READ: TEETH.

DEPRESSION A low area of ground is a depression; so is a low level of atmospheric pressure. Businesses depend on a certain level of demand for the goods and services they sell. If there is little or no demand, business suffers a depression.

To one family, a depression may mean buying no new clothes and eating small, low-cost meals without special treats. It may mean moving to a small, crowded apartment, getting along without a car, and worrying about whether the parents will find jobs or lose the ones they have.

To a country, a depression means a time when many small stores and businesses close because people cannot afford to buy goods or use serv-

ices. Large companies fire thousands of workers and cut their production sharply. Everything about the nation seems to be wrong.

The United States suffered serious depressions in the 1830's, the 1840's, the 1870's, and the 1890's. The most terrible depression of all began in 1929. This *Great Depression*, as it is called, paralyzed the country for 12 years. Many other countries have been struck by depressions, sometimes with horrible results. The Great Depression of the 1930's, for example, was nearly worldwide. Conditions in Germany were so terrible that the Germans were prepared to listen to the Nazis. Adolf Hitler came to power and led them into World War II. In the early 1990's many countries, including the United States, felt the pressures of a world recession.

Economists think that many things can help cause a depression. If too many people save too much of the money they earn, manufacturers have no customers for their products. This can cause depression. Or many manufacturers may spend money for new machines and buildings at the same time. Then a time follows when no one buys new machinery. Machine companies—and companies that make products needed to build machines—cannot find customers, so they fire workers. Soon mining and transportation companies have fewer customers, so they fire workers, too. Economists say that the way to avoid major depressions is to avoid major changes in the way a country spends its money.

ALSO READ: AMERICAN HISTORY; ECONOMICS; HOOVER, HERBERT; ROOSEVELT, FRANKLIN D.

DESERT A region so dry that most people, animals, and plants cannot live in it is called a desert. Many people think of deserts as being hot, burning areas covered with sand hills,

called *dunes*. However, deserts can be found in cooler regions far away from the equator. They may be covered with pebbles, large rocks, snow, or ice.

Low-latitude deserts (near the equator) and mid-latitude deserts (lying between 15 and 35 degrees in Northern and Southern Hemispheres) are alike in several ways. More moisture evaporates from the ground than enters it from rainfall. Infrequent rain usually pours in great torrents. Because the hard, dry ground cannot absorb the rainwater fast enough, flash floods often occur. Little soil exists because plant growth is needed for soil formation. Daytime temperatures may reach over 100° F (38° C). Nighttime temperatures may fall below the freezing point. The reason for the great variation in temperatures is that the ground is unable to hold the heat of the sun. Famous low-latitude deserts are the Sahara in

▲ *The Great Depression of the 1930's affected many countries. In Britain, as in the United States, people were reduced to lining up for food hand-outs.*

FAMOUS DESERTS OF THE WORLD			
DESERT	LOCATION	APPROXIMATE SIZE (square miles)	(square kilometers)
Antarctica	South Pole	5,500,000	14,245,000
Sahara	North Africa	3,500,000	9,065,000
Great Australian	Australia	1,500,000	3,885,000
Libyan	Libya	500,000	1,295,000
Gobi	Mongolia	300,000	777,000
Rub'al Khali	Arabia	250,000	647,500
Kalahari	Southern Africa	120,000	310,800
Khiva (Kara Kum)	Soviet Union	110,000	284,900
Atacama	Chile	25,000	64,750
Mohave	California, U.S.	15,000	38,850

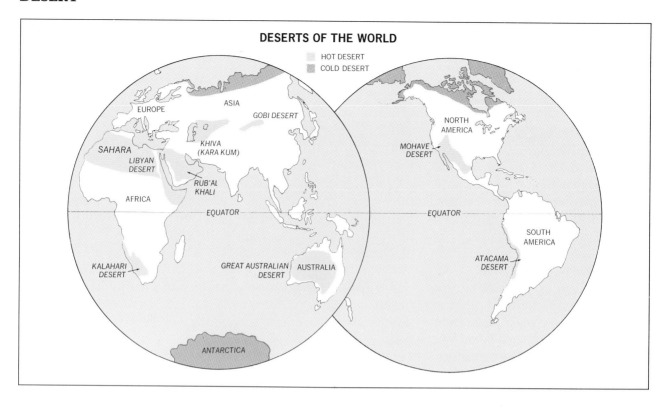

DESERTS OF THE WORLD

HOT DESERT
COLD DESERT

EUROPE
ASIA
GOBI DESERT
KHIVA
(KARA KUM)
SAHARA
LIBYAN
DESERT
RUB'AL
KHALI
AFRICA
EQUATOR
KALAHARI
DESERT
GREAT AUSTRALIAN
DESERT
AUSTRALIA
ANTARCTICA

NORTH
AMERICA
MOHAVE
DESERT
EQUATOR
SOUTH
AMERICA
ATACAMA
DESERT

northern Africa and the Arabian Desert in the Middle East. The Mohave Desert and the Painted Desert lie in the western United States. The Atacama and much of the Patagonia region in South America, as well as the Gobi in central Asia, are other mid-latitude deserts.

Another kind of desert is found in northern Canada, the northern Soviet Union, Greenland, and Antarctica. Very few plants and animals can survive in portions of these regions because they are so cold and icy. These areas are ice-cap and tundra regions, or *cold deserts*. Cold deserts are dry because they have no liquid water—it

▲ *A barrel cactus swells up after rain as its pleats fill with moisture* (left). *But after a drought it looks thinner because of loss of this stored moisture.*

is all in the form of ice. Two million years ago, Canada and most of Europe were cold deserts.

Certain plants are especially suited for desert living. Many hot and mid-latitude desert plants require very little moisture. Cacti, for example, store water in their thick stems. They do not have leaves that lose moisture. Some desert herbs and shrubs enter a sleeplike state during the driest periods. They drop their leaves and wither up, but their roots stay alive. During wetter periods, these plants turn green again and bear flowers.

▼ *The desert in bloom. Evening primroses of all kinds grow in North American hot deserts during the short, moist season. They have various ways of surviving the long, dry season.*

▲ *Part of the Sahara, the biggest hot desert. Its area is about 3,500,000 square miles (9,065,000 sq. km), nearly as large as the United States!*

Other kinds of plants have roots that go very deep underground to reach water. Certain mosses and lichens grow in parts of cold deserts during the short summer period.

Some animals are desert dwellers. Perhaps the camel is the most famous. It stores water in its stomach and can survive for a long period of time without drinking. The kangaroo rat does not drink water but gets enough from the seeds it eats. Other animals that may live in deserts include foxes, hares, and gazelles, as well as certain insects, birds, and reptiles.

People may live in parts of hot deserts where there are oases (there are no oases in cold deserts). An *oasis* is the area around a pool of surface water fed by an underground stream. People traveling through the desert

stop at oases to replenish their water supplies. Farmers are sometimes able to raise a few crops around larger oases.

ALSO READ: ANIMAL DISTRIBUTION, ANTARCTICA, CACTUS, CAMEL, GLACIER, GOBI DESERT, ICE AGE, MIRAGE, MOHAVE DESERT, PAINTED DESERT, SAHARA DESERT.

DESIGN Design is the arrangement of the different parts of something we can look at. Something looks pleasing when the parts fit together well. A cluster of buildings or the arrangement of furniture in a room is a design. The words and pictures in a book like this one, the clothes we wear, and all other man-made objects are designed. People who create designs for man-made products are called *industrial designers*. Industrial designers must be able to create designs that are attractive and practical. Well-designed objects suit their purpose in addition to pleasing the eye. A telephone should fit nicely in the

◄ *The addax, an animal that can survive in the Sahara desert. It gets all its water from dew and from the sparse plant life.*

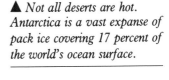

▲ *Not all deserts are hot. Antarctica is a vast expanse of pack ice covering 17 percent of the world's ocean surface.*

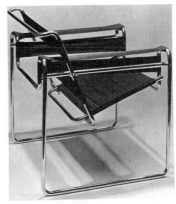

▲ *Marcel Breuer designed this chrome-plated steel tube chair in 1925. It would certainly put the design of some modern chairs to shame! Design is concerned not only with making things look good. It involves making them work well, too. This chair looks good and is comfortable to sit on.*

▲ *Design plays an important part in architecture. This is the Bonaventura Hotel in Los Angeles. The better a hotel looks from the outside the more likely people are to stay in it.*

hand. A chair should be comfortable to sit in. Another type of designer is one who designs clothes. Clothing designers try to create new and beautiful fashions. They select fabrics, furs, leathers, and other materials that they use for dresses, suits, coats, shoes, underclothing, and even jewelry.

Some excellent designs are not man-made. Much can be learned from natural objects. If you cut an apple in half, you will see how beautifully it is "designed." You could make a collection of objects from nature, such as milkweed pods, leaves, seeds from different plants, pinecones, or flowers. Notice the difference in shape, color, and feel. Look at your collection through a magnifying glass. You will see parts that you cannot usually see. Notice how well the parts fit together. Objects in nature not only look beautiful but also suit a particular purpose. The graceful shape of a bird is perfectly suited for flight. A gazelle is built for running, and a fish is created for swimming. Nature is constantly improving designs through evolution.

Variety is important in a design. The parts might be different in size, color, *tone* (darks and lights), or *texture* (the feel or look of the surface). These differences will make the design more interesting. But the parts of a design must be carefully chosen so

▲ *A beautiful example of a compact modern kitchen, well designed and with all up-to-date conveniences.*

that they look good when they are fitted together. A soaring skyscraper might be beautiful in itself. But if it is built in a street with tiny ancient houses, the design of the street will look odd. Everyone, though, will have an idea of what a good design is. Each artist will arrange shapes and colors in a way that looks best to him or her.

■ LEARN BY DOING

You might make a *collage* using different materials. Collect scrap materials that have different textures. Some might be rough (sandpaper or burlap), others smooth (silk) or soft (feather, cotton). Arrange pieces of these materials into a design on a piece of cardboard. You can cut them into different shapes and sizes if you wish. Also try to find differences in color and tone. Arrange the parts until they look best to you. Glue them down with colorless liquid glue.

You could make another collage using clippings of pictures from old magazines. Cut out parts that look rough, smooth, soft, and so on, and glue them down on cardboard. ■

ALSO READ: ARCHITECTURE, COMMERCIAL ART, EVOLUTION, INTERIOR DECORATING, PAINTING.

▶ *Clothes design is a major industry. Here models display the designer's latest creations by parading on a raised "catwalk" before a selected audience of trade buyers, press, and others. These clothes are by the Japanese designer, Kenzo.*

DE SOTO, HERNANDO (about 1500–1542)

Spain's desire for gold led Hernando de Soto to explore vast areas of southeastern North America. He sailed to the New World at age 19 and took part in the Spanish conquest of Central America.

De Soto joined Francisco Pizarro in 1532 in conquering the Incas of Peru. His share of the Incas' gold made him a rich man. But he was still restless for more wealth. Rumors of a land of gold to the north persuaded him to explore Florida. With an army of about 600 men, de Soto landed near what is now Tampa Bay, Florida, in 1539.

De Soto's expedition marched north through the wilderness to the Carolinas, then southwest to what is now Alabama, where de Soto and many of his men were wounded in a battle with Indians.

Marching westward, he became the first European to reach and cross the Mississippi. He and his dwindling army explored as far west as Oklahoma. Three years passed without a trace of gold. De Soto, discouraged, turned back to the banks of the Mississippi, where he died of a fever. He was buried in the river.

ALSO READ: CONQUISTADOR; EXPLORATION; PIZARRO, FRANCISCO.

DETECTIVE

Detectives are usually special kinds of police officers. Their job is to *investigate* (ask questions about) crimes and to gather *clues* (evidence) that will lead to the arrest of the suspect. A police detective works for the township, city, county, or state police department.

Police detectives often have to work in dangerous surroundings and investigate desperate individuals. They know that anything at the scene of a crime could be a clue—fingerprints, a strand of hair, a particle of clothing, the dirt on a person's shoes, or a tiny speck of blood. They work with *forensic scientists* of the police laboratory. A detective must search out people who can give information about a crime, and must be able to recognize any sign that would indicate a person is lying.

A *private investigator* is not a member of the police force. But former police detectives frequently become private detectives. They are often employed to trace missing persons, or hired by hotels or stores to keep down theft.

ALSO READ: CRIME, FEDERAL BUREAU OF INVESTIGATION, FINGERPRINT, FORENSIC SCIENCE, POLICE.

DETROIT

With 1,210,000 people, Detroit is the sixth largest city in the United States. It is a major inland port, standing on the Detroit River, a busy waterway separating the United States from Canada in southeastern Michigan. Called "Motor City" or the "Automobile Capital of the World," it is a great industrial center. Its large vehicle industry was founded in the early 1900's by such men as John and Horace Dodge, Henry Ford, and Ransom E. Olds. Besides vehicles, Detroit also makes many other things, including chemicals, machine tools, and medicines. Detroit contains Wayne State University. The Univer-

▲ *Hernando de Soto, Spanish explorer of the New World.*

▼ *The skyscrapers of Detroit make an impressive sight set against the deep blue of the Detroit River.*

▲ *Diamonds form deep underground in conditions of intense heat and pressure. Of the two diamonds shown above, one is cut and polished. The other is still uncut.*

Diamonds are made of very pure carbon that was squeezed by enormous pressure deep underground. Scientists believe that diamonds form at least 93 miles (150 km) underground. The diamonds have been slowly pushed up from these great depths.

sity of Michigan is at nearby Ann Arbor.

Detroit was founded in 1701, when Antoine de la Mothe Cadillac, leader of a group of French settlers, built a fort there. It was called Fort Pontchartrain d'Étroit. But most people shortened this long name to d'Étroit, which means "on the strait." The fort became British in 1760 and American in 1796. The modern city was built after 1805, when the original settlement was completely burned down.

The Detroit Museum of History has many items from the city's early days. The Henry Ford Museum at Dearborn has hundreds of antique vehicles. This museum is next door to Greenfield Village, where Henry Ford had more than 90 historical buildings restored. Detroit is also a sporting center. It contains the Joe Louis Arena for hockey and boxing, and the Pontiac Silverdome for basketball, baseball and football.

DEWEY DECIMAL SYSTEM
see LIBRARY.

DIAGHILEV, SERGEI see BALLET.

DIAMOND
Diamond is the hardest natural substance found on Earth. Diamonds are used for jewelry because of their brilliance. They are cut and polished to bring out their full beauty. When pure, a diamond is clear, but it often contains impurities that color it. Diamonds that are imperfect or too small to be used for jewelry are used in factories to cut and polish very hard metals and ceramics. Such diamonds are called *industrial* diamonds. Some diamonds used in industry are made artificially from graphite, a form of carbon.

Diamonds were first discovered in India and Borneo. Large deposits were found near Bahia (Salvador), Brazil, about 1670. The greatest

discovery of all was in Kimberley, South Africa, where "pipes" of blue earth containing many thousands of diamonds were found in 1870. This area is still the greatest diamond producer on Earth. The famous Jonker diamond comes from South Africa. Other famous diamonds are the Hope, Jubilee, Star of the South, Cullinan, and Koh-i-noor.

Diamonds are made of carbon. Coke is also made of carbon. But coke is black and softer than diamonds. The reason for the difference is that the carbon in diamonds is packed together much more tightly than it is in coke. Diamonds are formed below the Earth's crust at great pressure and heat. They are brought to the surface among other minerals in volcanic pipes.

ALSO READ: CARBON, GEM, MINERAL.

DIARY
Keeping a record of what happens each day can be interesting to do. People of all ages like to write down the things that they do. These records are called *diaries* or *journals*. Some children keep a diary of the things that happen to them or their families and friends. Others like to write about their own feelings and the way they think about certain problems and ideas.

When people keep diaries for several years, it is interesting to read them again and see how the people may have changed as they grew older. It is also fun for children to read diaries which were kept by their parents when they were young, to learn how they spent their time and how they thought about things back then.

Some well-known people of history kept diaries, such as Samuel Pepys, Jonathan Swift, Queen Victoria, and Sir Walter Scott. When we read these diaries today, we learn a lot about the writer and also about the way people lived when the writer was alive. *The Diary of a Young Girl* is a widely read book written by a 13-year-old girl named Anne Frank. Anne and her family lived in the Netherlands during World War II, and her diary tells about how they had to hide out from the Nazis.

■ LEARN BY DOING

Find an old notebook and write in it often about things that you see or think. Or go to the library and find a diary to read. What can you learn about a person's life or thoughts from such a book? ■

ALSO READ: AUTOBIOGRAPHY, BIOGRAPHY.

DIAS, BARTOLOMEU (about 1450–1500) In the 15th century, spices and other Asian treasures were carried overland from India to the Mediterranean Sea, then by ship to Europe. The cities of Italy controlled the trade through the Mediterranean. The king of Portugal wanted to find a direct water route to India. He wanted Portugal to have a share of the rich spice trade.

In 1487 the king commissioned Bartolomeu Dias (or Diaz) to look for a route around the southern end of Africa. Dias set sail with two ships. On New Year's Day of 1488, as he neared the Cape of Good Hope, at the southern tip of Africa, a storm blew his ships far to the south. After 13 days, he was able to turn east, but found no land in that direction. He then sailed north and reached the east coast of Africa well past the Cape of Good Hope. He realized he had circled the tip of Africa. Dias wanted to sail to India, but his men made him return to Portugal.

In 1500 Dias was one of the captains in the Portuguese fleet that discovered what we now call Brazil. He went down with his ship in a storm.

ALSO READ: EXPLORATION; GAMA, VASCO DA; HENRY THE NAVIGATOR.

DIATOM   see ALGAE, PLANKTON.

DICKENS, CHARLES (1812–1870) Who can imagine Christmas without Charles Dickens' famous story "A Christmas Carol" being shown on television? In the days before television, some member of the family would often read this story aloud. It is the tale of the miser Ebenezer Scrooge, who is visited by the Ghosts of Christmas Past, Present, and Future. The ghosts persuade Scrooge to change his cruel ways. He becomes a good, kind person, to the joy of the little lame boy, Tiny Tim, whose words at the end of the story are: "God bless us, every one!"

Dickens was one of the most famous storytellers of all time. He spent his childhood in Chatham and London, England. His family was very poor. Many of the most moving stories in his novels are drawn from his own experiences. He began his writing career as a newspaper reporter. His first novel, *Pickwick Papers* (1837), won him immediate popularity. *Oliver Twist* (1838), *Nicholas Nickleby* (1839), and *The Old Curiosity Shop* (1841) followed. Many of his novels were first published in monthly installments. Readers would wait in great excitement for the next part of the story.

His characters—with names such as the Artful Dodger, Uriah Heep, Mr. Micawber, and Jeremy Belcher—are often comic and always very human. He described in vivid detail the cold, hunger, beatings, illness, cruel treatment, and other injustices and discomforts that poor people of his time suffered. His books created an interest in social reform.

Dickens married and had ten children. He enjoyed traveling and went to the United States twice. Part of his novel *Martin Chuzzlewit* (1843) takes place in the United States. Dickens was a friendly man who loved people,

▲ *Bartolomeu Dias, Portuguese explorer.*

▲ *Charles Dickens, the great British novelist of the 19th century, whose books awakened Victorian social conscience to the plight of the poor.*

▲ *Emily Dickinson, U.S. poet, who retreated from the world at age 26 and spent almost the whole of the rest of her life alone.*

the theater, and writing to his friends. He is buried in Westminster Abbey in London. Some of his many other books are *David Copperfield* (1850), *A Tale of Two Cities* (1859), and *Great Expectations* (1861).

ALSO READ: LITERATURE, NOVEL.

DICKINSON, EMILY (1830–1886)

As a girl, Emily Dickinson was very lively, witty, and outgoing. She lived with her family in Amherst, Massachusetts. Her father was a lawyer and was elected to Congress. Emily received a good education. When she was 26, she began to spend most of her time alone. She lived with her family but stayed in her room, coming out only once in awhile. She wore white all the time. She lived this way for the rest of her life. No one is sure why she retreated from the world. Some scholars think that she had fallen in love with a man who was already married.

Emily Dickinson wrote more than 1,700 poems in her solitude. She used scraps of paper and the backs of envelopes for writing. Only seven of her poems were published in her lifetime. Her family did not know about most of her poems until she died. They are short, beautiful poems about nature, love, and death. Today many people believe that this solitary New England woman is one of the greatest U.S. poets. Many books have been written about her.

ALSO READ: POETRY.

DICTATOR

Sometimes a parent or a teacher will say that you must do a certain thing or else be punished. This is called *dictating*, or giving orders that must be obeyed.

A ruler of a country who behaves this way is called a dictator. Dictators have complete power over the people. They can make or unmake laws without consulting the people. They decide the policy of the government themselves. They have the power to put to death or imprison anyone who disobeys or criticizes them.

A country may benefit from the strong control of a single ruler at times of war or national emergency. But a dictator must limit the freedom of the people in order to retain complete power. Dictators were sometimes appointed in times of emergency in ancient Rome (Julius Caesar was one). But they were usually allowed to stay in power for only a limited time.

Dictators have ruled in several countries in recent times. Some came to power by gaining the support of a group, such as the army, and seizing control of a country by force. This is how Francisco Franco became dictator of Spain. But often dictators came to power legally and then took over complete control. Joseph Stalin of the Soviet Union, Adolf Hitler of Germany, François Duvalier ("Papa Doc") of Haiti, and Juan Perón of Argentina all became dictators by these methods. Most of these dictators promised their people a better life. But then they repressed all individual freedom. Newspapers were shut down, and radio and television controlled. They used secret police to enforce their laws. Often revolution is needed to remove a dictator from office. But revolution is almost impossible since the dictator controls the army and the police. However, in 1986 two dictators were successfully deposed, Ferdinand Marcos of the Philippines, and Jean-Claude Duvalier ("Baby Doc") of Haiti.

ALSO READ: CAESAR, JULIUS; FRANCO, FRANCISCO; HITLER, ADOLF; STALIN, JOSEPH.

DICTIONARY

The first time you print or write your name is a big day for you. You learn the importance of

▼ *Adolf Hitler* (right), *dictator of Germany, and Benito Mussolini, dictator of Italy, brought suffering and destruction to their own and other countries during World War II.*

spelling. As you learn to write more, you will probably use a reference book that has lots of words spelled correctly. This book is called a dictionary.

A dictionary is arranged alphabetically. The most common type of dictionary is a collection of most of the words used in one language. It shows the correct pronunciation of the words, generally by using small symbols above or below the words. It gives the *definition* or meaning of the words and may include a sentence or phrase to show how the word is used.

A dictionary tells the part of speech of each word listed, such as noun or adjective. This is usually shown by an abbreviation, as *n.* for noun or *adj.* for adjective. If a word has more than one definition, the separate definitions are listed.

Many different sizes and types of dictionaries are printed. The larger dictionaries tell the *etymology*, or origin and history, of words. Some words have come from other languages or have changed in spelling or meaning over the years. New words come into the language every day from science, technology, and many other sources. Dictionaries keep up-to-date with new words and also usually drop words if people stop using them.

A small dictionary is sometimes included in a storybook or a nonfiction book. This is usually done if difficult words or words of another language have been used in the book. The small dictionary is called a *glossary.*

Scholars in ancient Greece and Rome sometimes made lists of difficult or unusual words and gave their meanings. During the Middle Ages in Europe, most books were written in Latin. Students at this time used dictionaries that gave the meanings in Latin of difficult Latin words. By the 1600's, people had begun to write books in their own languages. The earliest English dictionaries gave the

ri·dent (rīd′ənt), *adj.* laughing; smiling; cheerful. [< L *rīdent-* (s. of *rīdēns*, prp. of *rīdēre*) = *rīd-* laugh + *-ent-* -ENT]

rid·er (rī′dər), *n.* **1.** a person who rides a horse or other animal, a bicycle, or the like. **2.** that which rides. **3.** any object or device that straddles, is mounted upon, or is attached to something else. **4.** a rail or stake used to brace the corners in a snake fence. **5.** an additional clause attached to a legislative bill in passing it. **6.** an addition or amendment to a document. [ME, OE *ridere*] —**rid′er·less,** *adj.*

rid·er·ship (rī′dər ship′), *n.* **1.** the people who ride a particular train, bus, subway, etc. **2.** the estimated number of such people.

ridge (rij), *n., v.,* **ridged, ridg·ing.** —*n.* **1.** a long, narrow elevation of land; a chain of hills or mountains. **2.** the long and narrow upper edge, angle, or crest of something, as a hill, wave, vault, etc. **3.** the back of an animal. **4.** any raised, narrow strip, as on cloth. **5.** the horizontal line in which the tops of the rafters of a roof meet. **6.** (on a weather chart) a narrow, elongated area of high pressure. —*v.t.* **7.** to provide with or form into a ridge or ridges. **8.** to mark with or as with ridges. —*v.i.* **9.** to form ridges. [ME *rigge,* OE *hrycg* spine, crest, ridge; c. OIcel *hryggr,* D *rug,* G *Rücken,* L *crux*] —**ridge′like′,** *adj.*

ridge·ling (rij′ling), *n. Vet. Med.* a colt with undescended testicles. Also, **ridg′ling.** Also called **ridg·el, ridg·il** (rij′əl). [? RIDGE + -LING², from the belief that the undescended organs were in the animal's back]

ridge·pole (rij′pōl′), *n.* the horizontal timber or member at the top of a roof, to which the upper ends of the rafters are fastened. Also, **ridge′ pole′.** Also called **ridge·piece** (rij′pēs′), **ridge′ board′.** —**ridge′poled′,** *adj.*

Ridge·wood (rij′wŏŏd′), *n.* a city in NE New Jersey. 27,547 (1970).

Ridg·way (rij′wā), *n.* **Matthew (Bun·ker)** (bung′kər), born 1895, U.S. general: chief of staff 1953–55.

ridg·y (rij′ē), *adj.,* **ridg·i·er, ridg·i·est.** rising in a ridge or ridges.

rid·i·cule (rid′ə kyool′), *n., v.,* **-culed, -cul·ing.** —*n.* **1.** speech or action intended to cause contemptuous laughter at a person or thing; derision. —*v.t.* **2.** to make fun of. [< L

definitions of only difficult English words. One of the first scholars to try to list most of the words in the English language was Samuel Johnson, in 1747–1755.

The first large U.S. dictionary was published by Noah Webster in 1828. It included the U.S. spelling and pronunciation of English words. It also included words of American Indian origin, such as "wampum" and "tomahawk," which Americans were using. Webster's name is still used for many U.S. dictionaries. The most complete U.S. dictionary is *Webster's International Dictionary.* Another one is the *Dictionary of Americanisms,* edited by Mitford M. Matthews.

Dictionaries that translate words of one language into another language are often used in schools, for example a "French-English dictionary." The *Oxford English Dictionary* is a very large and scholarly book that gives the complete etymology of each word. It has more than 400,000 entries. Dictionaries are also written for particular

▲ *An excerpt from a Funk & Wagnalls dictionary. Notice that some words have more than one meaning. The dictionary also gives synonyms for some words (abbreviation "syn"). A synonym is a word meaning the same, or almost the same, as another word.*

▲ *A technician inspects coins from a die-stamping machine.*

▼ *Molds are used in the making (casting) of many things, even some statues. First a clay version of the statue is made. A mold of this is made by covering the clay figure with plaster. Carefully the plaster is removed. The middle of the mold is almost filled with a core of material. Molten metal is poured between the core and the mold. When the metal cools and hardens it forms a hollow metal version of the original clay statue.*

subjects, such as history, science, or music. The work of updating them goes on all the time.

ALSO READ: JOHNSON, SAMUEL; REFERENCE BOOK; WEBSTER, NOAH.

DIES AND MOLDS Tom's mother made delicious cookies called gingerbread men. She mixed the dough and spread it out on a board with a rolling pin. Then she took a little metal cutter made in the shape of a man and pressed it down on the dough. Each time she pressed it down, the figure of a gingerbread man was cut out of the dough, ready to be baked into a cookie.

The cookie cutter Tom's mother used is one kind of die. A *die* is a metal pattern that stamps or cuts out something. Our coins are made by dies. Steel dies with coin designs in reverse are put into a coining press. These dies are patterns for the coins. One die is for the face of the coin, the other is for the back. The two dies come together under great pressure and strike a sheet of metal that is sandwiched between them. They press the metal into the shape of a coin.

Another kind of die is used to cut the threads on nuts and bolts. A block of metal with holes through it can also

serve as a die. Strips of copper, aluminum, or another metal are forced into the holes on one side and come out the other side as wire of the same width as the holes. This process is called *extrusion*.

Another way to shape materials is to use a mold. A mold is simply a form that gives a desired shape to fluids or plastic materials that are poured or pressed into it. Perhaps you have used a mold in the kitchen to shape a gelatin dessert.

Molds are also used in *foundries*. Foundries are shops that make metal *castings*. For example, some workers in a foundry might want to make an iron wheel. First they make a model, or *pattern*. That is, they make a wheel out of wood in just the shape they want. They put this pattern wheel in an iron box full of wet sand and press it down. Next they lift the wheel out of the sand. The shape of the wheel is left in the wet sand, like a footprint on the beach. The wet sand is the mold. The workers make two molds, one for each side of the wheel. After the sand hardens, they fasten the two molds together. The foundry workers pour molten iron into the space left by the pattern and let it cool. When the iron hardens, they remove the sand. There is an iron wheel just like the pattern.

Other types of molds are used to make pottery, dishes, candles, and plastic goods.

ALSO READ: IRON AND STEEL, PLASTIC.

DIESEL ENGINE A German engineer and inventor, Rudolf Diesel, built a new type of engine in the 1890's. His first version of the engine exploded and knocked him unconscious, but Diesel was not discouraged. He continued to work and completed his first working engine in 1897. It produced 25 horsepower (18,640 watts) with only one cylinder. During the following few years Diesel perfected his engine. Soon thousands

CASTING A METAL MODEL

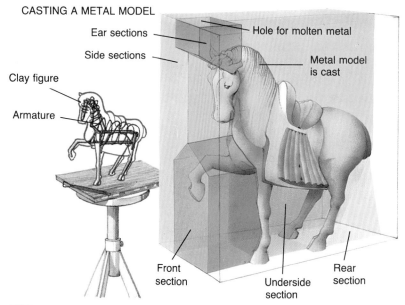

Ear sections
Side sections
Clay figure
Armature
Hole for molten metal
Metal model is cast
Front section
Underside section
Rear section

of diesel engines were being made in many different sizes.

Modern diesel engines are used to power trucks, buses, construction equipment, locomotives, large ships, and some automobiles. These engines can be enormous, weighing as much as 2 million pounds (907,000 kg) and delivering 25,000 horsepower (18,640 kW) or more—200 times the power produced by most automobile engines.

The diesel engine works much like a gasoline engine, except it has no carburetor or spark plug. Instead, the piston is used to squeeze the air into a very small volume. The air becomes very hot when tightly compressed. Fuel is simply sprayed into the cylinder, and the extremely hot air causes an explosion. The air must be tremendously compressed to become hot enough to ignite the fuel, so the cylinders of diesel engines must be very strong.

The diesel engine can use fuel more efficiently than the gasoline (*internal combustion*) engine, so a properly working diesel causes less air pollution than a gasoline engine. And diesel fuel oil is cheaper to produce than gasoline. Diesels are therefore more economical to use, although a diesel costs more to buy than a comparable gasoline engine.

Diesel engines are used to power electric generators in many ships and locomotives. The electricity is then used by the electric motors that actu-

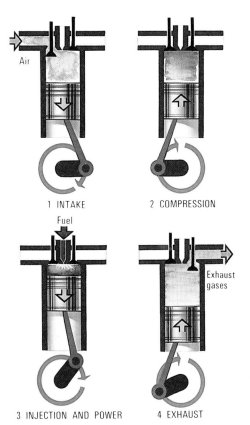

1 INTAKE   2 COMPRESSION

3 INJECTION AND POWER   4 EXHAUST

◄ *How a diesel engine works. (1) Air is drawn downward into the cylinder through a valve. (2) The air is put under pressure and becomes very hot. (3) Fuel is injected into the hot air and catches fire. This explosion forces the piston back and thus turns the wheel. (4) The piston pushes the exhaust gases out through another valve. Then the whole cycle begins again.*

ally turn the propellers or wheels. This is called the *diesel-electric system*.

ALSO READ: AUTOMOBILE, ENGINE, PETROLEUM.

DIET   see FOOD, NUTRITION.

DIGESTION   The food you eat gives you energy and helps to build and repair the cells of your body. But food must be digested before it can be used. The process of digestion takes the large molecules of proteins, carbohydrates, and fats in the food and breaks them down into smaller molecules and simpler chemical forms. These smaller molecules can then be carried by the blood throughout the body. Body cells absorb these molecules, which provide them with vitamins and minerals, through the walls of the blood vessels. (If you do not know the word "molecule," read the article on CHEMISTRY.)

Digestion takes place in the *alimen-*

The crocodile's digestion juices contain so much hydrochloric acid that they have been known to dissolve large metal objects such as spearheads.

▼ *This huge diesel engine, for use on ships, can produce far more power than any gasoline engine.*

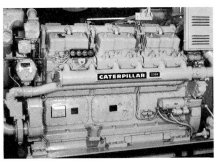

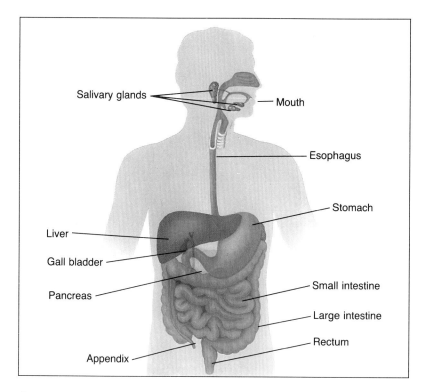

Salivary glands — Mouth
Esophagus
Stomach
Liver
Gall bladder
Pancreas
Small intestine
Large intestine
Rectum
Appendix

▲ *Digestion starts in the mouth, where saliva mixes with food as it is chewed. Food travels down the esophagus to the stomach and is churned and partly digested. Most digestion occurs in the small intestine. Here the food is mixed with bile and digestive juices from the pancreas. Proteins and fats are broken down by enzymes and absorbed into the body. The rest passes to the large intestine and the water is taken back into the body. The waste goes to the rectum.*

▼ *Food is pushed along in the esophagus by waves of tightenings of the muscle walls. This is called peristalsis.*

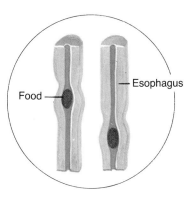

Food — Esophagus

tary canal, a long coiled tube extending from the mouth to the anus. The main parts of the tube are the mouth, esophagus, stomach, small intestine, and large intestine. The final part of the large intestine is called the rectum. Here undigested food is stored before being expelled through the anus.

Food passing through the alimentary canal is moistened, ground up, churned, broken down by acids and enzymes (chemicals that make other chemicals change), temporarily stored, and finally, absorbed (passed through the walls of the intestine into the blood). The parts of food that cannot be digested or used are eliminated (thrown out) from the body via the anus.

In the Mouth Many organs, glands, and muscles work together to complete digestion. Digestion begins in the mouth. When you take a bite of bread, for example, *saliva* pours into your mouth from three pairs of glands, located under your tongue, beneath your jaw, and in the sides of your mouth. In fact, just looking at, smelling, or imagining your favorite

food can "make your mouth water," or produce saliva.

Saliva contains water and a sticky substance called *mucin*, which makes food soft and moist so that it can be swallowed. It also contains the enzyme *ptyalin*, which begins the digestion of starch (a carbohydrate). Ptyalin changes the starch in your bite of bread into a simpler chemical form—a sugar called *maltose*. Other enzymes will break down the maltose into simpler forms of sugar as the food moves through the alimentary canal.

Chewing plays an important part in digestion for many mammals. A cow, for example, chews its food, swallows it, then brings it back into its mouth and chews it again. You may have seen cows in a field chewing their "cuds" steadily even when they are not cropping grass. Some other animals, such as cats and dogs, do not chew, but bite or tear at their food. They then swallow it down in unchewed lumps.

Humans both tear and chew their food. You use your front teeth for biting or tearing and your flat-topped back teeth for chewing. The chewing helps break down solid food into small pieces. A lump of food is ready for swallowing when it is thoroughly coated with saliva. Then the tongue forces the food to the back of the mouth and down the throat. A flap called the *epiglottis* closes off the windpipe so that no food can get caught there and cause choking or loss of breath. Muscles in the wall of the throat move the food into the next area, the *esophagus*. No digestion takes place in the esophagus. It is simply a tunnel that leads to the stomach. The wavelike movements (*peristalsis*) of small muscles in the walls of the esophagus are so strong that your food would be forced into your stomach even if you were standing on your head while eating!

The Stomach The *stomach* is a hollow, baglike organ, shaped rather like the letter J. The lining of the stomach has glands that pour out *gastric juice*. This juice contains enzymes that continue the breaking down of food. Gastric juice also contains *hydrochloric acid*. It combines with protein in the food, making it easier for the enzyme *pepsin* to break down protein. Powerful muscles in the wall of the stomach churn the food so that it is well mixed with the gastric juice.

Food, depending on its nature, stays in the stomach for varying periods, as long as one to four hours or even more. Liquids pass through very quickly. When the stomach digests meat, it produces more gastric juice than it does in digesting potatoes or sugars. Fats, however, slow down the production of gastric juice, so that a meal containing a large amount of fat stays longest in the stomach—and holds off hunger for longer periods, too.

Food is in a thick, liquid form by the time it is ready to leave the stomach. Small quantities at a time are moved from the stomach into the *small intestine*. The small intestine is the most important organ of the digestive system. Here the final steps are taken to prepare the food for absorption. More enzymes come into the small intestine from an organ called the *pancreas*. Bile from the liver is added after having been collected in the gall bladder. Bile is useful in breaking up fat into small drops, or globules, that enzymes can get at more easily. Squeezing movements of the small intestine break up and knead the food, mixing it thoroughly with the intestinal juices and enzymes. At the same time, continuous wavelike movements push the food along. The small intestine is about 21 feet (6 m) long in an adult human.

Millions of tiny, fingerlike projections called *villi* line the small intestine. The nutrients in the digested food pass through the surfaces of the villi and into the blood and lymph. (Lymph is an important body fluid

that helps "clean up" your body.)

The food finally reaches the end of the small intestine about 6½ hours after a meal. It now enters the *large intestine*. All the nutrients have been taken from the food by this time. What remains is waste matter of indigestible material.

A tubelike organ called the *appendix* is attached to the large intestine. It does no known job for us but can cause trouble. It can become infected by bacteria and may need to be removed by surgery. This is called an *appendectomy*.

In the large intestine, most of the water is removed from the waste matter. This reduces the waste to a firm mass, which collects at the end of the large intestine. The waste matter moves out of the large intestine from time to time. It enters the *rectum* and is pushed out of the *anus*. This elimination of waste material is known as *defecation*.

Carnivores (meat-eating animals) have much shorter digestive tracts (tubes) than herbivores (plant-eating animals), who have much roughage to digest. For example, a cow has a small intestine 100 feet (30.5 m) long. Animals like us that eat both plants and meat—*omnivores*—have digestive tracts longer than those of carnivores but shorter than those of herbivores.

ALSO READ: BIOCHEMISTRY, ENZYME, FOOD, HUMAN BODY, KIDNEY, LIVER, NUTRITION.

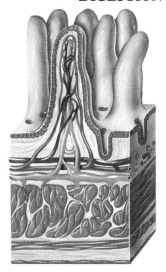

▲ *The lining of the intestine has fingerlike* villi *(singular "villus"; the word is Latin for "shaggy hair"). Through these villi, food goes into tiny blood vessels called* capillaries *(blue and red) and into the vessels of the lymph system (green).*

▼ *The digestive system of a cow. Its long intestine enables tough plant material to be broken down before it reaches the end of the intestine. A cow's stomach has four chambers. The first is called the* rumen. *The cow eats grass and swallows it whole into the rumen. After a while the cow coughs up the grass and chews it in the mouth. This chewing the cud* helps digestion.

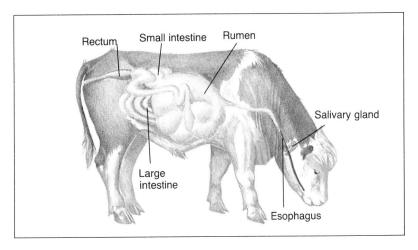

Some scientists now believe that a few of the dinosaurs were warm-blooded (that is, they could control their body temperature). They think that these dinosaurs were the ancestors of the birds. However, this has not yet been definitely proved.

▼ The School of Athens, *by Raphael, an Italian painter. This work is an example of how painters often try to make their paintings appear three-dimensional by using perspective and shading.*

DIMENSION If a man wants to build a garage for his car, he must be sure that it will be large enough to hold his car. It has to be longer, wider, and higher than the car is. *Length*, *width*, and *height* are called dimensions.

In measuring objects, however, some dimensions may be more important than others. For example, if a farmer wishes to measure a field, only the dimensions of length and width are important. It makes no sense to measure the height of the field. From this, you can see that "two-dimensional" means that only the length and width of the object are to be measured. Two-dimensional objects are flat, like a picture or a page of this book. Three-dimensional objects are solid, and their height or thickness is as important as length or width.

A property of a two-dimensional figure is its *area*, the space within its boundaries. *Square feet* and *acres* are both common units of area. A two-dimensional object that is 5 feet wide and 5 feet long has an area of 25 square feet ($5 \times 5 = 25$). A property of a three-dimensional object is its *volume*, the space within its boundaries. The boundaries of a solid object are called *surfaces*. *Cubic inches* and *gallons* are units used to measure volume. Not all measuring units may be familiar to you. The *metric system* uses different units. For example, lengths may be expressed in meters (a meter is about 3¼ feet), and areas in square meters or in hectares (a hectare is about 2½ acres). Volumes may be given in liters (a liter is just over two pints).

Mathematicians label figures according to how many dimensions they have. A *solid* figure, such as a cube, has three dimensions. A flat figure, with only two dimensions, is called a *plane* figure, or a *surface*. A straight *line* is a figure with only one dimension, that of length. A *point* is a figure with no dimensions.

ALSO READ: GEOMETRY, MEASUREMENT, METRIC SYSTEM, PHYSICS, RELATIVITY, TIME.

DINOSAUR Nearly everyone has heard of dinosaurs. But no one has ever seen one of these reptiles. Scientists believe that they all died out about 65 million years ago. Before then, giant dinosaurs and other reptiles were the lords of the land. The time in which they lived—thought to have lasted perhaps 150 million years—is known as the "Age of Reptiles." Scientists call this age the *Mesozoic era.*

We know that dinosaurs existed because fossil remains of their bodies have been found. Dinosaur bones and teeth that were turned to stone (became fossils) have been discovered embedded in rocks in all parts of the world. If you visit a natural history museum, you can see how scientists have put these bones and teeth together to make skeletons. These skeletons help us imagine what dinosaurs looked like. By studying the bones and teeth, scientists have learned about how the dinosaurs lived. For example, sharp teeth show that a dinosaur was a meat-eater (*carnivore*). Dull, flattened teeth show that a certain dinosaur was a plant-eater (*herbivore*).

The word "dinosaur" means "terrible lizard." Many dinosaurs were quite fierce-looking. Although they were not really lizards, some of them did look like lizards. Others looked like alligators; still others, like birds.

Several thousand different kinds of dinosaurs roamed the earth, although they did not all live at the same time, or even in the same parts of the world. Some walked on all fours, while others walked on their hind legs. Some were plant-eaters, while others were meat-eaters who preyed on the plant-eaters. Some roamed the land, while others spent most of their time in water. Our planet was hot and steamy then, and much of the land was marshy.

The earliest dinosaurs were small. One kind looked something like a turkey without feathers. It could run swiftly along the ground on its two large hindlegs. It had two smaller forelegs, which it used to grab things. The early dinosaurs gradually developed into many other kinds. Some changed into giants.

Brachiosaurus, one of the biggest dinosaurs we know about, was 40 feet (12 m) high and up to 90 feet (27 m) long from nose to tail. It had a tiny head at the end of a very long neck. This dinosaur weighed well over 50 tons (51 metric tons)—more than eight elephants! Brachiosaurs were so heavy that they could not move about easily on land. Only water could support their weight, so they lived mainly in swamps and fed on tender plants found there. Brachiosaurs had to keep eating continually in order to nourish their huge body.

Brontosaurus, also called *Apatosaurus*, was a giant plant-eater. It looked something like *Brachiosaurus* but was smaller, growing to a length of 67 feet (20 m) and weighing about 35 tons (35.5 metric tons). Like many other dinosaurs, *Brontosaurus* must have been very stupid. In spite of its huge body, it had a tiny brain that weighed only a pound (about 0.45 kg).

One of the scariest-looking plant-

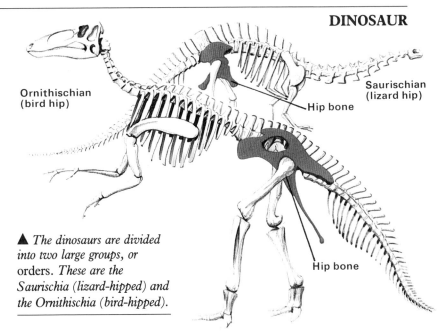

▲ *The dinosaurs are divided into two large groups, or* orders. *These are the Saurischia (lizard-hipped) and the Ornithischia (bird-hipped).*

Ornithischian (bird hip)

Saurischian (lizard hip)

Hip bone

Hip bone

eating dinosaurs was *Stegosaurus*. Rows of bony plates, like armor, ran down its back. It is thought these were used to help control the animal's body temperature. Its heavy tail bore four pointed spikes. Another armored plant-eater was *Triceratops*. It had a bony frill around its neck and three sharp horns for armor. The longest dinosaur was *Diplodocus* at some 88 feet (27 m) long.

Probably the most fearsome dinosaur of all was a meat-eater called *Tyrannosaurus rex*. It was about 20 feet (6 m) high and 47 feet (14 m) long. It had long, powerful hindlegs that allowed it to run after and catch other dinosaurs for food. Its head was enormous, and its mouth was full of daggerlike teeth that were 6 inches (15 cm) long. Probably even the armored dinosaurs fell prey to this fierce creature.

Why did these beasts become extinct? No one knows for sure, but many scientists now think that about 65 million years ago, a comet hit Earth. The impact was so huge that vast quantities of debris were thrown up into the atmosphere. There they stayed for many years, blocking out the heat from the sun and so chilling our planet. The dinosaurs just could not stand the cold!

ALSO READ: EVOLUTION, FOSSIL, REPTILE.

▼ *Two sworn enemies, Edward Drinker Cope (top) and Othniel Marsh, (bottom), made huge collections of dinosaur bones in North America in the late 1800's. Their bitter rivalry to identify new types of dinosaurs has been called the "Bone Wars"!*

HADROSAURUS
HAD-roe-SAW-rus

—— 33 feet (10 m) ——

TYRANNOSAURUS
tie-RAN-oh-SAW-rus

—— 50 feet (15 m) ——

TRICERATOPS
try-SER-a-tops

—— 30 feet (9 m) ——

SILVISAURUS
SIL-vih-SAW-rus

⌐— 13 feet (4 m) —⌐

STEGOSAURUS
STEG-oh-SAW-rus

⌐— 30 feet (9 m) —⌐

IGUANODON
ig-WA-no-DON

⌐— 30 feet (9 m) —

LAMBEOSAURUS
LAM-bee-oh-SAW-rus

⌐— 50 feet (15 m) —⌐

BRONTOSAURUS
BRON-toh-SAW-rus

⌐— 70 feet (21 m) —⌐

▲ *Organizations such as the British CND (campaign for Nuclear Disarmament–shown here demonstrating outside the U.S. Air Base at Greenham Common in England–attempt to influence government decisions about disarmament.*

DIRIGIBLE   see AIRSHIP.

DISARMAMENT   Armaments are weapons of war. When nations agree to disarm, they agree to reduce the numbers of their armaments, or even get rid of certain weapons altogether. This is called "disarmament." Another term for limited disarmament is "arms control."

During the 1800's new and more powerful weapons were invented. The strongest nations, or "Great Powers" as they were known, met to try to set limits to the use of such deadly weapons as poison gas. But these meetings, at The Hague (Netherlands) in 1906 and 1907, did not succeed, and poison gas was used during World War I. After this war, Germany was forbidden such weapons as tanks and submarines. The Great Powers met in Washington to discuss naval disarmament. The League of Nations held a disarmament conference in 1932. But these talks accomplished little.

After World War II, the United Nations urged the Great Powers to disarm. But the "cold war" between East and West led instead to an arms race, with both sides spending huge amounts of money on armaments. The invention of nuclear weapons posed a new, and much greater, threat to world peace.

Since the 1950's there have been various attempts at disarmament agreements. The nations have agreed to ban nuclear tests in the atmosphere, and in Antarctica. The United States is a signatory to these treaties and to the *nuclear nonproliferation treaty* signed in 1968. During the 1970's and 1980's the strategic arms limitation talks between the United States and the Soviet Union made slow progress. In 1986 there was an agreement on military maneuvers in Europe. This importantly included provision for inspection, to ensure that both sides obeyed the agreement. Talks continued on such questions as the banning of chemical weapons and the introduction of space weapons, following the United States' unveiling of its strategic defense initiative (SDI or "Star Wars") proposals. In December 1987, U.S. President Ronald Reagan and Soviet leader Mikhail Gorbachev signed a treaty eliminating all medium-and shorter-range nuclear missiles. This led to a treaty ending the cold war between West and East in 1990.

DISCRIMINATION   If pupils in your school start a club for stamp collectors, anyone who is not a stamp collector is excluded. We say that the club's members are *discriminating* against non-stamp collectors. That is a harmless form of discrimination, but many kinds are bad. One of the oldest forms of discrimination is in religion. For example, until 1829 Roman Catholics in Britain could not vote or become members of Parliament.

Two forms of discrimination are being fought today. One is *racism*, discriminating against people on account of their race. In the United States, blacks were discriminated against for many years. The other form is by sex. In some countries, women are barred from many jobs just because they are women.

ALSO READ: BLACK AMERICANS; CIVIL RIGHTS.

DISEASE   A disease is a condition that prevents a living thing from functioning in a normal, healthy way.

If you think of the diseases you know about, you will realize that each one is different from the others. When you are sick, something has gone wrong in your body. The doctor examines you and finds *symptoms* (signs) of disease. The combination of symptoms you have tells the doctor what disease you have. For example, if you have a very itchy rash on your stomach that also spreads over your body and a mild fever, the doctor will probably say that you have chicken pox. The most common symptoms of disease include fever, chills, pain in some part of the body (such as sore throat, headache, or muscle aches), swelling, rash, coughing, weakness, and loss of weight.

A very important part of medicine is *diagnosing* (finding out) what disease a person has. This special kind of detective work is not easy to do.

Kinds of Disease Doctors classify diseases (place them into groups) in several ways. For example, sometimes diseases are classified according to what part of the body they affect. Thus there are bone diseases, eye diseases, skin diseases, and many other kinds. But the most important and useful way to group diseases is by their causes. This helps doctors know how to treat a specific disease.

INFECTIONS. An infection is caused by living things (organisms) that grow inside the body. Most infections are caused by "germs," several different kinds of living things so tiny they can be seen only with a microscope. There are several different kinds of germs, including bacteria, viruses, and fungi.

Bacteria cause many diseases, including pneumonia, strep throat, tuberculosis, scarlet fever, and whooping cough. Bacterial diseases were once among the most feared of all diseases, but today most diseases caused by bacteria are easy to treat with modern antibiotics. Some bacterial diseases are also prevented by vaccines. A *vaccine* consists of dead or weakened bacteria of a disease. It causes the body to develop antibodies to that disease.

Viruses cause the common cold and many other diseases, including yellow fever, measles, mumps, a type of influenza, and poliomyelitis. Many virus diseases can be prevented by vaccines. But virus diseases are hard to treat because antibiotics do not stop most viruses.

Fungi cause several diseases. Most, such as athletes' foot, are skin diseases. Fungus diseases are usually not affected by antibiotics, so they are difficult diseases to treat.

Many of these infectious diseases are also *contagious*—they spread through the air from one person to another. Some infectious diseases are not contagious. The organisms that cause these diseases must be passed from person to person by animal carriers. The germs that cause typhus and bubonic plague, two of our most horrible diseases, are spread by certain lice and fleas. Malaria is another disease. Malaria germs can be carried only by certain mosquitoes. When there are none of these mosquitoes, the disease cannot spread.

Some infectious diseases, including malaria, are caused by certain *protozoans* (protists), single-celled animals. These diseases occur mostly in the tropics, where these tiny animals are not killed by cold weather.

Still other infectious diseases are caused by organisms much larger than germs, certain kinds of worms. These worms are *parasites*, animals that live on or in *hosts*, plants or other animals. Parasites harm the host on which they live. Worms cause many serious human infections. The tapeworm, for example, attaches itself to the intestine of its human host, where it can grow to be 15 feet (4.6 m) long. A tapeworm drains food that its host needs, and it can cause stomach pains and weakness.

NEOPLASMS. A neoplasm is a *tumor*, a sudden growth of body tissue that is not normal. "Neoplasm" comes from Greek words meaning "new form" or "new shape."

There are two main kinds of tumors, benign and malignant. *Malignant* tumors, or cancers, are extremely serious. Malignant tumors

▲ *Edward Jenner, a great British physician, developed a way of treating disease. He called this vaccination. He had heard an old rural saying that people who had a much milder disease, cowpox, never caught smallpox. He took fluid from a blister of a person with cowpox and injected it into a young boy. Two months later he injected the boy with smallpox. The boy did not get smallpox.*

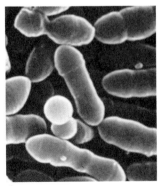

▲ *Bacteria come in all sorts of shapes. This microscope slide shows rod-shaped bacteria, like the ones that cause tuberculosis (TB).*

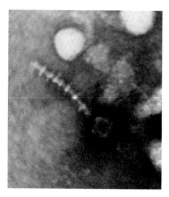

▲ *Viruses are specific—that is, they usually affect only one type of host (e.g., human beings). Often they affect only particular types of bodily tissues.*

▲ *The mold from which penicillin is made. Penicillin is an* antibiotic. *Antibiotics are able to kill bacteria without affecting the body's cells.*

are found in plants and in humans, as well as other animals. A cancer can kill healthy tissue around it, and it can spread throughout the body of the host. Different kinds of cancers grow and spread at different rates. But any cancer will grow and spread until it kills its host, unless it is treated. Treatment may involve use of radiation and chemicals or cutting out the diseased tissue in surgery. *Benign* tumors do not spread, and they do not kill healthy tissue. They are usually treated if doctors aren't sure what kind of tumors they may be or if they cause pain. One way doctors can determine if a tumor is malignant or not is to perform a *biopsy* (the removal and examination of tissues, cells, or fluid from the body). X-rays also help doctors identify the kinds of tumors people may have.

ALLERGIES. An allergy is a strong reaction or resistance to something that touches your body or gets inside it. Some "allergies" are good. Your body often "fights" germs that get into it, and thus can keep you from getting a disease. But when your body fights something that will not harm you, you may be annoyed. Allergic reactions can be very serious. A person who is allergic to bee stings can become very sick, and even die.

HEREDITARY DISEASES. These diseases are present at birth and inherited from one or both parents. For example, some boys and men suffer from the disease called hemophilia. The blood of persons with this disease does not clot, so bleeding goes on and on. If you cut yourself, a small scab forms quickly, and the bleeding stops. But when hemophiliacs cut themselves, the cut continues to bleed—even a tiny cut is very dangerous. Some sons inherit this disease from their mothers, even though their mothers do not show signs of the disease. Other diseases, such as allergies and diabetes, may also be hereditary. Doctors now think that some cancers also belong to this group of *genetic* diseases.

CONGENITAL DISEASES. Congenital diseases attack unborn babies. They are not inherited but happen when the embryo (developing baby in the womb) is disturbed. For example, if a pregnant woman has German measles (*rubella*)—especially during the first three months of her pregnancy—her unborn baby may also suffer from the effects of the illness. The baby may be born with a defect such as deafness or blindness. Some heart defects, as well as other physical problems, are also congenital.

NUTRITIONAL DISEASES. People who do not eat correctly may develop special diseases. People who always overeat may gain so much weight that they strain the heart, blood vessels, or kidneys. Overweight people get diseases such as diabetes and high blood-pressure more often than people of normal weight. People who do not eat the right food develop *deficiency* diseases (diseases due to a lack). A person who does not get enough calcium may have bones so weak that they bend into peculiar shapes. If vitamin C is not part of the diet, scurvy may develop, so that cuts heal slowly, skin bruises easily, capillaries (tiny blood vessels) break, and gums bleed.

ENVIRONMENTAL DISEASES. Our environment sometimes contains disease-causing elements. For example, coal miners work in an environment in which the air often contains tiny particles of coal dust. The miners breathe in these particles, which get stuck in the lungs, so many coal miners suffer from the serious disease called "black lung." We sometimes pollute our environment, causing disease. Thousands of people have become seriously ill from breathing smog, a poisonous mixture of smoke and fog. Being around cigarette smokers is thought to be dangerous to a person's health, too.

OTHER TYPES. Some other serious kinds of diseases attack human beings. *Hormonal* diseases occur when the functions of the endocrine glands are disturbed. These glands control body shape, growth, how the body uses food, and how the body adjusts to the world. Dwarfism and giantism are two diseases that occur when people's glands do not work properly. Several other serious diseases are also hormonal diseases.

Circulatory diseases happen if blood cannot flow normally. A clot (block) in a blood vessel may cause pain. If the clot forms in the heart, a heart attack may result.

Metabolic diseases occur when the normal chemical activities of the body are disturbed. Such diseases include diabetes, in which the victim cannot use sugar properly.

Degeneration includes diseases of old age, when parts of the body begin to wear out and break down (degenerate). Such ailments may cause blindness or deafness or attack bones, muscles, or joints.

Mental illness includes many problems that affect the way in which a person lives. Some problems are minor. But some mental illnesses may make a person completely unable to live a normal life and may even cause physical illness.

Prevention and Treatment Many diseases can be prevented. The means of prevention depends on how the disease is spread. Diseases carried by animals can be stopped if the animals that spread the diseases are controlled. Nutritional diseases are prevented when people eat properly. And many very serious diseases are prevented when sanitary conditions are improved.

Just as many kinds of diseases exist, there are many cures. Antibiotics cure most bacterial diseases. Other kinds of diseases have other cures.

Germs are everywhere in the world. They are constantly in contact with the human body. Did you ever wonder why people are not sick all the time? The answer to this question is that the best and most wonderful

▲ *A child being vaccinated against German measles. The vaccination will protect the child from getting this disease. Notice that an injection gun is being used instead of a needle.*

prevention and cure of disease is the human body! The skin keeps out most germs. Eyebrows, eyelashes, and eyelids protect the eyes, and tears wash out anything that slips past these "fences." Tiny hairlike structures that line the breathing passage trap most germs that are breathed in. Saliva and acid in the stomach kill most germs eaten in food. Sneezing and coughing push irritating substances out of the body.

When illness occurs, the body usually cures itself. White blood cells and body proteins called *antibodies* may quickly bring the disease under control and then force it out of the body. This happens when you have a cold. There is no known cure for the common cold. You do not take medicine to cure the cold, although it may help you feel more comfortable. Your body stops the cold. Your body is usually the best "medicine" for disease. Your doctor gives you medicine only when the body's defenses are not enough.

Doctors now realize that there is a close link between "mind" and "body." They know that if someone is worried or unhappy, this could bring about physical or mental ill health.

For further information on:
Causes of Disease, *see* BACTERIA, FLY, FUNGUS, GENETICS, GLAND, HEART, INSECT PEST, PARASITE, PROTIST, VIRUS, VITAMINS AND MINERALS, WORM.
Cures and Preventions, *see* ANTIGEN AND ANTIBODY, IMMUNITY, MEDICINE, MENTAL HEALTH, PUBLIC HEALTH, SANITATION, SURGERY.

▲ *Walt Disney, creator of some of the best animated cartoons of all time.*

▼ *Mickey Mouse, probably the most famous cartoon character of all. Here Mickey is shown in what is usually believed his best-ever role—as the Sorcerer's Apprentice in* Fantasia *(1940).*

Diseases, *see* ALLERGY, CANCER, CHILDHOOD DISEASES, COMMON COLD, CONTAGIOUS DISEASES, FEVER, PLANT DISEASE, RABIES.

Drugs, *see* ANESTHETIC, ANTIBIOTIC, ANTISEPTIC, DRUGS.

DISNEY, WALT (1901–1966) As a young artist, Walt Disney would often work late at night in his studio. The story goes that he heard some mice in his wastebasket one night. He captured them and kept them in little cages on his desk. One of them was his particular friend. This mouse was to give Disney the idea for his famous cartoon character, Mickey Mouse. Disney and his friend Ub Iwerks invented new ways of making cartoon movies; Disney received more than 100 awards for his work.

Walter Elias Disney was born in Chicago, but he spent most of his boyhood in Missouri. His family later returned to Chicago. Disney studied at the Chicago Academy of Fine Arts. He began his career as an artist in Kansas City, Missouri, and made his first cartoon movie there. He and his brother Roy moved to Hollywood in 1923 and started the Disney Studio. Many of Disney's cartoons deal with *fantasy* (the world of make-believe). Mickey Mouse first appeared in 1928 in a cartoon called *Steamboat Willie*. Disney's first full-length cartoon, *Snow White and the Seven Dwarfs*, was released in 1937. *Fantasia* and *Pinocchio* followed. Some of Disney's

other full-length cartoons were *Cinderella, Peter Pan, Bambi, Lady and the Tramp*, and *Sleeping Beauty*. Disney also made non-cartoon films, including many comedies and nature films. *The Living Desert* and *The Vanishing Prairie* were two of his "True Life Adventures."

In 1955, Walt Disney opened a fabulous amusement park, called Disneyland, in Anaheim, California. The jungle-river ride and Cinderella's castle are two of its many attractions. A similar park, called Walt Disney World, opened near Orlando, Florida, in 1971. It, too, has many rides and shows based on Disney's movies and characters. This park is a vacation resort, with several hotels and a man-made beach.

DISTANCE see MEASUREMENT.

DISTILLATION When a liquid boils, it becomes a gas, or *vapor*. If vapor is cooled, it condenses, or becomes a liquid again. If boiling and condensing take place in an apparatus that contains the boiling liquid and also cools the vapor, the process is called *distillation*. The apparatus in which a liquid is distilled is commonly called a *still*.

■ LEARN BY DOING

Heat a teakettle of water to boiling. You will see a clear space above the kettle spout and below the cloud of

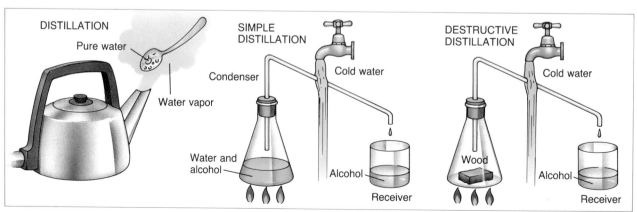

DISTILLATION
Pure water
Water vapor

SIMPLE DISTILLATION
Condenser
Cold water
Water and alcohol
Alcohol
Receiver

DESTRUCTIVE DISTILLATION
Cold water
Wood
Alcohol
Receiver

"steam" that is pouring out. The clear space is actually the steam, or water vapor, which is water in the form of a gas. The cloud of "steam" is not water vapor, but actually a mass of condensed water droplets. Carefully place the bowl of a spoon in the cloud. Droplets of distilled water will form on the spoon, as the steam condenses. ■

Distillation is often used to separate two or more liquids that are mixed together. When these liquids are heated together in a simple still, the liquid that boils at the lowest temperature evaporates more quickly than the other liquids. The temperature at which a liquid boils is the *boiling point*. The vapor then passes through a *condenser*. The condenser is cooled. This lowers the temperature of the vapor inside the condenser. The vapor condenses back into a liquid called a *distillate*, which collects in a *receiver*. Mixtures of liquids that have greatly different boiling points are distilled by a process called *simple distillation*. *Fractional distillation* is the process by which mixtures of liquids that have close boiling points are distilled into separate portions, or fractions.

Destructive distillation is used to separate liquids, such as wood alcohol, from solid substances (wood). When the solid is heated in a closed container, the liquid that forms boils away. The vapor is collected and condensed into a liquid again (wood alcohol). A solid substance (charcoal) is left behind in the still.

Distillation has been used for centuries to make perfumes, flavorings, and alcoholic beverages such as whiskey, and to purify water. Fractional distillation is used to make alcoholic beverages and to separate gasoline, kerosene, fuel oil, and other useful products from petroleum.

ALSO READ: ALCOHOLIC BEVERAGE, PETROLEUM.

DISTRICT OF COLUMBIA

Many students from all parts of the United States make a special trip to Washington, D.C., to see the nation's capital. The government buildings, national monuments, and cultural attractions in the nation's capital make the trip an exciting one. The white-domed Capitol and the White House are among the city's most famous buildings. The Lincoln Memorial, the Washington Monument, and the Jefferson Memorial honor three great Presidents. The Smithsonian Institution, a center of scientific learning, has world-famous collections. Other attractions of Washington, D.C., are the John F. Kennedy Center for the Performing Arts, which opened in 1971, and the National Gallery of Art.

This great city began as a small area of marshy land. Congress had decided in 1790 that the United States should have a brand-new city as its capital. The city would not be in a state. It would be in a district belonging to the nation.

Maryland and Virginia agreed to give land for the district. The district was to be a square, with each side 10 miles (16 km) long. The square would lie on both sides of the Potomac River.

George Washington was President then. He chose Pierre Charles L'Enfant, a French architect, to draw up careful plans for the capital. President Washington spoke of it as "the Fed-

◄ *An aerial view of the District of Columbia. Can you spot the Capitol and other famous points of interest?*

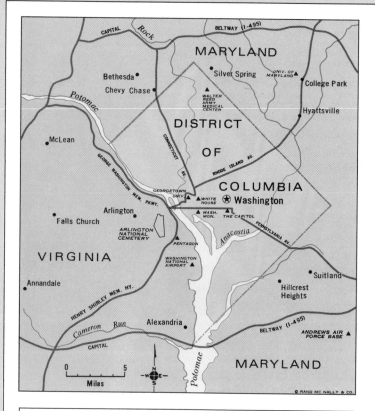

DISTRICT OF COLUMBIA

Area: 69 square miles (178 sq. km).
Population: 625,000
Principal river: Potomac (383 miles/616 km)
Highest Point: 420 feet (128 m)
Motto: (Justica omnibus) "Justice for all"
Song: "Washington"
Famous People: Duke Ellington, J Edgar Hoover, John Philip Sousa

District of Columbia

STATE EMBLEMS

▲ *The White House, in Washington, D.C., is the home of the President of the United States.*

Scarlet Oak

American Beauty Rose

Wood Thrush

eral City." But Congress decided to call it "the City of Washington in the District of Columbia," to honor both President Washington and Christopher Columbus.

President John Adams moved the Federal Government from Philadelphia to the new capital in 1800. Thomas Jefferson was the first President inaugurated there, in 1801.

For many years Washington City was a forlorn little cluster of buildings on Capitol Hill. Muddy roads led to the White House a mile away. A few miles away was the prosperous port town of Georgetown on the Potomac River. The British and Americans went to war in 1812. Two years later, the British invaded Washington. The White House was burned, and important government buildings were destroyed.

Washington was completely rebuilt immediately after the war. It remained a small, quiet community. Congressmen and other government officials did not like to come to this undeveloped little capital city. They fled to the cultural centers of Baltimore and Philadelphia whenever they could for concerts and plays.

Congress voted in 1846 to return to Virginia the District of Columbia lands south of the Potomac River. It appeared that the city would never need all that land. Besides, slave trading was not allowed in the District of Columbia, and some Virginians wanted slave markets there.

After the Civil War, Washington grew rapidly into a large and beautiful city. Many new government office buildings were built of white or gray stone in the classical style. The city developed around the original plan of architect L'Enfant, using his "spokes of a wheel" city plan, with circles at street intersections. Broad, tree-shaded avenues and large parks were also built. Universities, museums, and embassies of foreign countries were established in the city. The lovely area of Georgetown became

part of Washington in 1895. Georgetown's picturesque old houses, many dating back to the 1700's, gave charm to the city.

In 1874, Congress took control of Washington's government. City officials were chosen by Congress and the President. The 23rd Amendment to the Constitution, ratified in 1961, gave Washingtonians the right to vote in Presidential elections. City residents sought more national political representation and local self-government. They won a nonvoting delegate to the House of Representatives in 1970 and the right to elect their own mayor and a 13-member city council in 1974. The city also won the right to levy its own taxes.

ALSO READ: BANNEKER, BENJAMIN; CAPITOL, UNITED STATES; CONGRESS, UNITED STATES; LIBRARY OF CONGRESS; SMITHSONIAN INSTITUTION; UNITED STATES GOVERNMENT; WHITE HOUSE.

DIVING Have you tried diving from the side of a pool or from a diving board? You can accidentally hit the water with your chest first instead of your head. This is called a "belly flop," and it hurts. But once you get the swing of it, diving is great fun.

Good diving is exciting, especially when it is done from a high platform or diving board. Competitive divers—such as the persons who take part in the Olympic Games—are as skillful as acrobats. They practice hard to perfect their timing, coordination, and grace of movement.

There are five basic types of dives used in competitions. In a *forward dive*, divers stand on the diving board, facing straight ahead. (They may begin by taking a few running steps.) They then dive from the board, plunging into the water in a forward position, head first. In a *back dive*, they start out facing the board

▲ *Cox's Row, one of the elegant rows of houses that stand in Georgetown in the northwest section of the District of Columbia. Georgetown became part of the District in 1895. With its old houses, narrow streets, and tiny shops, Georgetown retains much of the charm of a small village of the 1800's.*

▼ *All the grace and beauty of diving is seen in this dive performed by U.S. springboard champion, Jennifer Chandler.*

DIVING

Swan dive

Back dive

Jackknife or Pike   Half gainer   Half twist

▲ *The diagram shows five stylish dives often used in competitions.*

▲ *Dorothea Dix, champion of reform in the care of the mentally ill.*

is the *swan dive*. The diver arches his or her body up and out when leaving the springboard. The body is horizontal for a brief time. The legs are stretched out straight, with the feet together, while the head is up and the arms extended. The diver seems to be flying through the air like a bird.

A dive commonly used in swimming competitions is the *racing dive*. It is done at the beginning of a race. The swimmer dives straight into the water from the edge of the pool. He or she tries to go as far as possible in the air and to skim the surface of the water as he or she hits it, already kicking the legs. This way the swimmer can begin to swim at full speed as soon as his or her body touches the water.

ALSO READ: SWIMMING.

DIVISION see ARITHMETIC.

DIX, DOROTHEA (1802–1887) In 1841, Dorothea Lynde Dix visited a jail in East Cambridge, Massachusetts, and was horrified to see that mentally ill people were being treated in the same way as criminals. They were chained and often beaten. She visited other jails in Massachusetts and found the same kind of conditions. She pleaded with the state legislature to do something about the problem.

Dorothea Dix was born in Hampden, Maine, and grew up in Massachusetts. She founded a school for girls in Boston in 1821 and was its head for 16 years. She spent almost 40 years of her life campaigning for better treatment of the mentally ill. She traveled throughout the United States, Canada, and Europe, talking to many people and raising money. Her work resulted in the founding of special institutions for the mentally ill and the poor in more than 20 U.S. states.

ALSO READ: MENTAL HEALTH.

and then flip over backward into the water. In a *full gainer*, they start out facing forward, but enter the water in a backward position. A *cutaway* is just the opposite. Divers start out facing the board, but turn in the air and enter the water in a forward position. In a *twisting dive*, the diver twists in the air before plunging into the water.

Divers do some fancy movements in the air as part of these basic dives. In a *pike*, or *jackknife*, divers bend their body at the hips. They keep their knees rigid and touch their ankles with their fingertips. In a *tuck*, they bring their knees up against their chest. In a *layout*, they straighten their body and hold it parallel to the water. These positions are held for only a short time before the diver straightens out and enters the water head-first.

An example of the layout position

DJIBOUTI The small republic of Djibouti lies on the northeast coast of Africa, at the southern entrance to the Red Sea. The country, the size of Massachusetts, is largely a stony desert, with some highlands. Its climate is hot and dry.

In 1862 France gained control of the area and in 1896 named it *French Somaliland*. France renamed it the Territory of Afars and Issas in 1967, for the territory's two largest native tribes. The Issa tribe is one of the tribes of the people called the *Somalis*, who also live in nearby Somalia. (See the map with the article on AFRICA.)

The country took the name of its capital and largest city, Djibouti, on attaining independence from France in 1977. Many of neighboring Ethiopia's exports are carried by railroad to the port of Djibouti, where oceangoing vessels dock. Most people beyond the city are nomadic herders of goats and cattle.

ALSO READ: AFRICA, ETHIOPIA, SOMALIA.

DOG Dogs are very popular pets. They are loving, loyal, obedient, playful, and intelligent. They can be house pets, working dogs, show dogs, and sporting dogs. The same qualities that make dogs wonderful pets also make them useful working animals. Guard dogs and sentry dogs protect property. They have been used in wartime to carry coded messages. Guide dogs lead and protect people who are blind. Dogs are used by narcotics officials to smell out drugs hidden in packages and luggage. Some dogs herd sheep, goats, or cattle. Dogs can also be trained to save lives in the water or in snowy mountains, and to track down lost people.

Dogs have well-developed senses. They hear and smell better than we can. That is why hunting dogs find game better than the hunter could. Whistles pitched so high that people cannot hear them are sometimes used to call dogs. Sharp teeth, powerful jaws, and speed for running away are the defenses a dog uses.

Types of Dogs An ancestor of the dog, which probably looked like a wolf, began to live and hunt with people about 12,000 years ago. It was the first *domesticated*, or tame, dog.

It is easy to see how dogs first began their association with primitive peoples: scavenging packs of dogs would follow the early nomadic tribes and feed off scraps and bones. The dogs, in turn, would provide warning if anything unusual approached. Eventually, both dogs and groups of humans began to hunt together.

The dog of today is the result of centuries of breeding and close association with humans. Foxes, wolves, coyotes, and jackals are among the wild cousins of the dog. Few wild

▲ *The German shepherd dog is popular throughout the world. They are big and powerful, and also intelligent. They are much used as guard dogs and in police work.*

▲ *The collie is a beautiful working dog that was first bred to herd sheep in Scotland. It makes a wonderful pet for children because of its loyal, gentle nature.*

DJIBOUTI

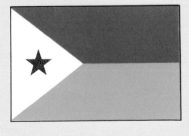

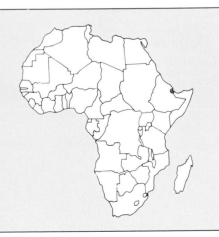

Capital City: Djibouti (205,000 people).

Area: 8,508 square miles (22,000 sq. km).

Population: 415,000.

Government: Republic.

Natural Resources: Sugar, coffee.

Export Products: Sugar, coffee, cattle, hides, skins.

Unit of Money: Djibouti franc.

Official Language: French.

BREEDS OF DOGS
ELIGIBLE FOR REGISTRATION IN
AMERICAN KENNEL CLUB STUD BOOK

SPORTING GROUP
Brittanys
Pointers
Pointers, German
  Shorthaired
Pointers, German
  Wirehaired
Retrievers, Chesapeake
  Bay
Retrievers, Curly-Coated
Retrievers, Flat-Coated
Retrievers, Golden
Retrievers, Labrador
Retrievers, English
Setters, English
Setters, Gordon
Setters, Irish
Spaniels, American Water
Spaniels, Clumber
Spaniels, Cocker
Spaniels, English Cocker
Spaniels, English Springer
Spaniels, Field
Spaniels, Irish Water
Spaniels, Sussex
Spaniels, Welsh Springer
Vizslas
Weimaraners
Wirehaired Pointing
  Griffons

HOUND GROUP
Afghan Hounds
Basenjis
Basset Hounds
Beagles
Black & Tan Coonhounds
Bloodhounds
Borzois
Dachshunds
Foxhounds, American
Foxhounds, English
Greyhounds
Harriers
Ibizan Hounds
Irish Wolfhounds
Norwegian Elkhounds
Otter Hounds
Pharaoh Hounds
Rhodesian Ridgebacks
Salukis

Scottish Deerhounds
Whippets

WORKING GROUP
Akitas
Alaskan Malamutes
Bernese Mountain Dogs
Boxers
Bullmastiffs
Doberman Pinschers
Giant Schnauzers
Great Danes
Great Pyrenees
Komondorok
Kuvaszok
Mastiffs
Newfoundlands
Portuguese Water Dogs
Rottweilers
St. Bernards
Samoyeds
Siberian Huskies
Standard Schnauzers

TERRIER GROUP
Airedale Terriers
American Staffordshire
  Terriers
Australian Terriers
Bedlington Terriers
Border Terriers
Bull Terriers
Cairn Terriers
Dandie Dinmont Terriers
Irish Terriers
Kerry Blue Terriers
Lakeland Terriers
Manchester Terriers
Miniature Schnauzers
Norfolk Terriers
Norwich Terriers
Scottish Terriers
Sealyham Terriers
Skye Terriers
Smooth Fox Terriers
Soft-Coated Wheaten
  Terriers
Staffordshire Bull
  Terriers
Welsh Terriers

West Highland White Terriers
Wire Fox Terriers

TOY GROUP
Affenpinschers
Brussels Griffons
Chihuahuas
English Toy Spaniels
Italian Greyhounds
Japanese Chin
Maltese
Manchester Terriers
Miniature Pinschers
Papillons
Pekingese
Pomeranians
Poodles (Toy)
Pugs
Shih Tzu
Silky Terriers
Yorkshire Terriers

**NON-SPORTING
GROUP**
Bichons Frises
Boston Terriers
Bulldogs
Chow Chows
Dalmatians
French Bulldogs
Keeshonden
Lhasa Apsos
Poodles
Schipperkes
Tibetan Spaniels
Tibetan Terriers

HERDING GROUP
Australian Cattle Dogs
Bearded Collies
Belgian Malinois
Belgian Sheepdogs
Belgian Tervuren
Bouviers des Flandres
Briards
Collies
German Shepherd Dogs
Old English Sheepdogs
Pulik
Shetland Sheepdogs
Welsh Corgis, Cardigan
Welsh Corgis, Pembroke

PARTS OF A DOG

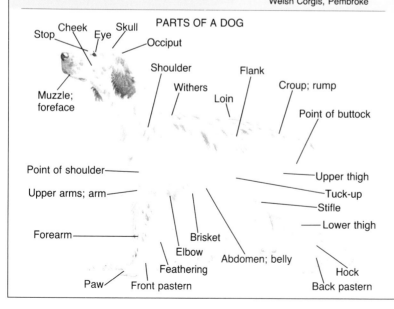

Stop · Cheek · Eye · Skull · Occiput · Shoulder · Withers · Flank · Loin · Croup; rump · Point of buttock · Muzzle; foreface · Point of shoulder · Upper arms; arm · Upper thigh · Tuck-up · Stifle · Lower thigh · Forearm · Brisket · Elbow · Abdomen; belly · Feathering · Hock · Paw · Front pastern · Back pastern

dogs exist today. One that does is the dingo of Australia, which is really a domesticated dog that ran wild. Many dogs are mixed breeds. Some people think that these dogs make the best pets. But other people prefer to own a dog of one breed—a *purebred*. A purebred has a pedigree (a list of the dogs in its ancestry), and it can be registered with the American Kennel Club.

Sporting dogs are a group of medium-sized to large dogs that are used for hunting game and as pets. Setters, retrievers, spaniels, and pointers are sporting dogs. Most of them are slim, with long legs and a keen sense of smell.

The golden retriever and the Irish setter are probably the best-known sporting dogs. The golden retriever is a medium-sized hunting dog, which is also popular as a guide dog for the blind. It has a rich golden coat and a very friendly personality. The Irish setter is often used in hunting birds. It has a bright, coppery-red coat. Chesapeake Bay retrievers, German short-haired pointers, cocker spaniels, and Weimaraners are some other sporting dogs.

Working dogs are many different sizes and shapes. They also have many different abilities. All of them are useful to people in some way, but they make good pets, too. Some working dogs, such as the collie and the Belgian sheepdog, were first bred to herd sheep. The strong, and sometimes fierce, Doberman pinscher and German shepherd make good guard dogs. Despite their great size, the Great Dane and the Saint Bernard are among the calmest of breeds. Siberian huskies and other working breeds are used as sled dogs in cold climates.

The *hound* breeds are quick, graceful, and lively. They love to romp and play. Many hounds are used in hunting and in dog racing. The basset hound and the dachshund have very short legs and long bodies. Greyhounds and whippets can run faster than other dogs. Police use bloodhounds for tracking because of their keen sense of smell. The saluki is probably the oldest breed of dog. They were the royal dogs of Egypt.

Terriers were first bred to hunt rodents by going down into their underground burrows. Many terriers are wire-haired, with coarse, wavy coats. Most of the terrier breeds are medium or small in size. They can run very fast, and they are frisky. Terriers were first brought to the United States from Britain. Another terrier, the Bedlington, resembles a fluffy white sheep. The Scottish terrier and the Cairn terrier have alert expressions and whiskers. Skye terriers have long fur, hiding the body and eyes. The Airedale terrier is one of the bravest breeds.

Nonsporting dogs are usually pets or show dogs, and they are rarely used in sport or as working dogs. The Dalmatian has a white coat with black spots. It is sometimes a fire-department mascot and was once known as the "plum pudding" dog. Boston terriers are small dogs with pug noses. They are not true terriers. Bulldogs are slightly pigeon-toed and have many wrinkles on their faces. The most popular nonsporting breed is the poodle, which comes in several sizes. Poodles are intelligent and lively, and they love to show off.

All *toy dogs* are unusually small in size. They are brave and alert, but some of them are nervous. The smallest poodle is a toy. The Pekingese is a proud little dog, whose body and expression are lion-like. The Yorkshire terrier has long, silky hair and usually weighs less than nine pounds (4 kg). Pomeranians and pugs have courageous, independent characters. The littlest dog of all is the Chihuahua. An adult Chihuahua can sit in the palm of a man's hand. Although they are small, toy dogs often have loud barks.

Selection, Care, and Training A female dog carries its young for about two months before giving birth to puppies. Usually four to six puppies are in a litter, but a litter may have only one or many more than six. The puppies are cared for and nursed by the mother for about a month.

The best time to get a puppy is when it is between six and eight weeks old. Make sure that the puppy is healthy. It should have clear, bright eyes; a shiny coat; a cool, moist nose; and an alert personality. Pick the liveliest puppy in the litter. A new puppy should be taken to a veterinarian, who will check its health and give it shots against rabies and distemper. Get a dog license and a collar for your new

▲ *Toy dogs are bred in all parts of the world; like the tiny Chihuahua from Mexico and the Griffon from Belgium*

▲ *The Dalmatian is a nonsporting dog with a fine, sleek, spotted coat. Dalmatians have been used as mascots by fire fighters.*

◄ *What could be a more pleasing sight than a mother dog with her* litter (family) *of puppies? These beautiful dogs are cocker spaniels.*

DOG

▲ *Sporting dogs are both used in hunting and kept as pets. The Irish setter is one very popular breed.*

dog as soon as possible.

Dogs can get sick easily. For this reason, the dog owner must feed his pet a balanced diet, give it a dry and sheltered place to sleep, and brush it regularly. Find out what is the best diet for your dog from a veterinarian or a good book on dog care. Dogs need plenty of water, meat, and dog biscuits. Never give a dog a bone that might splinter. Big dogs need a lot of exercise and space in which to run.

All dogs need training. House-breaking (to teach a dog not to soil indoors) is the first training a puppy gets. Put down fresh newspapers and praise it when it uses them. Take your puppy outdoors often, especially after feeding, to encourage clean habits. Do not allow your dog to soil the sidewalk.

A young dog should learn to obey its owner. It should learn to walk on a leash, come when you call, sit, stay, and lie down. After it has mastered the basic commands, it can also learn tricks. Even though dogs are anxious to please, it takes a lot of time to train them. Teach your dog one thing at a time. Never rush it or get impatient. Praise and tidbits of food when it behaves correctly are more effective than punishment when it is bad. Use the same word or command every time you tell a dog to do something. For example, do not say "down" one time and "lie" another time. After the dog has perfectly mastered one command, it can then learn another one. With patience, a dog can be taught many tricks and become an important member of the household.

ALSO READ: AESOP; CARNIVORE; COY-OTE; DOMESTICATED ANIMALS; FOX; LONDON, JACK; MAMMAL; PET; WOLF.

TRAINING A DOG

1 Heel Do not let your dog pull on the lead. Praise it when it is in the right position and jerk it back when it is not.

2 Sit To position your dog, hold its head up with one hand while pushing its rear down with the other.

3 Down This should be taught once the "sit" has been learned. Gently slide the dog's forepaws out from under it.

4 Stay Stand in front of your dog to stop it moving until you tell it to come. Gradually increase the distance between you and your dog.

5 Come With a disobedient dog teach this on the lead so that the dog has no choice but to come up to you.

6 Do's and Don'ts Do praise your dog for every success however small. Don't ever get irritable or lose your temper.